The Pearson Textbook Reader

Third Edition

Compiled by

Cheryl Novins

Longman

Boston   Columbus   Indianapolis   New York   San Francisco   Upper Saddle River
Amsterdam   Cape Town   Dubai   London   Madrid   Milan   Munich   Paris   Montreal   Toronto
Delhi   Mexico City   Sao Paulo   Sydney   Hong Kong   Seoul   Singapore   Taipei   Tokyo

Acquisitions Editor: Kate Edwards
Senior Supplements Editor: Donna Campion
Marketing Manager: Thomas DeMarco
Electronic Page Makeup: Grapevine Publishing Services, Inc.
Cover Designer: Teresa M. Ward
Cover Photo: www.iStockphoto.com

The Pearson Textbook Reader, Third Edition, compiled by Cheryl Novins.

Copyright © 2003, 2008, 2011 Pearson Education, Inc.

All rights reserved. Printed in the United States of Americia. This publication is protected by Copyright and permission should be obtained from the publisher prior to any prohibited reproduction, storage in a retrieval system, or transmission in any form or by any means, electronic, mechanical, photocopying, recording, or likewise. To obtain permission(s) to use material from this work, please submit a written request to Pearson Education, Inc., Permissions Department, One Lake Street, Upper Saddle River, New Jersey 07458 or you may fax your request to 201-236-3290.

2 3 4 5 6 7 8 9 10–QGD–13 12 11

Longman
is an imprint of

www.pearsonhighered.com

ISBN 13: 978-0-205-75118-1
ISBN 10:   0-205-75118-0

Contents

Unit III: Mathematics   67

Unit IV: History   107

Unit V: Humanities and the Visual Arts   145

Unit VI: Psychology   167

Credits   207

Introduction for Instructors

Reading courses offer college students many opportunities. In addition to helping students increase literal comprehension skills, such courses provide a basis for further college study in a wide variety of disciplines. Students who master the skills taught in their reading courses are well on their way to success in college and in the workplace.

A large part of success in any endeavor involves understanding the expectations of the situation. College students are expected to be independent learners, to take charge of their studies, and to find motivation from within. They are expected to attend lectures, take exams, and read their textbooks. Developmental reading texts often stress the importance of attending class and usually offer some tips on how to prepare for and take tests. They also include various excerpts from college texts to prepare students for the material they will encounter in their other college courses.

Unfortunately, such textbook excerpts (which often beautifully illustrate such important concepts as main idea, supporting details, and patterns of organization) tend to be fairly short—no more than a paragraph or two, or three or four pages at most. Such material tends to give ample drill and practice in the all-important reading skills, but often does not match the assignments that students will receive in their other courses, where they will be expected to read one or two complete textbook chapters per week.

In the interests of providing students with longer, chapter-length readings, Pearson is pleased to offer *The Pearson Textbook Reader, 3e*. This paperback volume features complete textbook chapters from freshman textbooks representing six different course areas. The six course areas are:

- **Business:** Chapter 3, "Communicating in a World of Diversity." From Bovee and Thill. *Business Communication Today*, 10/e. ©2010, Prentice Hall.
- **Allied Heath:** Chapter 45, "Sleep." From Berman, Snyder, Kozier, and Erb. *Fundamentals of Nursing: Concepts, Process, and Practice*, 8/e. ©2008, Prentice Hall.
- **Mathematics:** Chapter 11, "Mathematics and the Arts." From Bennett and Briggs. *Using and Understanding Mathematics: A Quantitative Reasoning Approach*, 4/e. ©2008, Pearson Education.
- **History:** Chapter 2, "American Society in the Making." From Carnes and Garraty. *The American Nation: A History of the United States Volume One To 1877*, 13/e. ©2008, Prentice Hall.
- **Humanities and the Visual Arts:** "Orientation," by Daniel Orozco, and "The Other Two," by Elizabeth Wharton.
- **Psychology:** Chapter 10, "Health and Stress." From Wood, Wood, and Boyd. *Mastering the World of Psychology*, 3/e. ©2008, Allyn & Bacon.

These chapters were also chosen to represent the most commonly required and/or selected courses taken by incoming college freshmen. Each chapter is reproduced in its entirety; the complete original text, all photographs and graphic art, and pedagogical features are included. In addition, a series of exercises, group activities, and critical thinking activities have been prepared specially for this edition.

We hope *The Pearson Textbook Reader, 3e* will be an asset to you and your students.

Kate Edwards
Acquisitions Editor, Reading and Study Skills
Pearson Education
Kate.Edwards@pearson.com

Unit 1: Business

From

Courtland L. Bovée

John V. Thill

Business Communication Today

Ninth Edition

Chapter 3:
Communicating in a World of Diversity

An Introduction to Business Communications

Business communications focuses on the unique communication processes that are at work in business environments. Many factors influence the effectiveness of business communications. Factors such as diversity, technology, organizational structures, and communication barriers are faced by companies in today's global marketplace. It is critical in business to ensure that all communication, whether written or verbal, is subject to appropriate business etiquette.

Business communication is a mandatory class in most undergraduate business programs. There are many career opportunities that include this field of study, such as advertising, marketing, international business, mass media, and public administration.

Strategies for Reading Business Texts

Prior to reading a business textbook, take the time to preview each chapter, paying close attention to the headings, subheadings, margin notes, and visuals. To ensure comprehension when reading the chapter, annotating and outlining the material is suggested. Pay attention to any technical concepts and terminology. It is important that as you read you distinguish between the fact and opinion of the authors and continually compare and contrast like concepts. In addition, take the time to carefully interpret supporting graphic material, including examples of business correspondences and documents.

3

Communicating in a World of Diversity

Learning Objectives

After studying this chapter, you will be able to

1 Discuss the opportunities and challenges of intercultural communication

2 Define *culture* and explain how culture is learned

3 Define *ethnocentrism* and *stereotyping* and give three suggestions for overcoming these limiting mindsets

4 Explain the importance of recognizing cultural variations and list eight categories of cultural differences

5 Identify steps you can take to improve your intercultural communication skills

6 List seven recommendations for writing clearly in multilanguage business environments

Communication Close-up at IBM

Ron Glover oversees IBM's efforts to build competitive advantage by capitalizing on the benefits of a diverse workforce.

www.ibm.com

The *I* in IBM stands for *International*, but it could just as easily stand for *Intercultural*, as a testament to the computer giant's long-standing commitment to embracing diversity. Ron Glover, IBM's vice president of global workforce diversity, knows from years of experience that communicating successfully across cultures is no simple task, however—particularly in a company that employs more than 350,000 people and sells to customers in roughly 175 countries around the world.

Language presents a formidable barrier to communication when you consider that IBM's employees speak more than 165 languages. But language is just one of many elements that play a role in communication between cultures. Differences in age, ethnic background, gender, sexual orientation, physical ability, and economic status can all affect the communication process. Glover emphasizes that "to operate successfully, we must be especially mindful of how we respect and value differences among people in countries and regions." He recognizes that these differences represent both a challenge and an opportunity, and a key part of his job is helping IBM executives and employees work together in a way that transforms their cultural differences into a critical business strength. Diversity, he explains, is "an essential aspect of IBM's broader business strategy."

Throughout its long history of employing and working with people from a variety of cultures, IBM has learned some powerful lessons. Perhaps the most significant is its conclusion that successfully managing a diverse workforce and competing in a diverse marketplace starts with embracing those differences, not trying to ignore them or pretending they don't affect interpersonal communication. Take Ron Glover's advice when he says that even if your company never does business outside the United States, "you will need to effectively engage differences to remain viable in the economy of the future."[1]

UNDERSTANDING THE OPPORTUNITIES AND CHALLENGES OF COMMUNICATION IN A DIVERSE WORLD

IBM's experience (profiled in the chapter-opening Communication Close-up) illustrates both the challenges and the opportunities for business professionals who know how to communicate with diverse audiences. Although the concept is often framed in terms of ethnic background, a broader and more useful definition of **diversity** "includes all the characteristics and experiences that define each of us as individuals."[2] As you'll learn in this chapter, these characteristics and experiences can have a profound effect on the way businesspeople communicate.

Diversity includes all the characteristics that define people as individuals.

Intercultural communication is the process of sending and receiving messages between people whose cultural backgrounds could lead them to interpret verbal and nonverbal signs differently. Every attempt to send and receive messages is influenced by culture, so to communicate successfully, you need a basic grasp of the cultural differences you may encounter and how you should handle them. Your efforts to recognize and bridge cultural differences will open up business opportunities throughout the world and maximize the contributions of all the employees in a diverse workforce.

The Opportunities in a Global Marketplace

You might be a business manager looking for new customers or fresh talent. You might be an employee looking for new work opportunities. Either way, chances are good that you'll be looking across international borders sometime in your career.

Thanks to communication and transportation technologies, natural boundaries and national borders are no longer the impassable barriers they once were. Local markets are opening to worldwide competition as businesses of all sizes look for new growth opportunities outside their own countries. Thousands of U.S. businesses depend on exports for significant portions of their revenues. Every year, these companies export hundreds of billions of dollars worth of materials and merchandise, along with billions more in personal and professional services. If you work in one of these companies, you may well be called on to visit or at least communicate with a wide variety of people who speak languages other than English and who live in cultures quite different from what you're used to (see Figure 3.1). Of the top 10 export markets for U.S. products, only two, Canada and Great Britain, speak English as an official language—and Canada also has French as an official language.[3]

1 LEARNING OBJECTIVE

Discuss the opportunities and challenges of intercultural communication

You will communicate with people from other cultures throughout your career.

The Advantages of a Diverse Workforce

Even if you never visit another country or transact business on a global scale, you will interact with colleagues from a variety of cultures, with a wide range of characteristics and life experiences. Over the past few decades, many innovative companies have changed the way they approach diversity, from seeing it as a legal requirement (providing equal opportunities for all) to seeing it as a strategic opportunity to connect with customers and take advantage of the broadest possible pool of talent.[4] Smart business leaders such as IBM's Ron Glover recognize the competitive advantages of a diverse workforce that offers a broader spectrum of viewpoints and ideas, helps companies understand and identify with diverse markets, and enables companies to benefit from a wider range of employee talents. According to Glover, more diverse teams tend to be more innovative over the long term than more homogeneous teams.[5]

The diversity of today's workforce brings distinct advantages to businesses:
- *A broader range of views and ideas*
- *A better understanding of diverse, fragmented markets*
- *A broader pool of talent from which to recruit*

FIGURE 3.1 Languages of the World

This map illustrates the incredible array of languages used around the world. Each dot represents the geographic center of one of the more than 6,900 languages tracked by the linguistic research firm SIL International. Even if all your business communication takes place in English, you will interact with audience members who speak a variety of other native languages.

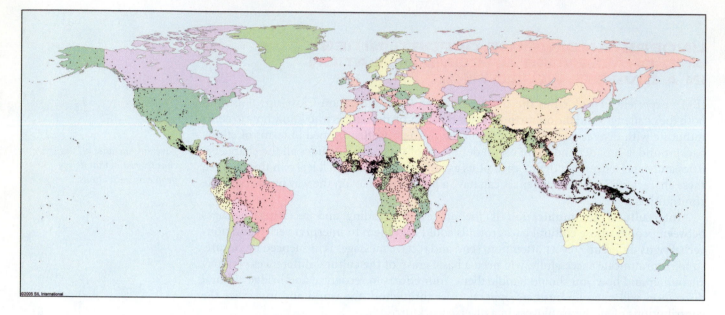

©2005 SIL International

Diversity is simply a fact of life for all companies. The United States has been a nation of immigrants from the beginning, and that trend continues today. The western and northern Europeans who made up the bulk of immigrants during the nation's early years now share space with people from across Asia, Africa, eastern Europe, and other parts of the world. Even the term *minority*, as it applies to nonwhite residents, makes less and less sense every year: In two states (California and New Mexico), in several dozen large cities, and in several hundred counties across the United States, Caucasian Americans make up less than half the population.[6] This pattern of immigration isn't unique to the United States. For example, workers from Africa, Asia, and the Middle East are moving to Europe in search of new opportunities, while workers from India, the Philippines, and Southeast Asia contribute to the employment base of the Middle East.[7]

However, you and your colleagues don't need to be recent immigrants to constitute a diverse workforce. Differences in everything from age and gender to religion and ethnic heritage to geography and military experience enrich the workplace. Both immigration and workforce diversity create advantages—and challenges—for business communicators throughout the world.

The Challenges of Intercultural Communication

A company's cultural diversity affects how its business messages are conceived, composed, delivered, received, and interpreted.

Culture influences everything about communication, including
- *Language*
- *Nonverbal signals*
- *Word meaning*
- *Time and space issues*
- *Rules of human relationships*

Today's increasingly diverse workforce encompasses a wide range of skills, traditions, backgrounds, experiences, outlooks, and attitudes toward work—all of which can affect communication in the workplace. Supervisors face the challenge of connecting with these diverse employees, motivating them, and fostering cooperation and harmony among them. Teams face the challenge of working together closely, and companies are challenged to coexist peacefully with business partners and with the community as a whole.

The interaction of culture and communication is so pervasive that separating the two is virtually impossible. The way you communicate—from the language you speak and the nonverbal signals you send to the way you perceive other people—is influenced by the culture in which you were raised. The meaning of words, the significance of gestures, the importance of time and space, the rules of human relationships—these and many other aspects of communication are defined by culture. To a large degree, your culture influences the way you think, which naturally affects the way you communicate as both a sender and a receiver.[8] So you can see that intercultural communication is much more complicated than simply matching language between sender and receiver. It goes beyond mere words to beliefs, values, and emotions.

Think back to the communication process model you studied in Chapter 1 (page 10). Elements of human diversity can affect communication at every stage of the communication process, from the ideas a person deems important enough to share to the habits and expectations of giving feedback. In particular, your instinct is to encode your message using the assumptions of *your* culture. However, members of your audience decode your message according to the assumptions of *their* culture. The greater the difference between cultures, the greater the chance for misunderstanding.[9] For example, the American-made movie *Hollywood Buddha* was advertised with posters showing the star of the movie sitting on the head of a statue of Buddha. Such a depiction may have few spiritual implications for non-Buddhists, but it was a serious insult to many Buddhists—so much so that Buddhists in a number of countries took to the streets in protest, and the government of Thailand (where Buddhism is the predominant religion) was prompted to create a guidebook to help foreigners understand and respect Thai culture.[10]

Communication among people of diverse cultural backgrounds and life experiences is not always easy, but doing it successfully can create tremendous strategic advantages.

Throughout this chapter, you'll see numerous examples of how communication styles and habits vary from one culture to another. These examples are intended to illustrate the major themes of intercultural communication, not to give an exhaustive list of styles and habits of any particular culture. With an understanding of these major themes, you'll be prepared to explore the specifics of any culture.

ENHANCING YOUR SENSITIVITY TO CULTURE AND DIVERSITY

The good news is that you're already an expert in culture, at least in the culture in which you grew up. You understand how your society works, how people are expected to communicate, what common gestures and facial expressions mean, and so on. The bad news is that because you're such an expert in your own culture, your communication is largely automatic; that is, you rarely stop to think about the communication rules you're following. An important step toward successful intercultural communication is becoming more aware of these rules and of the way they influence your communication.

Understanding the Concept of Culture

Culture is a shared system of symbols, beliefs, attitudes, values, expectations, and norms for behavior. Your cultural background influences the way you prioritize what is important in life, helps define your attitude toward what is appropriate in a situation, and establishes rules of behavior.[11]

Actually, you belong to several cultures. In addition to the culture you share with all the people who live in your own country, you belong to other cultural groups, including an ethnic group, possibly a religious group, and perhaps a profession that has its own special language and customs. With its large population and long history of immigration, the United States is home to a vast array of cultures. As one indication of this diversity, the inhabitants of this country now speak more than 160 languages.[12] In contrast, Japan is much more homogeneous, having only a few distinct cultural groups.[13]

Members of a given culture tend to have similar assumptions about how people should think, behave, and communicate, and they all tend to act on those assumptions in much the

2 LEARNING OBJECTIVE

Define *culture* and explain how culture is learned

Culture is a shared system of symbols, beliefs, attitudes, values, expectations, and behavior norms.

You belong to several cultures, each of which affects the way you communicate.

same way. Cultures can differ widely and vary in their rate of change, their degree of complexity, and their tolerance toward outsiders. These differences affect the level of trust and openness that you can achieve when communicating with people of other cultures.

You learn culture both directly (by being instructed) and indirectly (by observing others).

People learn culture directly and indirectly from other members of their group. As you grow up in a culture, you are taught by the group's members who you are and how best to function in that culture. Sometimes you are explicitly told which behaviors are acceptable; at other times you learn by observing which values work best in a particular group. In these ways, culture is passed on from person to person and from generation to generation.[14]

Cultures tend to offer views of life that are both coherent (internally logical) and complete (answer all of life's big questions).

In addition to being automatic, culture tends to be *coherent*; that is, a culture appears to be fairly logical and consistent when viewed from the inside. Certain norms within a culture may not make sense to someone outside the culture, but they probably make sense to those inside. Such coherence generally helps a culture function more smoothly internally, but it can create disharmony between cultures that don't view the world in the same way.

Finally, cultures tend to be *complete*; that is, they provide most of their members with most of the answers to life's big questions. This idea of completeness dulls or even suppresses curiosity about life in other cultures. Not surprisingly, such completeness can complicate communication with other cultures.[15]

3 LEARNING OBJECTIVE

Define *ethnocentrism* and *stereotyping* and give three suggestions for overcoming these limiting mindsets

Ethnocentrism is the tendency to judge other groups according to the standards, behaviors, and customs of one's own group.

Stereotyping is assigning generalized attributes to an individual on the basis of membership in a particular group.

Cultural pluralism is the acceptance of multiple cultures on their own terms.

You can avoid ethnocentrism and stereotyping by avoiding assumptions and judgments and by accepting differences.

Overcoming Ethnocentrism and Stereotyping

Ethnocentrism is the tendency to judge other groups according to the standards, behaviors, and customs of one's own group. Given the automatic influence of one's own culture, when people compare their culture to others, they often conclude that their own group is superior.[16] An even more extreme reaction is **xenophobia**, a fear of strangers and foreigners. Clearly, businesspeople who take these views are not likely to communicate successfully across cultures.

Distorted views of other cultures or groups also result from **stereotyping**, assigning a wide range of generalized attributes to an individual on the basis of membership in a particular culture or social group. For instance, assuming that an older colleague will be out of touch with the youth market or that a younger colleague can't be an inspiring leader are examples of stereotyping age groups.

Those who want to show respect for other people and to communicate effectively in business need to adopt a more positive viewpoint, in the form of **cultural pluralism**—the practice of accepting multiple cultures on their own terms. When crossing cultural boundaries, you'll be even more effective if you move beyond simple acceptance and adapt your communication style to that of the new cultures you encounter—even integrating aspects of those cultures into your own.[17] A few simple habits can help:

- **Avoiding assumptions.** Don't assume that others will act the same way you do, use language and symbols the same way you do, or even operate from the same values and beliefs. For instance, in a comparison of the 10 most important values in three cultures, people from the United States had *no* values in common with people from Japanese or Arab cultures.[18]
- **Avoiding judgments.** When people act differently, don't conclude that they are in error or that their way is invalid or inferior.
- **Acknowledging distinctions.** Don't ignore the differences between another person's culture and your own.

Unfortunately, overcoming ethnocentrism and stereotyping is not a simple task, even for people who are highly motivated to do so. Moreover, research suggests that people often have beliefs and biases that they're not even aware of—and that may even conflict with the beliefs they *think* they have. (To see if you have some of these *implicit beliefs*, visit the Project Implicit website, at **https://implicit.harvard.edu/implicit**, and take some of the simple online tests.)[19]

4 LEARNING OBJECTIVE

Explain the importance of recognizing cultural variations and list eight categories of cultural differences

Recognizing Variations in a Diverse World

You can begin to learn how people in other cultures want to be treated by recognizing and accommodating eight main types of cultural differences: contextual, legal and ethical, social, nonverbal, age, gender, religious, and ability.

▌COMMUNICATING ACROSS CULTURES

Test Your Intercultural Knowledge

Even well-intentioned businesspeople can make mistakes if they aren't aware of simple but important cultural differences. Can you spot the erroneous assumptions in these scenarios?

1. You're tired of the discussion, and you want to move on to a new topic. You ask your Australian business associate, "Can we table this for a while?" To your dismay, your colleague ignores the request and keeps right on discussing the topic.

2. You finally made the long trip overseas to meet the new director of your German division. Despite slow traffic, you arrive only four minutes late. His door is shut, so you knock on it and walk in. The chair is too far away from the desk, so you pick it up and move it closer. Then you lean over the desk, stick out your hand and say, "Good morning, Hans. It's nice to meet you." Why is his reaction so chilly?

3. Your meeting went better than you'd ever expected. In fact, you found the Japanese representative for your new advertising agency to be very agreeable; she said yes to just about everything. When you share your enthusiasm with your boss, he doesn't appear very excited. Why?

Here's what went wrong in each situation:

1. To "table" something in Australia means to bring it forward for discussion, the opposite of the usual U.S. meaning.

2. You've just broken four rules of German polite behavior: punctuality, privacy, personal space, and proper greetings. In time-conscious Germany, guests should never arrive even a few minutes late. Also, Germans like their privacy and space, and many adhere to formal greetings of "Frau" and "Herr," even if the business association has lasted for years.

3. The word *yes* may not always mean "yes" in the Western sense. Japanese people may say *yes* to confirm that they have heard or understood something but not necessarily to indicate that they agree with it. You'll seldom get a direct no. Some of the ways that Japanese people say no indirectly include "It will be difficult," "I will ask my supervisor," "I'm not sure," "We will think about it," and "I see."

CAREER APPLICATIONS

1. Have you ever been on the receiving end of an intercultural communication error, such as when someone inadvertently used an inappropriate gesture or figure of speech? How did you respond?

2. After arriving late at the office of the German colleague, what would have been a better way to handle the situation?

Contextual Differences

Every attempt at communication occurs within a **cultural context**, the pattern of physical cues, environmental stimuli, and implicit understanding that convey meaning between two members of the same culture. However, cultures around the world vary widely in the role that context plays in communication (see Figure 3.2).

◄ In a **high-context culture**, people rely less on verbal communication and more on the context of nonverbal actions and environmental setting to convey meaning. For instance, a Chinese speaker expects the receiver to discover the essence of a message and uses indirectness and metaphor to provide a web of meaning.[20] In high-context cultures, the rules of everyday life are rarely explicit; instead, as individuals grow up, they learn how to recognize situational cues (such as gestures and tone of voice) and how to respond as expected.[21] The primary role of communication is building relationships, not exchanging information.[22]

◄ In a **low-context culture**, people rely more on verbal communication and less on circumstances and cues to convey meaning. In such cultures, rules and expectations are usually spelled out through explicit statements such as "Please wait until I'm finished" or "You're welcome to browse."[23] The primary task of communication in low-context cultures is exchanging information.[24]

Contextual differences are apparent in the way people approach situations such as decision making, problem solving, and negotiating. For instance, in low-context cultures, businesspeople tend to focus on the results of the decisions they face, a reflection of the cultural emphasis on logic and progress (for example, "Will this be good for our company? For my career?"). In comparison, higher-context cultures emphasize the means or the method by which a decision will be made. Building or protecting relationships can be as important as the facts and information used in making the decisions.[25] Consequently, negotiators working on business deals in such cultures may spend most of their time together building relationships rather than hammering out contractual details.

Cultural context is a pattern of physical cues, environmental stimuli, and implicit understanding that conveys meaning between members of the same culture.

High-context cultures rely heavily on nonverbal actions and environmental setting to convey meaning; low-context cultures rely more on explicit verbal communication.

Low-context cultures tend to value written agreements and interpret laws strictly, whereas high-context cultures view adherence to laws as being more flexible.

FIGURE 3.2   How Cultural Context Affects Business

Cultural context influences the nature of business communication in many ways. Note that these are generalized assessments of each culture; contextual variations can be found within each culture and from one individual to another.

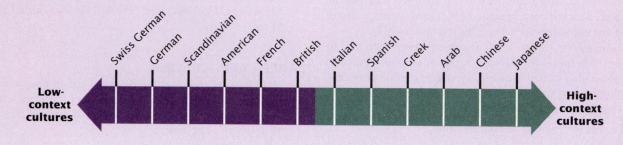

IN LOW-CONTEXT CULTURES	IN HIGH-CONTEXT CULTURES
Executive offices are separate with controlled access.	Executive offices are shared and open to all.
Workers rely on detailed background information.	Workers do not expect or want detailed information.
Information is highly centralized and controlled.	Information is shared with everyone.
Objective data are valued over subjective relationships.	Subjective relationships are valued over objective data.
Business and social relationships are discrete.	Business and social relationships overlap.
Competence is valued as much as position and status.	Position and status are valued much more than competence.
Meetings have fixed agendas and plenty of advance notice.	Meetings are often called on short notice, and key people always accept.

Low-context cultures ← Swiss German · German · Scandinavian · American · French · British · Italian · Spanish · Greek · Arab · Chinese · Japanese → High-context cultures

The distinctions between high and low context are generalizations, of course, but they are important to keep in mind as guidelines. Communication tactics that work well in a high-context culture may backfire in a low-context culture and vice versa.

Legal and Ethical Differences

Cultural context influences legal and ethical behavior, which in turn can affect communication. For example, because low-context cultures value the written word, they consider written agreements binding. But high-context cultures put less emphasis on the written word and consider personal pledges more important than contracts. They also tend to take a more flexible approach regarding adherence to the law, whereas low-context cultures adhere to the law strictly.[26]

Honesty and respect are cornerstones of ethical communication, regardless of culture.

As you conduct business around the world, you'll find that both legal systems and ethical standards differ from culture to culture. Making ethical choices across cultures can seem complicated, but you can keep your messages ethical by applying four basic principles:[27]

- **Actively seek mutual ground.** To allow the clearest possible exchange of information, both parties must be flexible and avoid insisting that an interaction take place strictly in terms of one culture or another.
- **Send and receive messages without judgment.** To allow information to flow freely, both parties must recognize that values vary from culture to culture, and they must trust each other.
- **Send messages that are honest.** To ensure that information is true, both parties must see things as they are—not as they would like them to be. Both parties must be fully aware of their personal and cultural biases.
- **Show respect for cultural differences.** To protect the basic human rights of both parties, each must understand and acknowledge the other's needs and preserve each other's dignity by communicating without deception.

Social Differences

The nature of social behavior varies among cultures, sometimes dramatically. Wal-Mart learned this lesson the hard way when the giant retailer tried to expand into Germany. Store clerks resisted the company requirement of always smiling at customers—a cornerstone of customer relationship strategies in the United States—because customers sometimes misinterpreted smiling as flirting. Wal-Mart dropped the requirement but, after a number of other cultural and strategic missteps, eventually left the German market.[28]

Some behavioral rules are formal and specifically articulated (table manners are a good example), and others are informal and learned over time (such as the comfortable distance to stand from a colleague during a discussion). The combination of formal and informal rules influences the overall behavior of most people in a society most of the time. In addition to the factors already discussed, social norms can vary from culture to culture in the following areas:

Formal rules of etiquette are explicit and well defined, but informal rules are learned through observation and imitation.

- **Attitudes toward work and success.** Many U.S. citizens hold the view that material comfort earned by individual effort is a sign of superiority and that people who work hard are better than those who don't. This view is reflected in the number of hours that U.S. employees work every year.
- **Roles and status.** Culture dictates, or at least tries to dictate, the roles that people play, including who communicates with whom, what they communicate, and in what way. For example, in some countries women still don't play a prominent role in business, so women executives who visit these countries may find that they're not taken seriously as businesspeople.[29] Culture also dictates how people show respect and signify rank. For example, people in the United States show respect by addressing top managers as "Mr. Roberts" or "Ms. Gutierrez." However, people in China are addressed according to their official titles, such as "President" or "Manager."[30]

  Respect and rank are reflected differently from culture to culture in the way people are addressed and in their working environment.

- **Use of manners.** What is polite in one culture may be considered rude in another. For instance, asking a colleague "How was your weekend?" is a common way of making small talk in the United States, but the question sounds intrusive to people in cultures in which business and private lives are seen as totally separate. Research a country's expectations before you visit and watch carefully and learn after you arrive.

  The rules of polite behavior vary from country to country.

- **Concepts of time.** People in high-context cultures see time as a way to plan the business day efficiently, often focusing on only one task during each scheduled period and viewing time as a limited resource. However, executives from low-context cultures often see time as more flexible. Meeting a deadline is less important than building a business relationship.[31] Trying to coax a team into staying on a strict schedule would be an attractive attribute in U.S. companies but could be viewed as pushy and overbearing in other cultures.

  Attitudes toward time, such as strict adherence to meeting schedules, vary throughout the world.

- **Future orientation.** Successful companies tend to have a strong *future orientation*, planning for and investing in the future, but national cultures around the world vary widely in this viewpoint (see Figure 3.3). Some societies encourage a long-term outlook that emphasizes planning and investing—making sacrifices in the short term for the promise of better outcomes in the future. Others are oriented more toward the present, even to the point of viewing the future as hopelessly remote and not worth planning for.[32]
- **Openness and inclusiveness.** At both the national level and within smaller groups, cultures vary on how open they are to accepting people from other cultures and people who don't necessarily fit the prevailing norms within the culture. An unwillingness to accommodate others can range from outright exclusion to subtle pressures to conform to majority expectations. IBM has long been a leader in the effort to create an inclusive environment that ensures fair opportunities for both employees and external business partners. Executive-led task forces at the company represent women; Asian American, African American, Hispanic American, and Native American people; people with disabilities; and gay, lesbian, bisexual, and transgender employees. Diversity is embraced at the employee level through more than 100 networking groups that unite people who have a variety of talents and interests.[33]

  Cultures around the world exhibit varying degrees of openness toward outsiders and people whose personal identities don't align with prevailing social norms.

FIGURE 3.3 Future Orientation and National Competitiveness
Countries vary widely in the degree to which they are willing to embrace and invest in
the future. As this graph shows, there appears to be a strong correlation between a
country's future orientation and its ability to compete in global markets. A culture's
attitude about the future is one of several social elements that influence the
communication process.

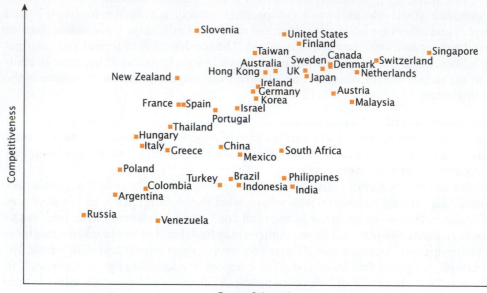

Future Orientation
(cultural support for delayed gratification, planning, and investment)

Nonverbal Differences

The meanings of nonverbal signals vary widely from culture to culture, so you can't rely on assumptions.

As discussed in Chapter 2, nonverbal communication can be a reliable guide to determining the meaning of a message—but this holds true only if the sender and receiver assign the same meaning to nonverbal signals. For instance, the simplest hand gestures have different meanings in different cultures. A gesture that communicates good luck in Brazil is the equivalent of giving someone "the finger" in Colombia.[34] Don't assume that the gestures you grew up with will translate to another culture; doing so could lead to embarrassing mistakes (see Figure 3.4).

When you have the opportunity to interact with people in another culture, the best advice is to study the culture in advance and then observe the way people behave in the following areas:

- **Greetings.** Do people shake hands, bow, or kiss lightly (on one side of the face or both)? Do people shake hands only when first introduced and every time they say hello or good-bye?
- **Personal space.** When people are conversing, do they stand closer together or farther away than you are accustomed to?
- **Touching.** Do people touch each other on the arm to emphasize a point or slap each other on the back to show congratulations? Or do they refrain from touching altogether?
- **Facial expressions.** Do people shake their heads to indicate "no" and nod them to indicate "yes"? This is what people are accustomed to in the United States, but it is not universal.
- **Eye contact.** Do people make frequent eye contact or avoid it? Frequent eye contact is often taken as a sign of honesty and openness in the United States, but in other cultures it can be a sign of aggressiveness or lack of respect.
- **Posture.** Do people slouch and relax in the office and in public, or do they sit up and stand up straight?
- **Formality.** In general, does the culture seem more or less formal than yours?

FIGURE 3.4 Avoiding Nonverbal Mishaps

The smile is about the only nonverbal gesture that has the same meaning in all cultures. But even a simple smile isn't all that simple. People in many cultures do not smile at strangers as much as people in the United States do, so travelers from the United States are sometimes put off by what they consider unfriendly responses from strangers. Conversely, people from other cultures can be put off by the U.S. habit of frequent smiling, which some view as insincere.

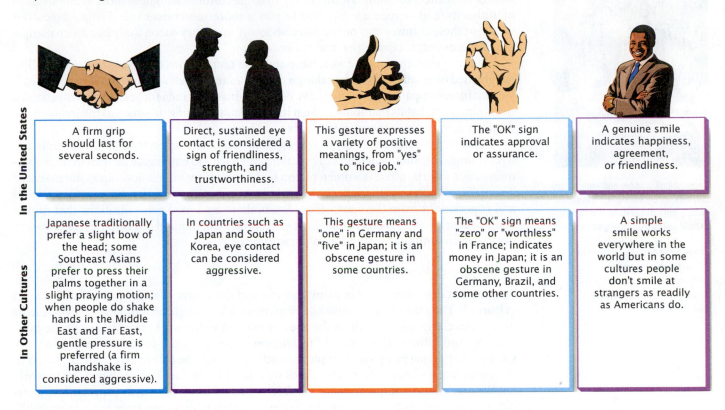

	In the United States	In Other Cultures
	A firm grip should last for several seconds.	Japanese traditionally prefer a slight bow of the head; some Southeast Asians prefer to press their palms together in a slight praying motion; when people do shake hands in the Middle East and Far East, gentle pressure is preferred (a firm handshake is considered aggressive).
	Direct, sustained eye contact is considered a sign of friendliness, strength, and trustworthiness.	In countries such as Japan and South Korea, eye contact can be considered aggressive.
	This gesture expresses a variety of positive meanings, from "yes" to "nice job."	This gesture means "one" in Germany and "five" in Japan; it is an obscene gesture in some countries.
	The "OK" sign indicates approval or assurance.	The "OK" sign means "zero" or "worthless" in France; indicates money in Japan; it is an obscene gesture in Germany, Brazil, and some other countries.
	A genuine smile indicates happiness, agreement, or friendliness.	A simple smile works everywhere in the world but in some cultures people don't smile at strangers as readily as Americans do.

Following the lead of people who grew up in the culture is not only a great way to learn but a good way to show respect as well.

Age Differences

In U.S. culture, youth is associated with strength, energy, possibilities, and freedom. In contrast, age is often associated with declining powers and a loss of respect and authority. However, older workers can offer broader experience, the benefits of important business relationships nurtured over many years, and high degrees of "practical intelligence"—the ability to solve complex, poorly defined problems.[35]

In contrast, in cultures that value age and seniority, longevity earns respect and increasing power and freedom. For instance, in many Asian societies, the oldest employees hold the most powerful jobs, the most impressive titles, and the greatest degrees of freedom and decision-making authority. If a younger employee disagrees with one of these senior executives, the discussion is never conducted in public. The notion of "saving face," of avoiding public embarrassment, is too strong. Instead, if a senior person seems to be in error about something, other employees will find a quiet, private way to communicate whatever information they feel is necessary.[36]

In addition to cultural values associated with various life stages, the multiple generations within a culture present another dimension of diversity. Today's workplaces can have as many as four distinct generations working side by side, generally defined as *traditionalists* (those born before 1946), *baby boomers* (born between 1946 and 1964), *generation X* (born between 1965 and 1980), and *generation Y* (born after 1980).[37] Each of these generations has been shaped by dramatically different world events and social trends, so it is not surprising

A culture's views on youth and aging affect how people communicate with one another.

Communication styles and expectations can vary widely among age groups, putting extra demands on teams that include workers of varying ages.

Broadly speaking, men tend to emphasize content in their messages, and woman tend to emphasize relationship maintenance.

that they often have different values, expectations, and communication habits. As with all other cultural matters, success in building bridges starts with understanding the gaps between the two sides.

Gender Differences

The perception of men and women in business varies from culture to culture, and these differences can affect communication efforts. In some cultures, men hold most or all positions of authority, and women are expected to play a more subservient role. Female executives who visit these cultures may not be taken seriously until they successfully handle challenges to their knowledge, capabilities, and patience.[38]

As more women enter the workforce and take on positions of increasing responsibility, enlightened company leaders are making a point to examine past assumptions and practices.[39] For instance, company cultures that have been dominated by men for years may have adopted communication habits that some women have difficulty relating to—such as the frequent use of sports metaphors or the acceptance of coarse language.

Whatever the culture, evidence suggests that men and women tend to have slightly different communication styles. Broadly speaking, men tend to emphasize content in their communication efforts, whereas women place a higher premium on relationship maintenance.[40] This difference can create friction when two parties in a conversation have different needs and expectations from the interchange. Again, these are broad generalizations that do not apply to every person in every situation, but keeping them in mind can help men and women overcome communication hurdles in the workplace.

Religious Differences

Religion is a dominant force in many cultures and the source of many differences between cultures.[41] The effort to accommodate employees' life interests on a broader scale has led a number of companies to address the issue of religion in the workplace. As one of the most personal and influential aspects of life, religion brings potential for controversy in a work setting. On the one hand, some employees feel they should be able to express their beliefs in the workplace and not be forced to "check their faith at the door" when they come to work. On the other hand, companies want to avoid situations in which openly expressed religious differences cause friction between employees or distract employees from their responsibilities. To help address such concerns, firms such as Ford, Intel, Texas Instruments, and American Airlines allow employees to form faith-based employee support groups as part of their diversity strategies. In contrast, Procter & Gamble is among the companies that don't allow organized religious activities at their facilities.[42]

U.S. law requires employers to accommodate employees' religious beliefs to a reasonable degree.

Religion in the workplace is a complex and contentious issue—and it's getting more so every year, at least as measured by a significant rise in the number of religious discrimination lawsuits.[43] Beyond accommodating individual beliefs to a reasonable degree, as required by U.S. law, companies occasionally need to resolve situations that pit one group of employees against another or against the company's policies.[44] As more companies work to establish inclusive workplaces, and as more employees seek to integrate religious convictions into their daily work, you can expect to see this issue being discussed at many companies in the coming years.

Ability Differences

Assistive technologies help employers create more inclusive workplaces and benefit from the contributions of people with physical or cognitive impairments.

Colleagues and customers with disabilities that affect communication represent an important aspect of the diversity picture. People whose hearing, vision, cognitive ability, or physical ability to operate computers is impaired can be at a significant disadvantage in today's workplace. As with other elements of diversity, success starts with respect for individuals and sensitivity to differences. Employers can also invest in a variety of *assistive technologies* that help people with disabilities perform activities that might otherwise be difficult or impossible. These technologies include devices and systems that help people communicate orally and visually, interact with computers and other equipment, and enjoy greater mobility in the workplace. For example, designers can emphasize *web accessibility*, taking steps to make websites more accessible to people whose vision is limited. Assistive technologies create a vital link for thousands of employees with disabilities, giving them opportunities to pursue a greater range of career paths and giving employers access to a broader base of talent. With the United States heading for a potentially serious shortage of workers in a few years, the economy will need all the workers who can make a contribution, and assistive technologies will be an important part of the solution.[45]

Adapting to Other Business Cultures

Culture is obviously a complex topic that requires a lifetime commitment to learning and growth. You'll find a variety of specific tips in "Improving Intercultural Communication Skills," starting on page 74, but here are four general guidelines that can help all business communicators improve their cultural competency:

- **Become aware of your own biases.** Successful intercultural communication requires more than just an understanding of the other party's culture; you need to understand your own culture and the way it shapes your communication habits.[46] For instance, knowing that you value independence and individual accomplishment will help you communicate more successfully in a culture that values consensus and group harmony.
- **Ignore the "Golden Rule."** You probably heard this growing up: "Treat people the way you want to be treated." The problem with the Golden Rule is that people *don't* always want to be treated the same way you want to be treated, particularly across cultural boundaries. The best approach: Treat people the way *they* want to be treated.
- **Exercise tolerance, flexibility, and respect.** As IBM's Ron Glover puts it, "To the greatest extent possible, we try to manage our people and our practices in ways that are respectful of the core principles of any given country or organization or culture."[47]
- **Practice patience and maintain a sense of humor.** Even the most committed and attuned business professionals can make mistakes in intercultural communication, so it is vital for all parties to be patient with one another. As business becomes ever more global, even the most tradition-bound cultures are learning to deal with outsiders more patiently and overlook occasional cultural blunders.[48] A sense of humor is a helpful asset as well, allowing people to move past awkward and embarrassing moments. When you make a mistake, simply apologize, if appropriate, ask the other person to explain the accepted way, and then move on.

An important step in understanding and adapting to other cultures is to recognize the influences that your own culture has on your communication habits.

Adapting to U.S. Business Culture

If you are a recent immigrant to the United States or grew up in a culture outside the U.S. mainstream, you can apply all the concepts and skills in this chapter to help adapt to U.S. business culture. Here are some key points to remember as you become accustomed to business communication in this country:[49]

The values espoused by U.S. culture include individualism, equality, and privacy.

- **Individualism.** In contrast to cultures that value group harmony and group success, U.S. culture generally expects individuals to succeed by their own efforts, and it rewards individual success. Even though teamwork is emphasized in many companies, competition between individuals is expected and even encouraged in many cases.
- **Equality.** Although the country's historical record on equality has not always been positive, and inequalities still exist, equality is considered a core American value. This applies to race, gender, social background, and even age. To a greater degree than people in many other cultures, Americans believe that every person should be given the opportunity to pursue whatever dreams and goals he or she has in life.
- **Privacy and personal space.** People in the Unites States are accustomed to a fair amount of privacy, and this

REAL-TIME UPDATES
Learn More

Overcoming culture shock

This entertaining five-part video series shares the experience of an Israeli journalist undergoing culture shock when coming to graduate school in New York City, and it offers help and encouragement to anyone living in a new culture for the first time. Go to **http://real-timeupdates.com/bct** and click on "Learn More." If you are using mybcommlab, you can access Real-Time Updates within each chapter or under Student Study Tools.

includes their "personal space" at work. For example, they expect you to knock before entering a closed office and to avoid asking questions about personal beliefs or activities until they get to know you well.

- **Time and schedules.** U.S. businesses value punctuality and the efficient use of time. For instance, meetings are expected to start and end at designated times.
- **Religion.** The United States does not have an official state religion. Many religions are practiced throughout the country, and people are expected to respect each other's beliefs.
- **Communication style.** Communication tends to be direct and focused on content and transactions, not relationships or group harmony.

These are generalizations, of course. Any nation of more than 300 million people will exhibit a wide variety of behaviors. However, following these guidelines will help you succeed in most business communication situations.

5 **LEARNING OBJECTIVE**

Identify steps you can take to improve your intercultural communication skills

IMPROVING INTERCULTURAL COMMUNICATION SKILLS

Communicating successfully between cultures requires a variety of skills (see Figure 3.5). You can improve your intercultural skills throughout your career by studying other cultures and languages, respecting preferences for communication styles, learning to write and speak

FIGURE 3.5   Components of Successful Intercultural Communication
Communicating in a diverse business environment is not always an easy task, but you can continue to improve your sensitivity and build your skills as you progress in your career.

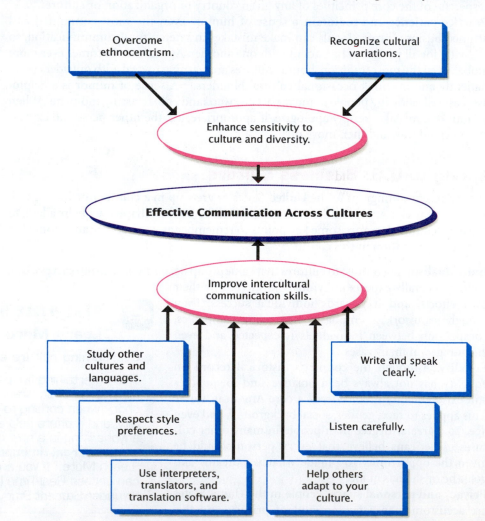

clearly, listening carefully, knowing when to use interpreters and translators, and helping others adapt to your culture.

Studying Other Cultures

Effectively adapting your communication efforts to another culture requires not only knowledge about the culture but also both the ability and the motivation to change your personal habits as needed.[50] Fortunately, you don't need to learn about the whole world all at once. Many companies appoint specialists for specific countries or regions, giving employees a chance to focus on just one culture at a time. Some firms also provide resources to help employees prepare for interaction with other cultures. On IBM's Global Workforce Diversity intranet site, for instance, employees can click on the "GoingGlobal" link to learn about customs in specific cultures.[51]

Even a small amount of research and practice will help you get through many business situations. In addition, most people respond positively to honest effort and good intentions, and many business associates will help you along if you show an interest in learning more about their cultures.

Numerous websites (such as www.culturecrossing.com) and books offer advice on traveling to and working in specific cultures. Also try to sample newspapers, magazines, and even the music and movies of another country. For instance, a movie can demonstrate nonverbal customs even if you don't grasp the language. (However, be careful not to rely solely on entertainment products. If people in other countries based their opinions of U.S. culture only on the silly teen flicks and violent action movies that the United States exports around the globe, what sort of impression do you imagine they'd get?) For some of the key issues to research before doing business in another country, refer to Table 3.1.

Successful intercultural communication can require the modification of personal communication habits.

Making an effort to learn about another person's culture is a sign of respect.

Studying Other Languages

Consider what it must be like to work at IBM, where the global workforce speaks more than 165 languages. Without the ability to communicate in more than one language, how could this diverse group of people ever conduct business? As commerce continues to become more globalized, the demand for multilingual communicators continues to grow as well. For instance, with so many U.S. and British companies outsourcing business functions to facilities in India, many Indians now view English skills as an important career asset. Conversely, China's continued growth as a manufacturing powerhouse is prompting many professionals in the United Sates and other countries to learn Mandarin, the official language in China.[52]

A number of U.S. companies are teaching their English-speaking employees a second language to facilitate communication with customers and co-workers. The Target retail chain is among those sponsoring basic Spanish classes for English-speaking supervisors of immigrant employees. Elsewhere around the country, enrollment is growing in specialized classes such as health-care Spanish and Spanish for professionals.[53] Informal coaching is helpful, too, such as having English- and Spanish-speaking employees teach each other a few business or technical terms every day.[54]

Even if your colleagues or customers in another country speak your language, it's worth the time and energy to learn common phrases in theirs. Learning the basics not only helps you get through everyday business and social situations but also demonstrates your commitment to the business relationship. After all, the other person probably spent years learning your language.

Finally, don't assume that people from two countries who speak the same language speak it the same way. The French spoken in Quebec and other parts of Canada is often noticeably different from the French spoken in France. Similarly, it's often said that the United States and the United Kingdom are two countries divided by a common language. For instance, *period* (punctuation), *elevator*, and *gasoline* in the United States are *full stop*, *lift*, and *petrol* in the United Kingdom.

English is the most prevalent language in international business, but don't assume that everyone understands it or speaks it the same way.

TABLE 3.1 Doing Business in Other Cultures

ACTION	DETAILS TO CONSIDER
Understand social customs	• How do people react to strangers? Are they friendly? Hostile? Reserved? • How do people greet each other? Should you bow? Nod? Shake hands? • How do you express appreciation for an invitation to lunch, dinner, or someone's home? Should you bring a gift? Send flowers? Write a thank-you note? • Are any phrases, facial expressions, or hand gestures considered rude? • How do you attract the attention of a waiter? Do you tip the waiter? • When is it rude to refuse an invitation? How do you refuse politely? • What topics may or may not be discussed in a social setting? In a business setting? • How do social customs dictate interaction between men and women? Between younger people and older people?
Learn about clothing and food preferences	• What occasions require special clothing? • What colors are associated with mourning? Love? Joy? • Are some types of clothing considered taboo for one gender or the other? • How many times a day do people eat? • How are hands or utensils used when eating? • Where is the seat of honor at a table?
Assess political patterns	• How stable is the political situation? • Does the political situation affect businesses in and out of the country? • Is it appropriate to talk politics in social or business situations?
Understand religious and social beliefs	• To which religious groups do people belong? • Which places, objects, actions, and events are sacred? • Do religious beliefs affect communication between men and women or between any other groups? • Is there a tolerance for minority religions? • How do religious holidays affect business and government activities? • Does religion require or prohibit eating specific foods? At specific times?
Learn about economic and business institutions	• Is the society homogeneous or heterogeneous? • What languages are spoken? • What are the primary resources and principal products? • Are businesses generally large? Family controlled? Government controlled? • What are the generally accepted working hours? • How do people view scheduled appointments? • Are people expected to socialize before conducting business?
Appraise the nature of ethics, values, and laws	• Is money or a gift expected in exchange for arranging business transactions? • Do people value competitiveness or cooperation? • What are the attitudes toward work? Toward money? • Is politeness more important than factual honesty?

Respecting Preferences for Communication Style

Communication style—including the level of directness, the degree of formality, preferences for written versus spoken communication, and other factors—varies widely from culture to culture. Knowing what your communication partners expect can help you adapt to their particular style. Once again, watching and learning are the best ways to improve your skills. However, you can infer some generalities by learning more about the culture. For instance, U.S. workers typically prefer an open and direct communication style; they find other styles frustrating or suspect. Directness is also valued in Sweden as a sign of efficiency; but, unlike with discussions in the United States, heated debates and confrontations are unusual. Italian, German, and French executives don't soften up colleagues with praise before they criticize—doing so seems manipulative to them. However, professionals from high-context cultures, such as Japan or China, tend to be less direct.[55] Finally, in general,

Business Communication 2.0

The Web 2.0 Way to Learn a New Language

Taking classes with a skilled teacher and getting real-life practice while living in another country are proven ways to learn a new language, but what if neither of these options is available to you? Thanks to the growth of social networking technology and other Web 2.0 communication tools, independent language learners now have a multitude of online learning options.

Palabea (www.palabea.net) is a great example of the possibilities of the Web 2.0 approach to learning. By adapting social networking concepts for the unique demands of language learning, this service offers numerous helpful features:

- **Online chat with other language learners.** No matter what language you're trying to learn, someone somewhere in the world speaks it—and is trying to learn your language. Palabea lets you connect and help each other with text, audio, or video chat.
- **Connections to native speakers in your local area.** Palabea can connect you with nearby native speakers of the language you're trying to learn.

- **User-generated content.** Palabea offers a growing collection of podcasts, video lectures, documents, and other learning tools, all contributed by members.
- **Virtual classrooms.** Just as online meeting systems let business colleagues collaborate in real time on reports and other documents, Palabea's virtual classrooms let members meet online to review and correct translations and other projects.

Palabea is just one of many online resources that can help language learners. The Free Language website (http://freelanguage.org) offers links to free resources for several dozen languages.

CAREER APPLICATIONS

1. How could a multinational company such as IBM benefit from the capabilities offered by Palabea and similar websites?
2. As a manager, would you be comfortable having employees use a free service such as Palabea before sending them on important overseas assignments? Why or why not?

---

business correspondence in other countries is often more formal than the style used by U.S. businesspeople (see Figure 3.6).

Writing Clearly

When sending written communication to businesspeople from another culture, familiarize yourself with their written communication preferences and adapt your approach, style, and tone to meet their expectations. Follow these recommendations:[56]

- **Use simple, clear language.** Use precise words that don't have the potential to confuse with multiple meanings. For instance, the word *right* has several dozen different meanings and usages, so look for a synonym that conveys the precise meaning you intend, such as *correct*, *appropriate*, *desirable*, *moral*, *authentic*, or *privilege*.[57]
- **Be brief.** Use simple sentences and short paragraphs, breaking information into smaller chunks that are easier for your reader to capture and translate. Remember that your messages need to be translated one word at a time.[58]
- **Use transitional elements.** Help readers follow your train of thought by using plenty of transitional words and phrases. Precede related points with expressions such as *in addition* and *first*, *second*, and *third*.
- **Address international correspondence properly.** Refer to Table A.1 through Table A.5 in Appendix A for an explanation of different address elements and salutations commonly used in certain foreign countries.
- **Cite numbers and dates carefully.** In the United States, 12-05-09 means December 5, 2009, but in many other countries, it means May 12, 2009. Dates in Japan and China are usually expressed with the year first, followed by the month and then the day; therefore, to write December 5, 2009, in Japan, write it as 2009-12-05. Similarly, 1.000 means one with three decimal places in the United States and Great Britain, but it means one thousand in many European countries.

---

6 LEARNING OBJECTIVE

List seven recommendations for writing clearly in multilanguage business environments

Clarity and simplicity are essential when writing to or speaking with people who don't share your native language.

FIGURE 3.6 Effective German Business Letter (Translated)

In Germany, business letters usually open with a reference to the business relationship and close with a compliment to the recipient. In this letter written by a supplier to a nearby retailer, you can see that the tone is more formal than would typically be used in the United States.

Literal translation of *Geschäftsführer* (Common English translation would be "managing director")

Refers to the ongoing business relationship

Uses language a bit more formally than U.S. letters do, such as "We give you a guarantee . . ."

Uses a complimentary close typical of German business letters (note the lack of punctuation)

Places the date to the right and below the address block (some German writers use the format 15 May 2009)

Shows concern for the audience

Ends with a compliment to the receiver

Does not include a title with the typed name

Furtwangen Handcrafts
Kussenhofstrasse 150
Furtwangen, Germany

Mister
Karl Wieland
Business Leader
Black Forest Gifts
Friedrichstrasse 98
70174 Stuttgart
GERMANY

15.5.2009

Very honorable Mister Wieland,

Because the tourist season will begin soon, we would like to take the opportunity to introduce our new line of hand-carved cuckoo clocks to you. Last year you were so friendly as to buy two dozen of our clocks. In recognition of our good business relationship, we now offer you the opportunity to select the new models before we offer this line to other businesses for purchase.

As you know, our artisans use only the best wood. According to time-honored patterns that are passed on from generation to generation, they carefully carve every detail by hand. Our clockworks are of superior quality, and we test every clock before it is painted and shipped. We give you a guarantee of five years on all Furtwangen Handcrafts clocks.

Enclosed you will find a copy of our newest brochure and an order form. To express our appreciation, we will take over the shipping costs if you order before 15 June 2009.

We continue to wish you a lot of success in your new Stuttgart location. We are convinced that you will continue to satisfy your regular clientele with your larger exhibition area and expanded stock and that you will also gain many new visitors.

With friendly greetings

Frederick Semper

Frederick Semper

- **Avoid slang, idiomatic phrases, and business jargon.** Everyday speech and writing are full of slang and **idiomatic phrases**, phrases that mean more than the sum of their literal parts. Many of these informal usages are so deeply ingrained, in fact, that you may not even be aware that you're using them. Examples from U.S. English include phrases such as "Off the top of my head" and "More bang for the buck." Your audience may have no idea what you're talking about when you use such phrases.

Humor does not "travel well" because it usually relies on intimate knowledge of a particular culture.

- **Avoid humor and other references to popular culture.** Jokes and references to popular entertainment usually rely on subtle cultural issues that might be completely unknown to your audience.

Although some of these differences may seem trivial, meeting the expectations of an international audience illustrates both knowledge of and respect for the other cultures (see Figure 3.7 and Figure 3.8).

FIGURE 3.7 Ineffective Intercultural Letter
This letter from a U.S. sales representative to a manager in France exhibits several intercultural mistakes, including the informal tone and use of U.S. slang. Compare this with the improved version in Figure 3.8.

La Cristallerie

Troy Halford, U.S. Sales Representative
163 Pico Boulevard
Los Angeles, CA 90032
Voice: (213) 975-8924
Fax: (213) 860-3489
halford@home.com

Uses the U.S. format for the date, rather than the international format typically used by French writers

April 7, 2009

Fails to follow French preferences for title and address format

Mr. Pierre Coll
Director of Accounting
La Cristallerie
22 Marne Blvd.
Beaune, France 21200

Uses reader's first name, which is much too informal for most French business correspondence

Dear Pierre:

I know you've had gorgeous spring weather, with sunny skies and balmy days. But here in the States, it's been a spring of another color. We've been hammered with storms, flooding, and even late snow. Travel over here has been a nightmare, which is why you'll find my expenses a bit elevated this month.

Wastes reader's time with unnecessarily dramatic and long description of weather problems

Uses slang and idioms throughout the message, creating the potential for confusion (e.g., hammered, bottlenecks, shut-eye, crunch, struck out, jam)

I realize that you've asked all the reps to reduce rather than increase our expenses, but there were extenuating circumstances this last month. All the bad weather we've been having has caused major bottlenecks, with flights canceled and people forced to sleep in the terminals wherever they could find a spot.

After being stuck in the Chicago airport for 18 hours straight, I was desperate for a hot shower and some shut-eye, so I decided to wait out the crunch in a hotel. I know that hotels near airports are expensive, but I struck out trying to book a cheaper room in town. The bottom line is I had to spend extra funds for a hotel at $877; meals, which came to some $175; $72 just in transportation from the terminal to the hotel, and extra phone calls totaling $38.

Buries specific information in awkward phrasing

Fails to provide a total of the extra expenses

I appreciate your understanding these unique circumstances. I was really in a jam.

Closes with a self-centered tone rather than trying to help the reader

Sincerely,

Troy Halford

Troy Halford
U.S. Sales Rep

Fails to alert the reader that other documents are enclosed

Speaking and Listening Carefully

Languages vary considerably in the significance of tone, pitch, speed, and volume. The English word *progress* can be a noun or a verb, depending on which syllable you accent. In Chinese, the meaning of the word *mà* changes, depending on the speaker's tone; it can mean *mother, pileup, horse,* or *scold.* Routine Arabic speech can sound excited or angry to an English-speaking U.S. listener.[59]

When talking with people whose native language is different from yours, remember that the processing of even everyday conversations can be difficult. For instance, speakers from the United States are notorious for stringing together multiple words into a single, mystifying pseudoword, such as turning "Did you eat yet?" into "Jeetyet?" The French language uses a concept known as *liaison,* in which one word is intentionally joined with the next. Without a lot

FIGURE 3.8 Effective Intercultural Letter
This version of the letter in Figure 3.7 follows French standards for correspondence and is also easier to read and to scan.

La Cristallerie

Troy Halford, U.S. Sales Representative
163 Pico Boulevard
Los Angeles, CA 90032
Voice: (213) 975-8924
Fax: (213) 860-3489
halford@home.com

7 April 2009

M. Pierre Coll
Commissaire aux Comptes
La Cristallerie
22, Boulevard de la Marne
21200 Beaune
FRANCE

Dear Monsieur Coll:

Enclosed are my expense statement and receipts for March 2009. My expenses are higher than usual this month because an unexpected snowstorm that closed the airport in Chicago left me stranded for nearly five days. I was able to get a hotel for the duration of the storm, although the only room available was far more expensive than my usual accommodations.

In addition to the regular expenses identified in the enclosed report, here are the additional expenditures caused by the weather delay:

Three nights at the Carlton-O'Hare Hotel	$ 877
Meals over four days	175
Transportation between hotel and terminal	72
Phone calls to reschedule meetings	38
Total extra expenses	**$1,162**

If you have any questions or need any more information about these expenses, please contact me.

Sincerely,

Troy Halford

Troy Halford
U.S. Sales Rep

Enclosures: Expense statement and receipts

Annotations:
- Follows French preferences for title and address format
- Addresses the reader more formally in the salutation, as is expected in most French correspondence
- Uses clear and conventional language that is easier for non-native English speakers
- Provides a total of the extra expenses
- Indicates that additional materials are enclosed with the letter
- Uses the international date format, which is preferred in French correspondence
- States the main idea directly and clearly in the opening, leaving no room for confusion about the letter's purpose
- Clearly identifies the extra expenses in a list that is easy to read
- Closes with an offer to help the reader with any further needs

Speaking clearly and getting plenty of feedback are two of the keys to successful intercultural conversations.

To listen more effectively in intercultural situations, accept what you hear without judgment and let people finish what they have to say.

of practice, new French speakers have a hard time telling when one word ends and the next one begins.

To be more effective in intercultural conversations, remember these tips: (1) Speak slowly and clearly; (2) don't rephrase until it's obviously necessary (immediately rephrasing something you've just said doubles the translation workload for the listener); (3) look for and ask for feedback to make sure your message is getting through; (4) don't talk down to the other person by overenunciating words or oversimplifying sentences; and (5) at the end of the conversation, double-check to make sure you and the listener agree on what has been said and decided.

As a listener, you'll need some practice to get a sense of vocal patterns. The key is simply to accept what you hear first, without jumping to conclusions about meaning or motivation. Let other people finish what they have to say. If you interrupt, you may miss something important. You'll also show a lack of respect. If you do not understand a comment, ask the person to repeat it. Any momentary awkwardness you might feel in asking for extra help is less important than the risk of unsuccessful communication.

Using Interpreters, Translators, and Translation Software

You may encounter business situations that require using an *interpreter* (for spoken communication) or a *translator* (for written communication). Interpreters and translators can be expensive, but skilled professionals provide invaluable assistance for communicating in other cultural contexts.[60] Keeping up with current language usage in a given country or culture is also critical in order to avoid embarrassing blunders. Landor Associates, a leading marketing agency, usually engages three native-language speakers to review translated materials to make sure the sense of the message is compatible with current usage and slang in a given country.[61] Some companies use *back-translation* to ensure accuracy. Once a translator encodes a message into another language, a different translator retranslates the same message into the original language. This back-translation is then compared with the original message to discover any errors or discrepancies.

Experienced international speakers, such as Dr. Eric Schmidt, Google's chairman and CEO, are careful to incorporate culture and language variations into their communication efforts.

The time and cost required for professional translation has encouraged the development of **machine translation**, any form of computerized intelligence used to translate one language to another. Dedicated software tools and online services such as WorldLingo (**www.worldlingo.com**) offer various forms of automated translation. Major search engines let you request translated versions of the websites you find. Although none of these tools can translate as well as human translators, they can be quite useful with individual words and short phrases, and they can often give you the overall gist of a message.[62]

For important business communication, use a professional interpreter (for oral communication) or translator (for written communication).

Helping Others Adapt to Your Culture

Whether a younger person is unaccustomed to the formalities of a large corporation or a colleague from another country is working on a team with you, look for opportunities to help people fit in and adapt their communication style. For example, if a non-native English speaker is making mistakes that could hurt his or her credibility, you can offer advice on the appropriate words and phrases to use. Most language learners truly appreciate this sort of assistance, as long as it is offered in a respectful manner. Moreover, chances are that while you're helping, you'll learn something about the other person's culture and language, too.

Help others adapt to your culture; doing so will create a more productive workplace and teach you about their cultures as well.

✔ **CHECKLIST**   **Improving Intercultural Communication Skills**

- Understand your own culture so that you can recognize its influences on your communication habits.
- Study other cultures so that you can appreciate cultural variations.
- Study the languages of people with whom you communicate, even if you can learn only a few basic words and phrases.
- Help nonnative speakers learn your language.
- Respect cultural preferences for communication style.

- Write clearly, using brief messages, simple language, generous transitions, and appropriate international conventions.
- Avoid slang, humor, and references to popular culture.
- Speak clearly and slowly, giving listeners time to translate your words.
- Ask for feedback to ensure successful communication.
- Listen carefully and ask speakers to repeat anything you don't understand.
- Use interpreters and translators for important messages.

Document Makeover

Improve This Letter

To practice correcting drafts of actual documents, visit the "Document Makeovers" section in either mybcommlab or the Companion Website for this text.

If mybcommlab is being used in your class, see your User Guide for specific instructions on how to access the content for this chapter. If you are accessing this feature through the Companion Website, click on "Document Makeovers" and then select Chapter 3. You will find a letter that contains problems and errors related to what you've learned in this chapter about developing effective intercultural communication skills. Use the Final Draft decision tool to create an improved version of this letter. Check the message for a communication style that keeps the message brief; does not become too familiar or informal; uses transitional elements appropriately; and avoids slang, idioms, jargon, and technical language.

You can also take steps to simplify the communication process. For example, oral communication in a second language is usually more difficult than written forms of communication, so instead of asking a foreign colleague to provide information in a conference call, you could set up an intranet site where the person can file a written report. Similarly, using instant messaging, e-mail, or blogging is often easier for colleagues with different native languages than participating in live conversations.

Whatever assistance you can provide will be greatly appreciated because smart businesspeople recognize the value of intercultural communication skills. Moreover, chances are that while you're helping others, you'll learn something about other cultures, too.

For a brief summary of ideas to improve intercultural communication in the workplace, see "Checklist: Improving Intercultural Communication Skills." For additional information on communicating in a world of diversity, visit http://real-timeupdates.com/bct and click on Chapter 3.

Communication Challenges at IBM

Ron Glover is responsible for overall diversity planning and strategy at IBM, but every manager throughout the company is expected to foster a climate of inclusion and support for employees of every cultural background. As a team leader in one of IBM's software development labs, you're learning to exercise sound business judgment and use good listening skills to help resolve situations that arise within your diverse group of employees. How would you address these challenges?

Individual Challenge: Vasily Pevsner, a Russian immigrant, has worked in the department for five years. He works well alone, but he resists working with other employees, even in team settings where collaboration is expected. Given the importance that you place on teamwork, how should you handle the situation? List several alternatives for addressing this dilemma, identify which one you would choose, and explain why you would choose this one.

Team Challenge: Your employees are breaking into ethnically based cliques. Members of ethnic groups eat together, socialize together, and often chat in their native languages while they work. You appreciate how these groups give their members a sense of community, but you worry that these informal communication channels are alienating nonmembers and fragmenting the flow of information. How can you encourage a stronger sense of community and teamwork across your department? Brainstorm at least three steps you can take to encourage better cross-cultural communication in your group.

SUMMARY OF LEARNING OBJECTIVES

1 **Discuss the opportunities and challenges of intercultural communication.** The global marketplace spans natural boundaries and national borders, allowing worldwide competition between businesses of all sizes. Therefore, today's businesspeople are likely to communicate across international borders with people who live in different cultures. Moreover, even domestic workforces are becoming more and more diverse, with employees having different national, religious, and ethnic backgrounds. In this environment, companies can benefit from a broad range of viewpoints and ideas, get a good understanding of diverse markets, and recruit workers from the broadest possible pool of talent. However, intercultural communication presents challenges as well, including motivating diverse employees to cooperate and to work together in teams as well as understanding enough about how culture affects language to prevent miscommunication.

2 **Define** *culture*, **and explain how culture is learned.** Culture is a shared system of symbols, beliefs, attitudes, values, expectations, and norms for behavior. Culture is

learned by listening to advice from other members of a society and by observing their behaviors. This double-edged method uses direct and indirect learning to ensure that culture is passed from person to person and from generation to generation.

3 **Define *ethnocentrism* and *stereotyping*, and give three suggestions for overcoming these limiting mindsets.** Ethnocentrism is the tendency to judge other groups according to the standards, behaviors, and customs of one's own group. Stereotyping is assigning a wide range of generalized attributes to individuals on the basis of their membership in a particular culture or social group, without considering an individual's unique characteristics. To overcome ethnocentrism and stereotyping, follow three suggestions: (1) Avoid assumptions, (2) avoid judgments, and (3) acknowledge distinctions.

4 **Explain the importance of recognizing cultural variations, and list eight categories of cultural differences.** People from different cultures encode and decode messages differently, increasing the chances of misunderstanding. By recognizing and accommodating cultural differences, we avoid automatically assuming that everyone's thoughts and actions are just like ours. Begin by focusing on eight categories of differences: contextual differences (the degree to which a culture relies on verbal or nonverbal actions to convey meaning), legal and ethical differences (the degree to which laws and ethics are regarded and obeyed), social differences (how members value work and success, recognize status, define manners, and think about time), nonverbal differences (differing attitudes toward greetings, personal space, touching, facial expression, eye contact, posture, and formality), age differences (how members think about youth, seniority, and longevity), gender differences (how men and women communicate), religious differences (how beliefs affect workplace relationships), and ability differences (inclusive strategies that enable people with disabilities to more fully communicate with the rest of the workforce).

5 **Identify the steps you can take to improve your intercultural communication skills.** Communicating successfully between cultures requires a variety of skills, all of which you can continue to improve throughout your career. Make your intercultural communication effective by studying other cultures; studying other languages; respecting your audience's preferences for communication style; writing as clearly as possible; speaking as clearly as you can; listening carefully; using interpreters, translators, and translation software when necessary; and helping others adapt to your own culture.

6 **List seven recommendations for writing clearly in multilanguage business environments.** It's important to take extra care with your writing, adapting your approach, style, and tone to meet audience expectations. To write effectively to multilingual audiences, follow these recommendations: (1) Use simple, clear language; (2) be brief; (3) use transitional elements; (4) address international correspondence properly; (5) cite numbers and dates carefully; (6) avoid slang, idiomatic phrases, and unfamiliar jargon; and (7) minimize or avoid humor and references to popular culture.

PEARSON
mybcommlab™

Log on to **www.mybcommlab.com** to access the following study and assessment aids associated with this chapter:

- Video applications
- Real-Time Updates
- Peer review activity
- Quick Learning Guides

- Pre/post test
- Personalized study plan
- Model documents
- Sample presentations

If you are not using mybcommlab, you can access the Real-Time Updates and Quick Learning Guides through **http://real-timeupdates.com/bct**. The Quick Learning Guide (located under "Learn More" on the website) hits all the high points of this chapter in just two pages. This guide, especially prepared by the authors, will help you study for exams or review important concepts whenever you need a quick refresher.

Test Your Knowledge

1. How have market globalization and cultural diversity contributed to the increased importance of intercultural communication?
2. What are the potential advantages of a diverse workforce?
3. How do high-context cultures differ from low-context cultures?
4. In addition to contextual differences, what other categories of cultural differences exist?
5. What is ethnocentrism, and how can it be overcome in communication?

6. What four principles apply to ethical intercultural communication?
7. Why is it important to understand your own culture when attempting to communicate with people from other cultures?
8. What are some ways to improve speaking and listening skills when communicating with people of other cultures?
9. What are the risks of using computerized translation when you need to read a document written in another language?
10. What steps can you take to help someone from another culture adapt to your culture?

Apply Your Knowledge

1. What are some of the intercultural differences that managers of a U.S.-based firm might encounter during a series of business meetings with a China-based company whose managers speak English fairly well?
2. What are some of the intercultural communication issues to consider when deciding whether to accept a job in an overseas branch of a U.S. company? How about a job in the United States with a local branch of a foreign-owned firm? Explain.
3. How do you think company managers from a country that has a relatively homogeneous culture might react when they do business with the culturally diverse staff of a company based in a less homogeneous country? Explain your answer.
4. Make a list of the top five priorities in your life (for example, fame, wealth, family, spirituality, peace of mind, individuality, artistic expression). Compare your list with the priorities that appear to be valued in the culture in which you are currently living. (You can be as broad or as narrow as you like in defining *culture* for this exercise, such as overall U.S. culture or culture in your college or university.) Do your personal priorities align with the culture's priorities? If not, how might this disparity affect your communication with other members of the culture?
5. **Ethical Choices** Your office in Turkey desperately needs the supplies that have been sitting in Turkish customs for a month. Should you bribe a customs official to speed up delivery? Explain your decision.

Practice Your Knowledge

Message for Analysis

Your boss wants to send a brief e-mail message, welcoming employees recently transferred to your department from the company's Hong Kong branch. They all speak English, but your boss asks you to review his message for clarity. What would you suggest your boss change in the following e-mail message—and why? Would you consider this message to be audience centered? Why or why not?

> I wanted to welcome you ASAP to our little family here in the States. It's high time we shook hands in person and not just across the sea. I'm pleased as punch about getting to know you all, and I for one will do my level best to sell you on America.

Exercises

Active links for all websites in this chapter can be found online. If mybcommlab is being used in your class, see your User Guide for instructions on accessing the content for this chapter. Otherwise, visit **www.pearsonhighered.com/bovee**, locate *Business Communication Today*, Tenth Edition, click the Companion Website link, select Chapter 3, and then click on "Featured Websites." Please note that links to sites that become inactive after publication of the book will be removed from the Featured Websites section.

3.1 **Intercultural Sensitivity: Recognizing Variations** You represent a Canadian toy company that's negotiating to buy miniature truck wheels from a manufacturer in Osaka, Japan. In your first meeting, you explain that your company expects to control the design of the wheels as well as the materials that are used to make them. The manufacturer's representative looks down and says softly, "Perhaps that will be difficult." You press for agreement, and to emphasize your willingness to buy, you show the prepared contract you've brought with you. However, the manufacturer seems increasingly vague and uninterested. What cultural differences may be interfering with effective communication in this situation? Explain.

3.2 **Ethical Choices** A U.S. manager wants to ship machine parts to a West African country, but a government official there expects a special payment before allowing the shipment into the country. How can the two sides resolve their different approaches without violating U.S. rules against bribing foreign officials? On the basis of the information presented in Chapter 1, would you consider this situation an ethical dilemma or an ethical lapse? Please explain.

3.3 **Teamwork** Working with two other students, prepare a list of 10 examples of slang (in your own language) that might be misinterpreted or misunderstood during a business conversation with someone from another culture. Next to each example, suggest other words you might use to convey the same message. Do the alternatives mean *exactly* the same as the original slang or idiom?

3.4 **Intercultural Communication: Studying Cultures** Choose a specific country, such as India, Portugal, Bolivia, Thailand, or Nigeria, with which you are not familiar. Research the culture and write a brief summary of what a U.S. manager would need to know about concepts of personal space and rules of social behavior in order to conduct business successfully in that country.

3.5 **Multicultural Workforce: Bridging Differences** Differences in gender, age, and physical abilities contribute to the diversity of today's workforce. Working with a classmate, role-play a conversation in which
   a. a woman is being interviewed for a job by a male personnel manager.
   b. an older person is being interviewed for a job by a younger personnel manager.

c. an employee who is a native speaker of English is being interviewed for a job by a hiring manager who is a recent immigrant with relatively poor English skills.

How did differences between the applicant and the interviewer shape the communication? What can you do to improve communication in such situations?

3.6 Intercultural Sensitivity: Understanding Attitudes As the director of marketing for a telecommunications firm based in Germany, you're negotiating with an official in Guangzhou, China, who's in charge of selecting a new telephone system for the city. You insist that the specifications be spelled out in the contract. However, your Chinese counterpart seems to have little interest in technical and financial details. What can you do or say to break this intercultural deadlock and obtain the contract so that both parties are comfortable?

3.7 Cultural Variations: Ability Differences You are a new manager at K & J Brick, a masonry products company that is now run by the two sons of the man who founded it 50 years ago. For years, the co-owners have invited the management team to a wilderness lodge for a combination of outdoor sports and annual business planning meetings. You don't want to miss the event, but you know that the outdoor activities weren't designed for someone with your physical impairments. Draft a short memo to the rest of the management team, suggesting changes to the annual event that will allow all managers to participate.

3.8 Culture and Time: Dealing with Variations When a company knows that a scheduled delivery time given by an overseas firm is likely to be flexible, managers may buy in larger quantities or may order more often to avoid running out of product before the next delivery. Identify three other management decisions that may be influenced by differing cultural concepts of time and make notes for a short (two-minute) presentation to your class.

3.9 Intercultural Communication: Using Interpreters Imagine that you're the lead negotiator for a company that's trying to buy a factory in Prague, the capital of the Czech Republic. Although you haven't spent much time in the country in the past decade, your parents grew up near Prague, so you understand and speak the language fairly well. However, you wonder about the advantages and disadvantages of using an interpreter anyway. For example, you may have more time to think if you wait for an intermediary to translate the other side's position. Decide whether to hire an interpreter and write a brief e-mail message (two or three paragraphs) explaining your decision.

3.10 Internet: Translation Software Explore the powers and limitations of computer translation at Babel Fish, http://babelfish.yahoo.com. Click on "Translate" and enter a sentence such as "We are enclosing a purchase order for four dozen computer monitors." Select "English to Spanish" and click to complete the translation. Once

you've read the Spanish version, cut and paste it into the "text for translation" box, select "Spanish to English," and click to translate. Try translating the same English sentence into German, French, or Italian and then back into English. How do the results of each translation differ? What are the implications for the use of automated translation services and back-translation? How could you use this website to sharpen your intercultural communication skills? Summarize your findings in a brief report.

3.11 Intercultural Communication: Improving Skills You've been assigned to host a group of Swedish college students who are visiting your college for the next two weeks. They've all studied English, but this is their first trip to your area. Make a list of at least eight slang terms and idioms they are likely to hear on campus. How will you explain each phrase? When speaking with the Swedish students, what word or words might you substitute for each slang term or idiom?

3.12 Intercultural Communication: Podcasting Your company was one of the first to use podcasting (see page 191 for more information) as a business communication tool. Executives frequently record messages (such as monthly sales summaries) and post them on the company's intranet site; employees from the 14 offices in Europe, Asia, and North America then download the files to their music players and listen to the messages while riding the train to work, eating lunch at their desks, and so on. Your boss asks you to draft the opening statement for a podcast that will announce a revenue drop caused by intensive competitive pressure. She reviews your script and hands it back with a gentle explanation that it needs to be revised for international listeners. Improve the following statement in as many ways as you can:

> Howdy, comrades. Shouldn't surprise anyone that we took a beating this year, given the insane pricing moves our knucklehead competitors have been making. I mean, how those clowns can keep turning a profit is beyond me, what with steel costs still going through the roof and labor costs heating up—even in countries where everybody goes to find cheap labor—and hazardous waste disposal regs adding to operating costs, too.

Expand Your Knowledge

Exploring the Best of the Web

Cultural Savvy for Competitive Advantage

www.executiveplanet.com

Want to be more competitive when doing business across borders? Executive Planet offers quick introductions to expected business practices in a number of countries, from setting up appointments to giving gifts to negotiating deals. Visit www.executiveplanet.com and browse the country reports to answer the following questions.

1. What sort of clothes should you pack for a business trip to Mexico that will include both meetings and social events?
2. You've been trying to sell your products to a Saudi Arabian company whose executives treat you to an extravagant evening of dining and entertainment. Can you take this as a positive sign that they're likely to buy from you?
3. You collect antique clocks as a hobby, and you plan to give one of your favorites to the president of a Chinese company you plan to visit. Would such a gift likely help or hurt your relationship with this person?

Sharpening Your Career Skills Online

Bovée and Thill's Business Communication Web Search, at http://businesscommunicationblog.com/websearch, is a unique research tool designed specifically for business communication research. Use the Web Search function to find a website, video, podcast, or PowerPoint presentation that offers advice on communicating with business contacts in another country or culture. Write a brief e-mail message to your instructor, describing the item that you found and summarizing the career skills information you learned from it.

Testing Your Understanding—Unit I

Business Communication Today
Chapter 3: Communicating in a World of Diversity

Pages 4–10
CHECKING YOUR COMPREHENSION

Choose the best answer for each of the following questions.

1. When Americans travel for business, it is necessary that they
   a. explain to their business counterparts that they are ignorant of their culture.
   b. have a strong feeling of ethnocentrism.
   c. learn the culture of the country that they are visiting.
   d. carefully stereotype their business counterparts.

2. According to Figure 3.2, what two cultures would have the hardest time communicating in a business setting?
   a. French and Spanish
   b. Scandinavian and Greek
   c. American and Italian
   d. German and Arab

3. Which of the following cultural contexts affect business communication in high-context companies?
   a. Position and status are valued much more than competence.
   b. Workers rely on detailed background information.
   c. Meetings have fixed agendas and plenty of advance notice.
   d. Information is highly centralized and controlled.

4. According to the text, which of the following is considered a cultural group?
   a. professional group
   b. religious group
   c. country of origin
   d. all of the above

Identify the following statements as true or false.

5. It is possible to learn information regarding other cultures both directly and indirectly.

6. People in high-context cultures explicitly share their expectations verbally.

7. The best approach when communicating with people in other cultures is to treat others the way you want to be treated.

Answer each of the following questions.

8. Explain what is meant by the fact that cultures are both coherent and complete.

9. List the three contextual differences that cultures use to approach situations.

10. Identify the competitive advantages of a diverse workforce.

11. Explain why the word "minority" has a different connotation today than it did in the past.

Define each term as it is used in the chapter.

12. cultural pluralism

13. spectrum

14. xenophobia

15. constitute

16. essence

Discussion and Critical Thinking Questions

1. Discuss how stereotypes that you have heard others make about different cultures could be a detriment to working with people of these cultures in the workplace.

2. Based on the strategies IBM utilizes to manage its diverse workforce, what suggestions do you have for smaller companies with global workforces?

3. To what category does the United States belong in terms of cultural context? What does this mean in terms of decision making, problem solving, and negotiating?

Pages 11–18
CHECKING YOUR COMPREHENSION

1. Which of the following statements is NOT true regarding older employees in Asia?
   a. They hold the most powerful positions.
   b. Younger employees often challenge their knowledge in public.
   c. Decision-making authority is often given to them.
   d. The notion of "saving face" is strong regarding the older employees.

2. The authors suggest that the main reason Wal-Mart was not successful in the German market was because
   a. the retailer was not able to overcome informal and formal cultural differences.
   b. the workers in Wal-Mart were against smiling when welcoming customers.
   c. the merchandise being sold could be manufactured cheaper in Germany.
   d. they had opened too many stores at once throughout the country.

3. According to Figure 3.3, what three countries show an inability to compete in global markets?
   a. The Netherlands, Switzerland, and Singapore
   b. Slovenia, the United States, and New Zealand
   c. Russia, Venezuela, and Argentina
   d. South Africa, Mexico, and Brazil

4. The text suggests that you should do all of the following to improve intercultural communication skills in another culture EXCEPT:
   a. conduct research on the culture.
   b. apologize for making cultural mistakes.
   c. become fluent in the language.
   d. read newspapers and magazines from the country.

Identify the following statements as true or false.

5. Non-verbal communication is a reliable guide for communicators in other cultures to determine the meaning of a message.

6. There is a law that prohibits companies from banning their employees from forming organized religious activities at their facilities.

7. Employees from the same country may vary in cultural values due to their age differences.

Answer each of the following questions.

8. List the four basic principles that are necessary to use when making ethical choices across cultures.

9. Identify the generalization noted in the text regarding men's and women's communication styles.

10. Explain what is meant by the term "assistive technologies" and how they are useful to the workplace.

11. Explain why it is important to ignore "The Golden Rule" when dealing with other cultures.

Define each term as it is used in the chapter.

12. cornerstone

13. assumptions

14. coarse

15. contentious

Discussion and Critical Thinking Questions

1. What advice regarding the business culture in the United States would you give a foreign company that was planning to move its offices from Japan to this country?

2. Discuss the challenges older workers face in the United States. How are these challenges different from the ones older workers face in other countries mentioned in the text?

3. Discuss the different problems that may arise that would not allow your company to follow the advice of IBM's Ron Glover: "To the greatest extent possible, we try to manage our people and our practices in ways that are respectful of the core principles of any given country or organization or culture."

Pages 18–28
CHECKING YOUR COMPREHENSION

1. What inference can be made regarding back translation?
   a. Landon Associates is a premier company because they use back translation.
   b. Back translation is more cost effective than machine translation.
   c. Communication using back translation reduces message inconsistencies.
   d. Interpreters often use back translation to decrease communication errors.

2. When addressing a letter to a company in Japan, the date would be expressed as
   a. October 14, 2009.
   b. 2009-10-14.
   c. 10-14-09.
   d. 2009-14-10.

3. Which of the following facts is not given in the text regarding writing clearly in multilanguage business environments?
   a. Use longer sentences to continually reiterate your thoughts and ideas.
   b. Use the address elements and salutations used by your business associate's culture.
   c. Eliminate the use of such phrases as "a day late and a dollar short."
   d. Increase the use of transitional words to help your reader follow your thoughts.

Identify the following statements as true or false.

4. It is important not to rely on machine translations for important messages.

5. Reading and writing are harder in a second language than speaking and listening.

6. Vocal patterns are consistent between cultures.

7. It is not necessary to speak the language of the country in which you are doing business.

Answer each of the following questions.

8. Explain why the author of the text included both Figure 3.7 and Figure 3.8.

9. According to the text, what are the two main keys to successful intercultural conversations?

10. Explain the differences between an interpreter and a translator.

Define each term as it is used in the chapter.

11. idiomatic phrases

12. liaison

13. blunder

14. cliques

Discussion and Critical Thinking Questions

1. What is the greatest challenge when learning conventional English in the United States? What does this indicate about the difficulties in learning to converse in other languages?

2. Discuss the implications of sending a letter to a colleague in another country that does not follow the noted suggestions included in the chapter.

3. Discuss why you feel multilanguage communication has recently become a topic that is taught to both students in school and employees of business.

Chapter Review
END OF CHAPTER ANALYSIS

1. The author employs all of the following techniques for making the material easier to read and understand EXCEPT:
   a. boldface.
   b. marginal notations.
   c. graphics.
   d. chapter outline.

2. After reading this chapter, you should be able to answer all of the following questions EXCEPT:
   a. What are some strategies for studying other cultures?
   b. What is the correct way to respect other cultures' communication styles?
   c. What are some solutions to overcoming ethnocentrism and stereotyping?
   d. What is the correct way to give and receive constructive feedback?

3. What is the overall purpose of this chapter?
   a. To understand the challenges and potential opportunities of intercultural communication.
   b. To provide an analysis of the ethical and legal issues of doing business globally.
   c. To understand the importance of customizing verbal and written correspondence for international companies.
   d. To learn how to help others adapt to different cultures.

Group Project

1. Choose another culture and use the questions in Table 3.1 to research the proper protocol to do business in that country. What details does your group feel would be the most important to follow in regards to respecting the culture and communicating with the people?

Journal Ideas

1. Using the information and guidelines in the chapter regarding clear multilanguage correspondence, write a letter to a colleague in a different culture expressing interest in selling their product in the United States.

2. Depending on your future career, what specific factors noted in the chapter do you think you will have to face at work? What are some solutions to alleviate the problems you may face in your specific career regarding multilanguage and cross-culture communication?

Organizing Information

It is important to be able to recognize and organize main ideas, supporting details, and examples in text. Use the eight categories of cultural differences (which begins on p. 8) to create a graphic organizer. The first one, contextual differences, is done for you.

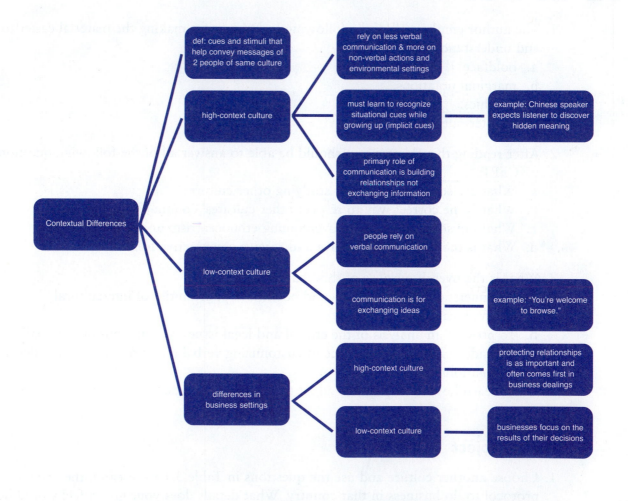

Unit II: Allied Health

From

Berman, Snyder, Kozier, and Erb

Fundamentals of Nursing:
Concepts, Process, and Practice

Eighth Edition

Chapter 45:
Sleep

An Introduction to Allied Health

Allied health pertains to the study needed for professional healthcare providers who are directly involved in the delivery of healthcare but are not physicians or dentists. They collaborate with physicians and other members of the healthcare team to deliver high-quality patient care services for the identification, prevention, and treatment of diseases, disabilities, and disorders. This course of study is highly specialized, depending on what specific career a person is training for since there are many educational standards for each discipline. Allied healthcare providers partake in formal education and clinical training.

Allied health professionals are expert in a multitude of therapeutic, diagnostic, and preventive health interventions and function in several diverse settings, including disease prevention and control, dietary and nutritional services, mental and physical health promotion, rehabilitation, and health systems management. Allied heath professions comprise more than 60 percent of the entire healthcare work force, and span over 200 distinct disciplinary groups. In the United States alone, approximately two million allied health professionals are employed.

Strategies for Reading Allied Health Texts

When reading an allied health textbook, it is necessary to define all unknown terms and pay close attention to illustrations and figures. Since there will be many facts and details, it is often necessary to note the reasons and explanations that support the relationships of specific concepts. Much of the material learned when studying this discipline will focus on the completion of tasks such as taking a patient's blood pressure or administering occupational therapy, which will involve the learning of different processes. To learn these procedures, it would be beneficial to use visual aids such as concept maps or flow charts.

Sleep

LEARNING OUTCOMES

After completing this chapter, you will be able to:

1. Explain the functions and the physiology of sleep.

2. Identify the characteristics of the sleep states: NREM and REM sleep.

3. Describe variations in sleep patterns throughout the life span.

4. Identify factors that affect normal sleep.

5. Describe common sleep disorders.

6. Identify the components of a sleep pattern assessment.

7. Develop nursing diagnoses, outcomes, and nursing interventions related to sleep problems.

8. Describe interventions that promote normal sleep.

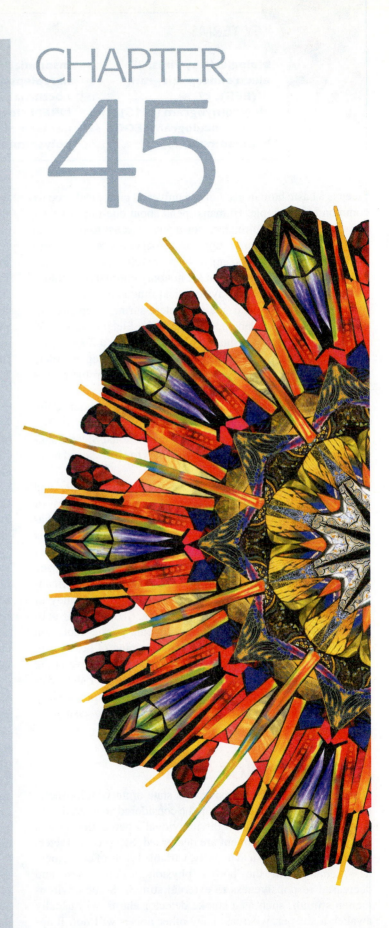

Sleep is a basic human need; it is a universal biological process common to all people. Humans spend about one-third of their lives asleep. We require sleep for many reasons: to cope with daily stresses, to prevent fatigue, to conserve energy, to restore the mind and body, and to enjoy life more fully. Sleep enhances daytime functioning. It is vital for not only optimal psychological functioning but also physiological functioning as the rate of healing of damaged tissue is greatest during sleep (Robinson, Weitzel, & Henderson, 2005, p. 263). Sleep is an important factor in a person's quality of life. And yet, a 2006 report from the Institute of Medicine (IOM) states that sleep disorders and sleep deprivation is an unmet public health problem. It is estimated that 50 million to 70 million Americans suffer from a chronic disorder of sleep and wakefulness that hinders daily functioning and adversely affects health (IOM, 2006, p. 24). Numerous *Sleep in America* polls by the National Sleep Foundation reflect that Americans, from infants to elders, need more sleep.

Furthermore, many members of the general public and health professionals are unaware of the consequences of chronic sleep loss (e.g., increased risk of hypertension, diabetes, obesity, depression, heart attack, and stroke). Almost 20% of all serious car crash injuries are associated with driver sleepiness (IOM, 2006, p. 25). As a result, the IOM report made a number of recommendations, including: (a) increasing financial investments in interdisciplinary **somnology** (the study of sleep) and sleep medicine research training; (b) increasing public awareness by establishing a multimedia public education campaign; (c) increasing education and training of health care professionals in somnology and sleep medicine; (d) developing new technologies for the diagnosis and treatment of sleep disorders; and (e) monitoring the American population's sleep patterns and the prevalence and health outcomes associated with sleep disorders (IOM, 2006).

PHYSIOLOGY OF SLEEP

Historically, sleep was considered a state of unconsciousness. More recently, **sleep** has come to be considered an altered state of consciousness in which the individual's perception of and reaction to the environment are decreased. Sleep is characterized by minimal physical activity, variable levels of consciousness, changes in the body's physiologic processes, and decreased responsiveness to external stimuli. Some environmental stimuli, such as a smoke detector alarm, will usually awaken a sleeper, whereas many other noises will not. It appears that individuals respond to meaningful stimuli while sleeping and selectively disregard nonmeaningful stimuli. For example, a mother may respond to her baby's crying but not to the crying of another baby.

The cyclic nature of sleep is thought to be controlled by centers located in the lower part of the brain. Neurons within the reticular formation, located in the brain stem, integrate sensory information from the peripheral nervous system and relay the information to the cerebral cortex (see Anatomy & Physiology Review). The upper part of the reticular formation consists of a network of ascending nerve fibers called the reticular activating system (RAS), which is involved with the sleep–wake cycle. An intact cerebral cortex and reticular formation are necessary for the regulation of sleep and waking states.

Neurotransmitters, located within neurons in the brain, affect the sleep–wake cycles. For example, serotonin is thought to lessen the response to sensory stimulation and gamma-aminobutyric acid (GABA) to shut off the activity in the neurons of the reticular activating system. Another key factor to sleep is exposure to darkness. Darkness and preparing for sleep causes a decrease in stimulation of the RAS. During this time, the pineal gland in the brain begins to actively secrete the natural hormone melatonin, and the person feels less alert. During sleep, the growth hormone is secreted and cortisol is inhibited.

With the beginning of daylight, melatonin is at its lowest level in the body and the stimulating hormone, cortisol, is at its highest. Wakefulness is also associated with high levels of acetylcholine, dopamine, and noradrenaline. Acetylcholine is released in the reticular formation, dopamine in the midbrain, and noradrenaline in the pons. These neurotransmitters are localized within the reticular formation and influence cerebral cortical arousal.

Circadian Rhythms

Biological rhythms exist in plants, animals, and humans. In humans, these are controlled from within the body and synchronized with environmental factors, such as light and darkness. The most familiar biological rhythm is the circadian rhythm. The term *circadian* is from the Latin *circa dies,* meaning "about a day." Although sleep and waking cycles are the best known of the circadian rhythms, body temperature, blood pressure, and many other physiologic functions also follow a circadian pattern.

Sleep is a complex biological rhythm. When a person's biological clock coincides with the sleep–wake cycles, the person is said to be in circadian synchronization; that is, the person is awake when the body temperature is highest, and asleep when the body temperature is lowest. Circadian regularity begins to develop by the sixth week of life, and by 3 to 6 months most infants have a regular sleep–wake cycle.

ANATOMY & PHYSIOLOGY REVIEW · Reticular Activating System

Nerve impulses from the senses reach the reticular activating system (RAS), which is in the reticular formation (located in the brain stem) with projections to the hypothalamus and cerebral cortex. The nerve fibers in the RAS relay impulses to the cerebral cortex for perception by the person.

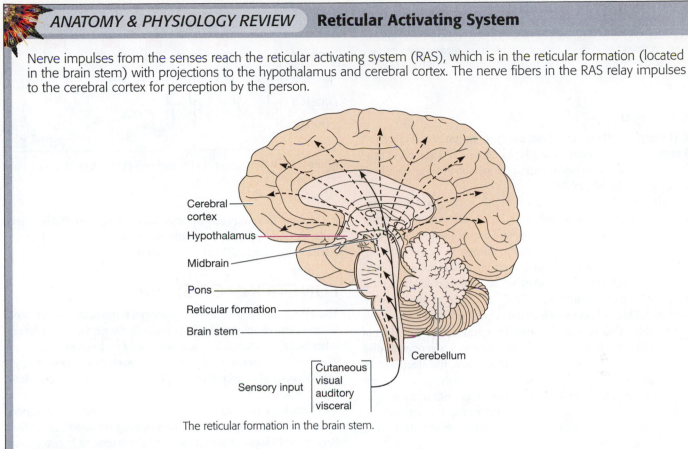

Cerebral cortex
Hypothalamus
Midbrain
Pons
Reticular formation
Brain stem
Cerebellum
Sensory input
Cutaneous
visual
auditory
visceral

The reticular formation in the brain stem.

QUESTIONS

1. How would you describe activity of the RAS in preparation for and during sleep?
2. What happens physiologically when your alarm clock wakes you in the morning?
3. What areas of the brain are affected by head trauma or stroke and affect an individual's level of alertness?

Types of Sleep

Sleep architecture refers to the basic organization of normal sleep. There are two types of sleep: **NREM** (non-rapid-eye-movement) **sleep** and **REM** (rapid-eye-movement) **sleep.** During sleep, NREM and REM sleep alternate in cycles. Irregular cycling and/or absent sleep stages are associated with sleep disorders (IOM, 2006, p. 42).

NREM Sleep

NREM sleep occurs when activity in the RAS is inhibited. About 75% to 80% of sleep during a night is NREM sleep. NREM sleep is divided into four stages, each associated with distinct brain activity and physiology. Stage I is the stage of very light sleep and lasts only a few minutes. During this stage, the person feels drowsy and relaxed, the eyes roll from side to side, and the heart and respiratory rates drop slightly. The sleeper can be readily awakened and may deny that he or she was sleeping.

Stage II is the stage of light sleep during which body processes continue to slow down. The eyes are generally still, the heart and respiratory rates decrease slightly, and body temperature falls. Stage II lasts only about 10 to 15 minutes but constitutes 44% to 55% of total sleep (IOM, 2006, p. 44). An individual in stage II requires more intense stimuli than in stage I to awaken.

Stages III and IV are the deepest stages of sleep, differing only in the percentage of delta waves recorded during a 30-second period. During *deep sleep* or *delta sleep,* the sleeper's heart and respiratory rates drop 20% to 30% below those exhibited during waking hours. The sleeper is difficult to arouse. The person is not disturbed by sensory stimuli, the skeletal muscles are very relaxed, reflexes are diminished, and snoring is most likely to occur. Even swallowing and saliva production are reduced during delta sleep (Orr, 2000). These stages are essential for restoring energy and releasing important growth hormones. See Box 45–1.

BOX 45–1 Physiologic Changes during NREM Sleep

- Arterial blood pressure falls.
- Pulse rate decreases.
- Peripheral blood vessels dilate.
- Cardiac output decreases.
- Skeletal muscles relax.
- Basal metabolic rate decreases 10% to 30%.
- Growth hormone levels peak.
- Intracranial pressure decreases.

REM Sleep

REM sleep usually recurs about every 90 minutes and lasts 5 to 30 minutes. Most dreams take place during REM sleep but usually will not be remembered unless the person arouses briefly at the end of the REM period.

During REM sleep, the brain is highly active, and brain metabolism may increase as much as 20%. For example, during REM sleep, levels of acetylcholine and dopamine increase, with the highest levels of acetylcholine release occurring during REM sleep. Since both of these neurotransmitters are associated with cortical activation, it makes sense that their levels would be high during dreaming sleep. This type of sleep is also called paradoxical sleep because electroencephalogram (EEG) activity resembles that of wakefulness. Distinctive eye movements occur, voluntary muscle tone is dramatically decreased, and deep tendon reflexes are absent. In this phase, the sleeper may be difficult to arouse or may wake spontaneously, gastric secretions increase, and heart and respiratory rates often are irregular. It is thought that the regions of the brain that are used in learning, thinking, and organizing information are stimulated during REM sleep.

Sleep Cycles

During a sleep cycle, people typically pass through NREM and REM sleep, the complete cycle usually lasting about 90 to 110 minutes in adults. In the first sleep cycle, a sleeper usually passes through all of the first three NREM stages in a total of about 20 to 30 minutes. Then, stage IV may last about 30 minutes. After stage IV NREM, the sleep passes back through stages III and II over about 20 minutes. Thereafter, the first REM stage occurs, lasting about 10 minutes, completing the first sleep cycle. It is not unusual for the first REM period to be very brief or even skipped entirely. The healthy adult sleeper usually experiences four to six cycles of sleep during 7 to 8 hours (see Figure 45-1 ■). The sleeper who is awakened during any stage must begin anew at stage I NREM sleep and proceed through all the stages to REM sleep.

The duration of NREM stages and REM sleep varies throughout the sleep period. During the early part of the night, the deep sleep periods are longer. As the night progresses, the sleeper spends less time in stages III and IV of NREM sleep.

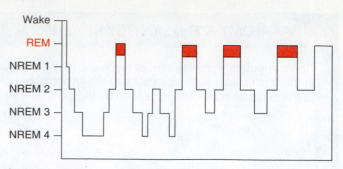

Figure 45-1 ■ Time spent in REM and non-REM stages of sleep in an adult.

REM sleep increases and dreams tend to lengthen. Before sleep ends, periods of near wakefulness occur, and stages I and II NREM sleep and REM sleep predominate.

FUNCTIONS OF SLEEP

The effects of sleep on the body are not completely understood. Sleep exerts physiologic effects on both the nervous system and other body structures. Sleep in some way restores normal levels of activity and normal balance among parts of the nervous system. Sleep is also necessary for protein synthesis, which allows repair processes to occur.

The role of sleep in psychological well-being is best noticed by the deterioration in mental functioning related to sleep loss. Persons with inadequate amounts of sleep tend to become emotionally irritable, have poor concentration, and experience difficulty making decisions.

NORMAL SLEEP PATTERNS AND REQUIREMENTS

Although it used to be believed that maintaining a regular sleep–wake rhythm is more important than the number of hours actually slept, recent research has shown that sleep deprivation is associated with significant cognitive and health problems. Although reestablishing the sleep–wake rhythm (e.g., after the disruption of surgery) is an important aspect of nursing, it is not appropriate to curtail or decrease daytime napping in hospitalized clients.

Newborns

Newborns sleep 16 to 18 hours a day, on an irregular schedule with periods of 1 to 3 hours spent awake. Unlike older children and adults, newborns enter REM sleep (called active sleep during the newborn period) immediately. Rapid eye movements are observable through closed lids, and the body movements and irregular respirations may be observed. NREM sleep (also called quiet sleep during the newborn period) is characterized by regular respirations, closed eyes, and the absence of body and eye movements. Newborns spend nearly 50% of their time in each of these states, and the sleep cycle is about 50 minutes.

It is best to put newborns to bed when they are sleepy but not asleep. Newborns can be encouraged to sleep less during the day by exposing them to light and by playing more with them during the day hours. As evening approaches, the environment can be less bright and quieter with less activity (National Sleep Foundation, n.d.d).

Infants

At first, infants awaken every 3 or 4 hours, eat, and then go back to sleep. Periods of wakefulness gradually increase during the first months. By 6 months, most infants sleep through the night (from midnight to 5 AM) and begin to establish a pattern of daytime naps. At the end of the first year, an infant usually takes two naps per day and should get about 14 to 15 hours of sleep in 24 hours.

About half of the infant's sleep time is spent in light sleep. During light sleep, the infant exhibits a great deal of activity, such as movement, gurgles, and coughing. Parents need to make sure that infants are truly awake before picking them up for feeding and changing. Putting infants to bed when they are drowsy but not asleep helps them to become "self-soothers." This means that they fall asleep independently and if they do awake at night, they can put themselves back to sleep. Infants who become used to parental assistance at bedtime may become "signalers" and cry for their parents to help them return to sleep at night (National Sleep Foundation, n.d.a).

Toddlers

Between 12 and 14 hours of sleep are recommended for children 1 to 3 years of age. Most still need an afternoon nap, but the need for midmorning naps gradually decreases. The toddler may exhibit a great deal of resistance to going to bed and may awaken during the night. Nighttime fears and nightmares are also common. A security object such as a blanket or stuffed animal may help. Parents need assurance that if the child has had adequate attention from them during the day, maintaining a daily sleep schedule and consistent bedtime routine will promote good sleep habits for the entire family.

Preschoolers

The preschool child (3 to 5 years of age) requires 11 to 13 hours of sleep per night, particularly if the child is in preschool. Sleep needs fluctuate in relation to activity and growth spurts. Many children of this age dislike bedtime and resist by requesting another story, game, or television program. The 4- to 5-year-old may become restless and irritable if sleep requirements are not met.

Parents can help children who resist bedtime by maintaining a regular and consistent sleep schedule. It also helps to have a relaxing bedtime routine that ends in the child's room. Preschool children wake up frequently at night, and they may be afraid of the dark or experience night terrors or nightmares. Often limiting or eliminating TV will reduce the number of nightmares.

School-Age Children

The school-age child (5 to 12 years of age) needs 10 to 11 hours of sleep, but most receive less because of increasing demands

---

RESEARCH NOTE **Are There Barriers to Following the Back-to-Sleep Recommendations for Infants?**

Research has shown that placing infants to sleep in the supine position decreases the risk of SIDS. The Back-to-Sleep educational initiative resulted in many more caregivers placing their infants in the supine position for sleep. The incidence of SIDS has decreased by 50%. In spite of this overall decrease, racial differences in the incidence of SIDS continue with African American infants having a higher incidence of SIDS than Caucasian and Latino infants. Previous studies found that it was more common for African American caregivers to place their infants in the prone position for sleep. Other factors associated with placing the infant in the prone position included having a grandmother living in the home, young age of the mother, and having previous child-rearing experience.

The researchers wanted to determine new barriers and more information about previously identified barriers that interfere with adherence to the Back-to-Sleep recommendations among inner-city caregivers, primarily African Americans. They conducted a qualitative research study using focus groups. Forty-nine caregivers participated, with 86% being African American, 6% Hispanic, 4% white, and 4% other.

Four themes were identified:

1. Safety. All were concerned about the safety of their infants while they slept, which prompted some of the participants to bring their infants into their beds for closer observation. Many believed that the infant would choke if placed in the supine position.
2. Comfort. Many of the participants made their decision about the position of the infant based on their perception of whether the baby seemed comfortable. Some felt that the infant looked more comfortable on its side or stomach and the baby slept longer in that position. Some felt that the infant seemed more comfortable close to them and had the infant sleep in bed with them.
3. Advice. Participants trusted the advice of older female family members with previous child-rearing experience. They also trusted their own instincts and their previous experience. Some did not trust health care providers as a reliable source of advice, especially about the care of infants. They recommended that advice from health professionals be delivered in a certain way: "Don't tell us. . . . Tell us why."
4. Knowledge. Some of the participants believed that SIDS could only happen if the infant slept in a crib (SIDS is sometimes called crib death) and, as a result, did not place their infant in a crib. Some doubted the existence of SIDS and others referred to religious beliefs (e.g., "it's an act of God . . . there is no way to really stop it").

IMPLICATIONS

The generalizability of this study is limited because the data were collected in only two cities. However, the study did identify barriers to following the Back-to-Sleep recommendations. Nurses need to assess a caregiver's knowledge about SIDS and use effective teaching strategies that will enhance the trust of the caregiver.

Note: Reprinted from "Barriers to Following the Back-to-Sleep Recommendations: Insights from Focus Groups with Inner-City Caregivers," by E. R. Colson, L. K. McCabe, K. Fox, S. Levenson, T. Colton, G. Lister, et al., 2005, *Ambulatory Pediatrics, 5*(6), 349–354. Copyright © 2005 with permission from the Ambulatory Pediatric Association.

(e.g., homework, sports, social activities). They may also be spending more time at the computer and watching TV. Some may be drinking caffeinated beverages. All of these activities can lead to difficulty falling asleep and fewer hours of sleep. Nurses can teach parents and school-age children about healthy sleep habits. A regular and consistent sleep schedule and bedtime routine need to be continued.

Adolescents

Adolescents (12 to 18 years of age) require 9 to 10 hours of sleep each night; however, few actually get that much sleep (IOM, 2006, p. 56). The National Sleep Foundation's 2006 *Sleep in America* poll found that teens are sleepy at times and places where they should be fully awake—at school, at home, and on the road. This can result in lower grades, negative moods (e.g., unhappy, sad, tense), and increased potential for car accidents. Interestingly, while more than half of the adolescents knew they were not getting enough sleep, 90% of the parents believed their adolescent was getting enough sleep. Nurses can teach parents to recognize signs and symptoms that indicate their teen is not getting enough sleep. See Clinical Manifestations.

As children reach adolescence, their circadian rhythms tend to shift. Research in the 1990s found that later sleep and wake patterns among adolescents are biologically determined; the natural tendency for teenagers is to stay up late at night and wake up later in the morning (National Sleep Foundation, n.d.a).

CLINICAL MANIFESTATIONS
SLEEP DEPRIVATION AND
SLEEP PROBLEMS IN TEENS

The teen:
- Has difficulty waking in the morning for school and yawns frequently throughout the day.
- Is continuously late for class and has trouble getting out the door in the morning.
- Can't seem to get through the day without drinking caffeinated beverages like coffee or cola.
- Is having difficulty in school, or a teacher notices that he or she falls asleep in class periodically.
- Is irritable, is anxious, and gets angry easily on days when he or she gets less sleep.
- Runs from one activity to the next—he or she participates in extra-curricular activities, has a job, and stays up late doing homework every night, cutting into sleep time.
- Takes naps during the week for more than 45 minutes and "sleeps in" for 2 hours or longer on the weekends than during the week.

Note: From "Parents of Teens: Recognize the Signs & Symptoms of Sleep Deprivation and Sleep Problems," by National Sleep Foundation (n.d.e). Retrieved July 2, 2006, from http://www.sleepfoundation.org/_content/hottopics/teensigns.pdf. Used with permission of the National Sleep Foundation. For further information, please visit http://www.sleepfoundation.org.

Figure 45-2 ■ Many adolescents do not get enough sleep.

Many schools, however, start at 7 AM which is in conflict with the adolescent's sleep patterns and needs and contributes to their sleep deprivation (Figure 45-2 ■). As a result, some members of Congress have introduced resolutions to encourage schools and school districts to reconsider the early school start times.

During adolescence, boys begin to experience **nocturnal emissions** (orgasm and emission of semen during sleep), known as "wet dreams," several times each month. Boys need to be informed about this normal development to prevent embarrassment and fear.

Adults

Most healthy adults need 7 to 9 hours of sleep a night (National Sleep Foundation, n.d.b). However, there is individual variation as some adults may be able to function well (e.g., without sleepiness or drowsiness) with 6 hours of sleep and others may need 10 hours to function optimally. Signs that may indicate that a person is not getting enough sleep include falling asleep or becoming drowsy during a task that is not fatiguing (e.g., listening to a boring or monotonous presentation), not being able to concentrate or remember information, and being unreasonably irritable with others.

The National Sleep Foundation (n.d.b) reports that certain adults are particularly vulnerable for not getting enough sleep: students, shift workers, travelers, and persons suffering from acute stress, depression, or chronic pain. Adults working long hours or multiple jobs may find their sleep less refreshing. Also, the sleep habits of children have an impact on the adults caring for them. Parents and caregivers whose children get the least amount of sleep are twice as likely to say they sleep less than 6 hours a night (National Sleep Foundation, n.d.b). Parents of infants lose the most sleep—nearly an hour on a typical night. Women may experience more disrupted sleep during pregnancy, menses, and the perimenopausal period.

Nurses need to teach adults the importance of obtaining sufficient sleep and tips on how to promote sleep that results in the client waking up feeling restored or refreshed. See the Client Teaching box later in this chapter.

Elders

A hallmark change with age is a tendency toward earlier bedtime and wake times. Older adults (65 to 75 years) usually awaken 1.3 hours earlier and go to bed approximately 1 hour earlier than younger adults (ages 20 to 30). Elders may show an increase in disturbed sleep that can create a negative impact on their quality of life, mood, and alertness. Although the ability to sleep becomes more difficult, the need to sleep does not decrease with age (IOM, 2006, pp. 57–59).

The National Sleep Foundation's 2003 *Sleep in America* poll was the first poll to look at the sleep habits of Americans between the ages of 55 and 84. It found that older adults are sleeping 7 to 9 hours on both weeknights and weekends. Of interest, however, was the striking relationship between the elder individual's health and quality of life and the person's sleep quantity and quality. The poll found that the better the health of older adults, the more likely they are to sleep well. And, conversely, the more diagnosed medical conditions, the more likely they were to report sleep problems (National Sleep Foundation, n.d.c). Elders who have several medical conditions and complain of having sleeping problems should discuss this with their primary care provider. The elder may have a major sleep disorder that is complicating treatment of the other conditions. It is important for the nurse to teach about the connection between sleep, health, and aging. See the Client Teaching box about sleep promotion later in this chapter.

Some elderly clients with dementia may experience *sundown syndrome*. Although not a sleep disorder directly, it refers to a pattern of symptoms (e.g., agitation, anxiety, aggression, and sometimes delusions) that occur in the late afternoon (thus the name). These symptoms can last through the night, further disrupting sleep (Arnold, 2004).

FACTORS AFFECTING SLEEP

Both the quality and the quantity of sleep are affected by a number of factors. *Sleep quality* is a subjective characteristic and is often determined by whether a person wakes up feeling energetic or not. *Quantity of sleep* is the total time the individual sleeps.

Illness

Illness that causes pain or physical distress (e.g., arthritis, back pain) can result in sleep problems. People who are ill require

LIFESPAN CONSIDERATIONS Sleep Disturbances

CHILDREN

Learning to sleep alone without the parent's help is a skill that all children need to master. Regular bedtime routines and rituals such as reading a book help children learn this skill and can prevent sleep disturbance. Some sleep disturbances seen in children include the following:

- Trained night feeder. Infants who are fed during the night, who are fed until they fall asleep and then put in bed, or who have a bottle left with them in their bed learn to expect and demand middle-of-the-night feedings. Infants who are growing well do not need night feeding after about 4 months of age. Infants who are failing to thrive may need feeding at night.
- Sleep refusal. Many toddlers and young children are resistant to settling down to sleep. This sleep refusal may be due to not being tired, anxiety about separation from the parent, stress (e.g., a recent move), lack of a regular sleep routine, the child's temperament, or changes in sleep arrangements (e.g., move from a crib to a "big" bed).
- Night terrors. Night terrors are partial awakenings from non-REM, stage III or IV sleep. They are usually seen in children 3 to 6 years of age. The child may sleepwalk, or may sit up in bed screaming and thrashing about. They usually cannot be wakened, but should be protected from injury, helped back to bed, and soothed back to sleep. Baby-sitters should be alerted to the possibility of a night terror occurring. Children do not remember the incident the next day, and there is no indication of a neurological or emotional problem. Excessive fatigue and a full bladder may contribute to the problem. Having the child take an afternoon nap and empty the bladder before going to sleep at night may be helpful.

ADULTS

- New jobs, pregnancy, and babies are common examples that often disrupt the sleep of a young adult.

- The sleep patterns of middle-aged adults can be disrupted by taking care of elderly parents and/or chronically ill partners in the home.
- See the Client Teaching box on page 1177 for healthy sleep tips for the adult.

ELDERS

The quality of sleep is often diminished in elders. Some of the leading factors that often are influential in sleep disturbances include the following:

- Side effects of medications
- Gastric reflux disease
- Respiratory and circulatory disorders, which may cause breathing problems or discomfort
- Pain from arthritis, increased stiffness, or impaired immobility
- Nocturia
- Depression
- Loss of life partner and/or close friends
- Confusion related to delirium or dementia

Interventions to promote sleep and rest can help enhance the rejuvenation and renewal that sleep provides. The following interventions can help promote sleep:

- Reduce or eliminate the consumption of caffeine and nicotine.
- Be sure their environment is warm and safe, especially if they get out of bed during the night.
- Provide comfort measures, such as analgesics if indicated, and proper positioning.
- Enhance the sense of safety and security by checking on clients frequently and making sure that the call light is within reach.
- If lack of sleep is caused by medications or certain health conditions, interventions should focus on resolving the underlying problem.
- Evaluate the situation and find out what the rest and sleep disturbances mean to the client. They may not perceive sleeplessness to be a serious problem, but will just do other activities and sleep when tired.

more sleep than normal, and the normal rhythm of sleep and wakefulness is often disturbed. People deprived of REM sleep subsequently spend more sleep time than normal in this stage.

Respiratory conditions can disturb an individual's sleep. Shortness of breath often makes sleep difficult, and people who have nasal congestion or sinus drainage may have trouble breathing and hence may find it difficult to sleep.

People who have gastric or duodenal ulcers may find their sleep disturbed because of pain, often a result of the increased gastric secretions that occur during REM sleep.

Certain endocrine disturbances can also affect sleep. Hyperthyroidism lengthens presleep time, making it difficult for a client to fall asleep. Hypothyroidism, conversely, decreases stage IV sleep. Women with low levels of estrogen often report excessive fatigue. In addition, they may experience sleep disruptions due, in part, to the discomfort associated with hot flashes or night sweats that can occur with reduced estrogen levels.

Elevated body temperatures can cause some reduction in delta sleep and REM sleep.

The need to urinate during the night also disrupts sleep, and people who awaken at night to urinate sometimes have difficulty getting back to sleep.

Environment

Environment can promote or hinder sleep. Any change—for example, noise in the environment—can inhibit sleep. The absence of usual stimuli or the presence of unfamiliar stimuli can prevent people from sleeping. Hospital environments can be quite noisy, and special care needs to be taken to reduce noise in the hallways and nursing care units. In fact, some hospitals have instituted "quiet times" in the afternoon on nursing units where the lights are lowered and activity and noise are purposefully decreased so clients can rest or nap.

Discomfort from environmental temperature (e.g., too hot or cold) and lack of ventilation can affect sleep. Light levels can be another factor. A person accustomed to darkness while sleeping may find it difficult to sleep in the light. Another influence includes the comfort and size of the bed. A person's partner who has different sleep habits, snores, or has other sleep difficulties may become a problem for the person also.

Lifestyle

Following an irregular morning and nighttime schedule can affect sleep. Moderate exercise in the morning or early afternoon usually is conducive to sleep, but exercise late in the day can delay sleep. The person's ability to relax before retiring is an important factor affecting the ability to fall asleep. It is best, therefore, to avoid doing homework or office work before or after getting into bed.

Night shift workers frequently obtain less sleep than other workers and have difficulty falling asleep after getting off work. Wearing dark wrap-around sunglasses during the drive home and light-blocking shades can minimize the alerting effects of exposure to daylight, thus making it easier to fall asleep when body temperature is rising.

Emotional Stress

Stress is considered by most sleep experts to be the number one cause of short-term sleeping difficulties (National Sleep Foundation, n.d.b). A person preoccupied with personal problems

---

RESEARCH NOTE   Can Clients Sleep in a Hospital?

Nurses know the importance of sleep. However, the researchers believe that sleep has been undervalued by nursing practice. For example, noise is a major disturbance in the hospital setting, making it difficult for clients to sleep. Clients are often awakened early for obtaining lab specimens, weights, assessments, and medication administration. Using a conceptual model developed by Dreher, the researchers implemented a nonpharmacological intervention to promote sleep on a 36-bed medical unit.

Guided by a nurse manager, clinical nurse IV, and gerontological clinical nurse specialist, the certified nursing assistants (CNAs) completed an educational program about how to implement nonpharmacological interventions that promote sleep. The program used "sleep baskets" which held materials needed for the interventions and a list of possible interventions to help remind the CNA (e.g., back rub, warm drink, aromatherapy, a warmed blanket, relaxation music, earplugs, and closed doors).

In preparation for bedtime, the CNA used the sleep basket and asked the client to select sleep interventions. In addition, other noise reduction strategies were used. Staff were reminded to use "quiet voices" after 10 PM and to avoid hallway discussions on the night shift. Doors to client rooms were closed when bedtime routines were completed (unless the client required close monitoring). And, the intercom was not used at night.

To evaluate the effectiveness of the project, the CNA who used a sleep basket on the evening shift completed a form as to which interventions were performed. The next morning, the day CNA asked the client to rate the quality and quantity of sleep, to identify which interventions were the most helpful, and if the nonpharmacological interventions helped them sleep. During the evaluation period, 40 clients (average age of 75) were evaluated. The warmed blanket was their favorite intervention. Seventy-five percent of the clients stated that the interventions helped them sleep, and 60% rated their sleep quality as "good."

IMPLICATIONS

Project interventions appear helpful for sleep improvement, especially during the retiring phase of sleep. The researchers state that the program is now being used on four nursing units. Nurses and CNAs are more aware of clients who have had an exhausting day and try to help these clients take a 45-minute nap by posting signs that say: "Do not disturb. Client napping between the hours of _____ and _____."

Note: From "The Sh-h-h-h Project. Nonpharmacological Interventions" by S. B. Robinson, T. Weitzel, & L. Henderson. (2005). *Holistic Nursing Practice, 19*(6), 263–266. Copyright Lippincott, Williams & Wilkins. Reprinted with permission.

(e.g., school- or job-related pressures, family or marriage problems) may be unable to relax sufficiently to get to sleep. Anxiety increases the norepinephrine blood levels through stimulation of the sympathetic nervous system. This chemical change results in less deep sleep and REM sleep and more stage changes and awakenings.

Stimulants and Alcohol

Caffeine-containing beverages act as stimulants of the central nervous system. Drinking beverages containing caffeine in the afternoon or evening may interfere with sleep. People who drink an excessive amount of alcohol often find their sleep disturbed. Alcohol disrupts REM sleep, although it may hasten the onset of sleep. While making up for lost REM sleep after some of the effects of the alcohol have worn off, people often experience nightmares. The alcohol-tolerant person may be unable to sleep well and become irritable as a result.

Diet

Weight gain has been associated with reduced total sleep time as well as broken sleep and earlier awakening. Weight loss, on the other hand, seems to be associated with an increase in total sleep time and less broken sleep. Dietary L-tryptophan—found, for example, in cheese and milk—may induce sleep, a fact that might explain why warm milk helps some people get to sleep.

Smoking

Nicotine has a stimulating effect on the body, and smokers often have more difficulty falling asleep than nonsmokers do. Smokers are usually easily aroused and often describe themselves as light sleepers. By refraining from smoking after the evening meal, the person usually sleeps better; moreover, many former smokers report that their sleeping patterns improved once they stopped smoking.

Motivation

Motivation can increase alertness in some situations (e.g., a tired person can probably stay alert while attending an interesting concert or surfing the Web late at night). Motivation alone, however, is usually not sufficient to overcome the normal circadian drive to sleep during the night. Nor is motivation sufficient to overcome sleepiness due to insufficient sleep. Boredom alone is not sufficient to cause sleepiness, but when insufficient sleep combines with boredom, sleep is likely to occur.

Medications

Some medications affect the quality of sleep. Most hypnotics can interfere with deep sleep and suppress REM sleep. Beta-blockers have been known to cause insomnia and nightmares. Narcotics, such as meperidine hydrochloride (Demerol) and morphine, are known to suppress REM sleep and to cause frequent awakenings and drowsiness. Tranquilizers interfere with REM sleep. Although antidepressants suppress REM sleep, this effect is considered a therapeutic action. In fact, selectively depriving a depressed client of REM sleep will result in an immediate but transient improvement in mood. Clients accustomed to taking hypnotic medications and antidepressants may experience a REM rebound (increased REM sleep) when these medications are discontinued. Warning clients to expect a period of more intense dreams when these medications are discontinued may reduce their anxiety about this symptom. Boxes 45–2 and 45–3 list drugs that can disrupt sleep or cause excessive daytime sleepiness.

COMMON SLEEP DISORDERS

A knowledge of common sleep disorders can help nurses assess the sleep complaints of their clients and, when appropriate, make a referral to a specialist in sleep disorders medicine. Although sleep

---

RESEARCH NOTE   Are Shortened Sleep Durations Contributing to the Growing Epidemic of Obesity?

Previous studies have shown that sleep deprivation results in decreased leptin levels and increased ghrelin levels (two hormones involved in the regulation of appetite and hunger), markedly elevated hunger and appetite ratings, and cravings for sweet, starch, and salty snacks. Sleep loss has also been linked to changes in decreased glucose tolerance and altered insulin responses to glucose challenges in healthy individuals.

To determine if the number of hours of sleep was associated with obesity and weight gain, the researchers used data from 9,588 adults who participated in the 1982–1984, 1987, and 1992 Epidemiologic Follow-up Studies of the First National Health and Nutrition Examination Survey (NHANES I). After controlling for depression, physical activity, education, ethnicity, alcohol consumption, cigarette smoking, gender, waking during the night, daytime sleepiness, and age, a longitudinal and cross-sectional analysis showed that participants who obtained less than 7 hours sleep were significantly more likely to be obese or overweight. Subjects obtaining 5 hours of sleep were 60% more likely to be obese, and subjects obtaining 6 hours of sleep per night were 27% more likely

to be obese than subjects obtaining 7 hours of sleep. Males who averaged over 9 hours of sleep per night, and females who averaged 8 hours of sleep per night were also more likely to be obese than those who averaged only 7 hours of sleep per night.

IMPLICATIONS

This very large study suggests that short sleep durations may be a contributing factor to the current epidemic of obesity in the country. The researchers acknowledge that the longer sleep times associated with obesity may relate to the presence of a pre-existing sleep disorder (e.g., sleep apnea), something that subjects were not screened for when the study began in 1982. The optimal sleep duration for adults, based on this study and others, appears to be 7 hours.

Note: From *Sleep* by J. E. Gangwisch, D. Malaspina, B. Boden-Albala, and S. B. Heymsfield. Copyright 2005 by *American Academy of Sleep Medicine.* Reproduced with permission of *American Academy of Sleep Medicine* in the format Textbook via Copyright Clearance Center.

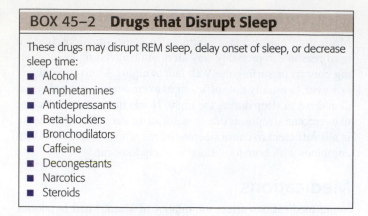

BOX 45–2 **Drugs that Disrupt Sleep**

These drugs may disrupt REM sleep, delay onset of sleep, or decrease sleep time:
- Alcohol
- Amphetamines
- Antidepressants
- Beta-blockers
- Bronchodilators
- Caffeine
- Decongestants
- Narcotics
- Steroids

CLINICAL MANIFESTATIONS **INSOMNIA**

- Difficulty falling asleep
- Waking up frequently during the night
- Difficulty returning to sleep
- Waking up too early in the morning
- Unrefreshing sleep
- Daytime sleepiness
- Difficulty concentrating
- Irritability

Note: From "Insomnia Symptoms" by National Sleep Foundation, 2005b. Retrieved July 2, 2006, from http://www.sleepfoundation.forg/sleeptionary/index.php?id=19&subsection=symptoms. Used with permission of the National Sleep Foundation. For further information, please visit http://www.sleepfoundation.org

disorders are typically categorized for the purpose of research as dysomnias, parasomnias, and disorders associated with medical or psychiatric illness, it is usually more appropriate for clinicians to focus on the client's symptoms (e.g., insomnia, excessive sleepiness, and abnormal events) occurring during sleep (parasomnias).

Insomnia

Insomnia is described as the inability to fall asleep or remain asleep. Persons with insomnia awaken not feeling rested.

Insomnia is the most common sleep complaint in America. Acute insomnia lasts one to several nights and is often caused by personal stressors and/or worry. If the insomnia persists for longer than a month, it is considered chronic insomnia. More often, people experience chronic-intermittent insomnia, which means difficulty sleeping for a few nights, followed by a few nights of adequate sleep before the problem returns (National Sleep Foundation, 2005a). See Clinical Manifestations for symptoms of insomnia. The two main risk factors of insomnia are older age and female gender (IOM, 2006, p. 91). Women suffer sleep loss in connection with hormonal changes (e.g., menstruation, pregnancy, and menopause). The incidence of insomnia increases with age, but it is thought that this is caused by some other medical condition.

Treatment for insomnia frequently requires the client to develop new behavior patterns that induce sleep and maintain sleep. Examples of behavioral treatments include the following:

- Stimulus control: creating a sleep environment that promotes sleep
- Cognitive therapy: learning to develop positive thoughts and beliefs about sleep
- Sleep restriction: following a program that limits time in bed in order to get to sleep and stay asleep throughout the night (National Sleep Foundation, 2005a).

BOX 45–3 **Drugs that May Cause Excessive Daytime Sleepiness**

These drugs may be associated with excessive daytime sleepiness:
- Antidepressants
- Antihistamines
- Beta-blockers
- Narcotics

The long-term efficacy of hypnotic medications is questionable. Such medications do not deal with the cause of the problem, and their prolonged use can create drug dependencies. Although antihistamines such as diphenhydramine (Benadryl) are thought to be safer for elderly clients than hypnotics, their side effects (i.e., atropine-like effects, dizziness, sedation, and hypotension) make them extremely hazardous. In fact, antihistamines should not be recommended for any client with a history of asthma, increased intraocular pressure, hyperthyroidism, cardiovascular disease, or hypertension.

Excessive Daytime Sleepiness

Clients may experience excessive daytime sleepiness as a result of hypersomnia, narcolepsy, sleep apnea, and insufficient sleep.

Hypersomnia

Hypersomnia refers to conditions where the affected individual obtains sufficient sleep at night but still cannot stay awake during the day. Hypersomnia can be caused by medical conditions, for example, central nervous system damage and certain kidney, liver, or metabolic disorders, such as diabetic acidosis and hypothyroidism. Rarely does hypersomnia have a psychological origin.

Narcolepsy

Narcolepsy is a disorder of excessive daytime sleepiness caused by the lack of the chemical hypocretin in the area of the central nervous system that regulates sleep. Clients with narcolepsy have sleep attacks or excessive daytime sleepiness, and their sleep at night usually begins with a sleep-onset REM period (dreaming sleep occurs within the first 15 minutes of falling asleep). The majority of clients also have cataplexy or the sudden onset of muscle weakness or paralysis in association with strong emotion, sleep paralysis (transient paralysis when falling asleep or waking up), hypnagogic hallucinations (visual, auditory, or tactile hallucinations at sleep onset or when waking up), and/or fragmented nighttime sleep. Their fragmented nocturnal sleep is not the cause of their excessive daytime sleepiness; many clients, particularly younger clients, have sound restorative nocturnal sleep but still cannot stay awake during the daytime. Onset of symptoms tends to occur between ages 15 and 30, and symptom severity usually stabilizes within the first 5 years of onset. Central nervous system stimulants such as methylphenidate (Ritalin) or amphetamines have been used to reduce excessive daytime sleepiness. Antidepressants, both older MAO inhibitors and the newer sertonergic antidepressants, are usually quite effective for controlling cataplexy. In 1999, the U.S. Food and Drug Administration (FDA), approved modafinil (Provigil) for control of excessive daytime sleepiness in narcoleptic clients. Although its exact mechanism of action is unknown, it has fewer side effects, and a lower potential for abuse. A second drug, sodium oxybate (Xyrem), approved in 2002 for the treatment of cataplexy, has also been shown to reduce excessive daytime sleepiness in clients with narcolepsy. Because Xyrem is difficult to administer (it is only available as a liquid and taken at bedtime and then again 2.5 to 4 hours after sleep onset) and its use is tightly controlled by the FDA, only those clients whose symptoms are not controlled by other medications are usually offered Xyrem. Only one pharmacy in the United States is allowed to dispense Xyrem. As a result, clients need to allow adequate time for obtaining their medications from the central pharmacy.

CLINICAL ALERT

Sodium oxybate is also known as gamma hydroxybutyrate or GHB—one of the drugs frequently associated with "date rapes." ■

Sleep Apnea

Sleep apnea is characterized by frequent short breathing pauses during sleep. Although all individuals have occasional periods of apnea during sleep, more than five apneic episodes or five breathing pauses longer than 10 seconds/hour is considered abnormal and should be evaluated by a sleep medicine specialist. Symptoms suggestive of sleep apnea include loud snoring, frequent nocturnal awakenings, excessive daytime sleepiness, difficulties falling asleep at night, morning headaches, memory and cognitive problems, and irritability. Although sleep apnea is most frequently diagnosed in men and postmenopausal women, it may occur during childhood.

The periods of apnea, which last from 10 seconds to 2 minutes, occur during REM or NREM sleep. Frequency of episodes ranges from 50 to 600 per night. Because these apneic pauses are usually associated with an arousal, clients frequently report that their sleep is nonrestorative and that they regularly fall asleep when engaging in sedentary activities during the day.

Three common types of sleep apnea are obstructive apnea, central apnea, and mixed apnea. Obstructive apnea occurs when the structures of the pharynx or oral cavity block the flow of air. The person continues to try to breathe; that is, the chest and abdominal muscles move. The movements of the diaphragm become stronger and stronger until the obstruction is removed. Enlarged tonsils and adenoids, a deviated nasal septum, nasal polyps, and obesity predispose the client to obstructive apnea. An episode of obstructive sleep apnea usually begins with snoring; thereafter, breathing ceases, followed by marked snorting as breathing resumes. Toward the end of each apneic episode, increased carbon dioxide levels in the blood cause the client to wake.

Central apnea is thought to involve a defect in the respiratory center of the brain. All actions involved in breathing, such as

chest movement and airflow, cease. Clients who have brain stem injuries and muscular dystrophy, for example, often have central sleep apnea. At this time, there is no available treatment. Mixed apnea is a combination of central apnea and obstructive apnea.

Treatment for sleep apnea is directed at the cause of the apnea. For example, enlarged tonsils may be removed. Other surgical procedures, including laser removal of excess tissue in the pharynx, reduce or eliminate snoring and may be effective in relieving the apnea. In other cases, the use of a nasal continuous positive airway pressure (CPAP) device at night is effective in maintaining an open airway. Weight loss may also help decrease the severity of symptoms.

Sleep apnea profoundly affects a person's work or school performance. In addition, prolonged sleep apnea can cause a sharp rise in blood pressure and may lead to cardiac arrest. Over time, apneic episodes can cause cardiac arrhythmias, pulmonary hypertension, and subsequent left-sided heart failure.

CLINICAL ALERT

Partners of clients with sleep apnea may become aware of the problem because they hear snoring that stops during the apneic period and then restarts. Surgical removal of tonsils or other tissue in the pharynx, if not the cause of the sleep apnea, can actually worsen the situation by removing the snoring and, thus, the warning that apnea is occurring. ■

Insufficient Sleep

Healthy individuals who obtain less sleep than they need will experience sleepiness and fatigue during the daytime hours. Depending on the severity and chronicity of this voluntary, albeit unintentional sleep deprivation, individuals may develop attention and concentration deficits, reduced vigilance, distractibility, reduced motivation, fatigue, malaise, and occasionally diplopia and dry mouth. The cause of these symptoms may or may not be attributed to insufficient sleep, since many Americans believe that 6.8 hours of sleep is sufficient to maintain optimal daytime performance. In fact, the sleep times of Americans have decreased dramatically over the past decade, with adults averaging only 6.8 hours of sleep on weekdays and 7.4 hours on weekends. All age groups, not just adults and adolescents, are getting less than the recommended amounts of sleep. Even 4 to 5-year-old children now average less than 9.5 hours of sleep, approximately 1.5 to 2.5 hours less than recommended.

Although the effects of obtaining less than optimal amounts of sleep are generally considered benign, there is growing evidence that insufficient sleep can have significant deleterious effects. Staying awake 19 consecutive hours produces the same impairments in reaction times and cognitive function as a blood alcohol level of 0.05, and staying awake for 24 consecutive hours has the same effects on reaction times and cognitive function as being legally drunk (with a blood alcohol level of 0.1). Nurses who report reduced hours of sleep are more likely to make an error, to have difficulty staying awake on duty, and to have difficulty staying awake while driving home from work than those who obtained more sleep.

When clients report obtaining more sleep on weekends or days off, it usually indicates that they are not obtaining sufficient sleep.

BOX 45–4 Parasomnias

- *Bruxism.* Usually occurring during stage II NREM sleep, this clenching and grinding of the teeth can eventually erode dental crowns, cause teeth to come loose, and lead to deterioration of the temporomandibular joint and TMJ syndrome.
- *Enuresis.* Bed-wetting during sleep can occur in children over 3 years old. More males than females are affected. It often occurs 1 to 2 hours after falling asleep, when rousing from NREM stages III and IV.
- *Periodic limb movements (PLMs) disorder.* In this condition, the legs jerk twice or three times per minute during sleep. It is most common among elders. This kicking motion can wake the client and result in poor sleep. The condition may be treated with medications such as those otherwise used for Parkinson's disease. PLMs differ from restless leg syndrome (RLS), which occurs whenever the person is at rest, not just at night when sleeping. RLS may occur during pregnancy or be due to other medical problems that can be treated.
- *Sleeptalking.* Talking during sleep occurs during NREM sleep before REM sleep. It rarely presents a problem to the person unless it becomes troublesome to others.
- *Somnambulism.* Somnambulism (sleepwalking) occurs during stages III and IV of NREM sleep. It is episodic and usually occurs 1 to 2 hours after falling asleep. Sleepwalkers tend not to notice dangers (e.g., stairs) and often need to be protected from injury.

Convincing the client to obtain more sleep may be difficult, but it can result in the resolution of their daytime symptoms.

Parasomnias

A **parasomnia** is behavior that may interfere with sleep and may even occur during sleep. The *International Classification of Sleep Disorders* (American Sleep Disorders Association, 2005) subdivides parasomnias into arousal disorders (e.g., sleepwalking, sleep terrors), sleep–wake transition disorders (e.g., sleep talking), parasomnias associated with REM sleep (e.g., nightmares), and others (e.g., bruxism). Box 45–4 describes examples of parasomnias.

NURSING MANAGEMENT

Assessing

A complete assessment of a client's sleep difficulty includes a sleep history, health history, physical exam, and, if warranted, a sleep diary and diagnostic studies. Only nurse practitioners with specialized training should investigate a complaint of excessive daytime sleepiness, investigate a sleep complaint lasting more than 6 months, or order and interpret diagnostic studies. All nurses, however, can take a brief sleep history and educate their clients about normal sleep.

Sleep History

A brief sleep history, which is usually part of the comprehensive nursing history, should be obtained for all clients entering a health care facility. It should, however, be deferred or omitted if the client is critically ill. Key questions to ask include the following:

- When do you usually go to sleep? And when do you wake up? Do you nap? If so, when? If the client is a child, it is also

important to ask about bedtime rituals. This information provides the nurse with information about the client's usual sleep duration and preferred sleep times, and allows for the incorporation of the client's preferences in the plan of care.
- Do you have any problems with your sleep? Has anyone ever told you that you snore loudly or thrash around a lot at night? Are you able to stay awake at work, when driving, or engaging in your usual activities?

  These questions elicit information about sleep complaints including the possibility of excessive daytime sleepiness. Loud snoring suggests the possibility of obstructive sleep apnea, and any client replying yes to this question should be referred to a specialist in sleep disorders medicine. Referrals should also be made if clients indicate they have difficulty staying awake during the day or that their movements disturb the sleep of their bed partners.
- Do you take any prescribed medications, over-the-counter medications, or herbal remedies to help you sleep? Or to stay awake?

  This information alerts the nurse to the use of prescription hypnotics and stimulants as well as the use of over-the-counter sleep aids and herbal remedies.
- Is there anything else I need to know about your sleep?

  This allows the client to voice any concerns or bring up topics that the nurse may not have asked about.

If the client is being admitted to a long-term care facility, it is also appropriate to ask about preferred room temperature, lighting (complete darkness versus using a night-light), and preferred bedtime routine.

A more detailed assessment is required if the client indicates any difficulty sleeping, difficulty remaining awake during the day, and/or recent changes in sleep pattern. This detailed history should explore the exact nature of the problem and its cause, when it first began and its frequency, how it affects daily living, what the client is doing to cope with the problem, and whether these methods have been effective. Questions the nurse might ask the client with a sleeping disturbance are shown in the accompanying Assessment Interview.

Health History

A health history is obtained to rule out medical or psychiatric causes of the client's difficulty sleeping. It is important to note that the presence of a medical or psychiatric illness (e.g., depression, Parkinson's disease, Alzheimer's disease, arthritis, or other disorders) does not preclude the possibility that a second problem (e.g., obstructive sleep apnea) may be contributing to the difficulty sleeping. Since medications can frequently cause or exacerbate sleep disturbances, information should be obtained about all of the prescribed and nonprescription medications, including herbal remedies that a client consumes.

Physical Examination

Rarely are sleep abnormalities noted during the physical exam unless the client has obstructive sleep apnea or some other health problem. Common findings among clients with sleep apnea include an enlarged and reddened uvula and soft palate, enlarged tonsils and adenoids (in children), obesity (in adults), and in male clients a neck size greater than 17.5 inches. Occasionally a deviated septum may be noted, but it is rarely the cause of obstructive sleep apnea.

Sleep Diary

A sleep specialist may ask clients to keep a sleep diary or log for 1 to 2 weeks in order to get a more complete picture of their sleep complaints. A sleep diary may include all or selected aspects of the following information that pertain to the client's specific problem:

- Time of (a) going to bed, (b) trying to fall asleep, (c) falling asleep (approximate time), (d) any instances of waking up and duration of these periods, (e) waking up in the morning, and (f) any naps and their duration
- Activities performed 2 to 3 hours before bedtime (type, duration, and time)
- Consumption of caffeinated beverages and alcohol and amounts of those beverages
- Any prescribed medications, over-the-counter medications, and herbal remedies taken during the day
- Bedtime rituals before sleep
- Any difficulties remaining awake during the day and times when difficulties occurred
- Any worries that the client believes may affect sleep
- Factors that the client believes have a positive or negative effect on sleep

If the client is a child, the sleep diary or log may be completed by a parent.

Diagnostic Studies

Sleep is measured objectively in a sleep disorder laboratory by **polysomnography:** An **electroencephalogram (EEG), electromyogram (EMG),** and **electro-oculogram (EOG)** are recorded simultaneously. Electrodes are placed on the scalp to record brain waves (EEG), on the outer canthus of each eye to record eye movement (EOG), and on the chin muscles to record the structural electromyogram (EMG). The electrodes transmit electric energy from the cerebral cortex and muscles of the face to pens that record the brain waves and muscle activity on graph paper. Respiratory effort and airflow, ECG, leg movements, and oxygen saturation are also monitored. Oxygen saturation is determined by monitoring with a pulse oximeter, a light-sensitive electric cell that attaches to the ear or a finger. Oxygen saturation and ECG assessments are of particular importance if sleep apnea is suspected. Through polysomnography, the client's activity (movements, struggling, noisy respirations) during sleep can be assessed. Such activity of which the client is unaware may be the cause of arousal during sleep.

Diagnosing

Insomnia, the NANDA (2007) diagnosis given to clients with sleep problems, is usually made more explicit with descriptions such as "difficulty falling asleep" or "difficulty staying asleep;" for example, *Insomnia* (delayed onset of sleep) related to overstimulation prior to bedtime.

Various factors or etiologies may be involved and must be specified for the individual. These include physical discomfort or pain; anxiety about actual or anticipated loss of a loved one, loss of a job, loss of life due to serious disease process, or worry about a family member's behavior or illness; frequent changes in sleep time due to shift work or overtime; and changes in sleep environment or bedtime rituals (e.g., noisy environment, alcohol or other drug dependency, drug withdrawal, misuse of sedatives prescribed for insomnia, and effects of medications such as steroids or stimulants). Examples of clinical applications of this diagnosis using NANDA, NIC, and NOC designations are shown in Identifying Nursing Diagnoses, Outcomes, and Interventions.

Sleep pattern disturbances may also be stated as the etiology of another diagnosis, in which case the nursing interventions are

IDENTIFYING NURSING DIAGNOSES, OUTCOMES, AND INTERVENTIONS
Clients with Sleep Problems

DATA CLUSTER Gillian Marks, 51, states she has had a problem falling asleep since her mastectomy 2 months ago. Says fears of prognosis become prominent when she is not active and busy. Has tried reading or watching TV but neither make her sleepy or relaxed. Appears agitated and restless.

NURSING DIAGNOSIS/ DEFINITION	SAMPLE DESIRED OUTCOMES*/ DEFINITION	INDICATORS	SELECTED INTERVENTIONS*/ DEFINITION	SAMPLE NIC ACTIVITIES
Insomnia/A disruption in amount and quality of sleep that impairs functioning	Personal Well-Being [2002]/Extent of positive perception of one's own health status and life circumstances	Very satisfied with • Ability to relax • Ability to express emotions	Coping Enhancement [5230]/Assisting a patient to adapt to perceived stressors, changes, or threats that interfere with meeting life demands and roles	• Appraise adjustment to changes in body image • Explore previous methods of dealing with life problems • Encourage verbalization of feelings, perceptions, and fears • Instruct on the use of relaxation techniques

DATA CLUSTER Thomas Strep states that a recent shortage of paramedics has resulted in extensive overtime and frequent "double shifts" and rotations from his usual two weekly 7–3 and 3–7 shifts. States, "All I want to do is go to sleep when I get home, but I can't. I guess I'm too riled up."

Sleep Deprivation/ Prolonged periods of time without sleep (sustained natural, periodic suspension of relative consciousness)	Rest [0003]/Quantity and pattern of diminished activity for mental and physical rejuvenation	Not compromised • Amount of rest • Rest pattern • Mentally rested	Progressive Muscle Relaxation [1460]/ Facilitating the tensing and releasing of successive muscle groups while attending to the resulting differences in sensation Simple Guided Imagery [6000]/ Purposeful use of imagination to achieve relaxation and/or direct attention away from undesirable sensations	• Choose quiet, comfortable setting • Have the client tense, for 5 to 10 seconds, each of 8 to 16 major muscle groups • Instruct client to focus on the sensations in the muscles when tensed and when relaxed • Discuss an image the client has experienced that is pleasurable and relaxing, such as lying on a beach, watching a snowfall, floating on a raft • Choose a scene that involves as many of the senses as possible • Have the client travel mentally to the scene and report how it smells, looks, feels, etc. • Assist the client to develop a method of ending the imagery such as counting while breathing deeply

*The NOC # for desired outcomes and the NIC # for nursing interventions are listed in brackets following the appropriate outcome or intervention. Outcomes, indicators, interventions, and activities selected are only a sample of those suggested by NOC and NIC and should be further individualized for each client.

directed toward the sleep disturbance itself. Examples include the following:

- *Risk for Injury* related to somnambulism
- *Ineffective Coping* related to insufficient quality and quantity of sleep
- *Fatigue* related to insufficient sleep
- *Risk for Impaired Gas Exchange* related to sleep apnea
- *Deficient Knowledge* (Nonprescription remedies for sleep) related to misinformation
- *Anxiety* related to sleep apnea and/or the diagnosis of a sleep disorder
- *Activity Intolerance* related to sleep deprivation or excessive daytime sleepiness

Planning

The major goal for clients with sleep disturbances is to maintain (or develop) a sleeping pattern that provides sufficient energy for daily activities. Other goals may relate to enhancing the client's feeling of well-being or improving the quality and quantity of the client's sleep. The nurse plans specific nursing interventions to reach the goal based on the etiology of each nursing diagnosis. These interventions may include reducing environmental distractions, promoting bedtime rituals, providing comfort measures, scheduling nursing care to provide for uninterrupted sleep periods, and teaching stress reduction, relaxation techniques, or good sleep hygiene.

Examples of NOC outcomes and NIC interventions to assist clients with sleep disturbances are shown in Identifying Nursing Diagnoses, Outcomes, and Interventions. Specific nursing activities associated with each of these interventions can be selected to meet the individual needs of the client. See the Nursing Care Plan and Concept Map at the end of the chapter.

Implementing

Sleep hygiene is a term referring to interventions used to promote sleep. Nursing interventions to enhance the quantity and quality of clients' sleep involve largely nonpharmacologic measures. These involve health teaching about sleep habits, support of bedtime rituals, the provision of a restful environment, specific measures to promote comfort and relaxation, and appropriate use of hypnotic medications.

For hospitalized clients, sleep problems are often related to the hospital environment or their illness. Assisting the client to sleep in such instances can be challenging to a nurse, often involving scheduling activities, administering analgesics, and providing a supportive environment. Explanations and a supportive relationship are essential for the fearful or anxious client. Different types of hypnotics may be prescribed depending on the type of sleep problem (e.g., difficulties falling asleep or difficulties maintaining sleep). Drugs with longer half-lives are often prescribed for difficulties maintaining sleep, but must be used with caution in the elderly.

Client Teaching

Healthy individuals need to learn the importance of sleep in maintaining active and productive lifestyles. They need to learn (a) the conditions that promote sleep and those that interfere with sleep, (b) safe use of sleep medications, (c) effects of other prescribed medications on sleep, and (d) effects of their disease states on sleep. Client teaching for promoting sleep is shown in Client Teaching.

Supporting Bedtime Rituals

Most people are accustomed to bedtime rituals or presleep routines that are conducive to comfort and relaxation. Altering or eliminating such routines can affect a client's sleep. Common prebedtime activities of adults include listening to music, reading, taking a soothing bath, and praying. Children need to be socialized into a presleep routine such as a bedtime story, holding onto a favorite toy or blanket, and kissing everyone goodnight. Sleep is also usually preceded by hygienic routines, such as washing the face and hands (or bathing), brushing the teeth, and voiding.

In institutional settings, nurses can provide similar bedtime rituals—assisting with a hand and face wash, providing a massage or hot drink, plumping of pillows, and providing extra blankets as needed. Conversing about accomplishments of the day or enjoyable events such as visits from friends can also help to relax clients and bring peace of mind.

Creating a Restful Environment

All people need a sleeping environment with minimal noise, a comfortable room temperature, appropriate ventilation, and appropriate lighting. Although most people prefer a darkened environment, a low light source may provide comfort for children or those in a strange environment. Infants and children need a

---

CLIENT TEACHING **Promoting Sleep**

SLEEP PATTERN
- If you have difficulty falling asleep or staying asleep, it is important to establish a regular bedtime and wake-up time for all days of the week to enhance your biological rhythm. A short daytime nap (e.g., 15 to 30 minutes), particularly among elders, can be restorative and not interfere with nighttime sleep. A younger person with insomnia should not nap.
- Establish a regular, relaxing bedtime routine before sleep such as reading, listening to soft music, taking a warm bath, or doing some other quiet activity you enjoy.
- Avoid dealing with office work or family problems before bedtime.
- Get adequate exercise during the day to reduce stress, but avoid excessive physical exertion at least 3 hours before bedtime.
- Use the bed for sleep or sexual activity, so that you associate it with sleep. Take work material, computers, and TVs out of the bedroom. Lying awake, tossing and turning, will strengthen the association between wakefulness and lying in bed (many people with insomnia report falling asleep in a chair or in front of the TV but having trouble falling asleep in bed).
- When you are unable to sleep, get out of bed, go into another room, and pursue some relaxing activity until you feel drowsy.

ENVIRONMENT
- Create a sleep-conducive environment that is dark, quiet, comfortable, and cool.

- Keep noise to a minimum; block out extraneous noise as necessary with white noise from a fan, air conditioner, or white noise machine. Music is not recommended as studies have shown that music will promote wakefulness (it is interesting and people will pay attention to it).
- Sleep on a comfortable mattress and pillows.

DIET
- Avoid heavy meals 2 to 3 hours before bedtime.
- Avoid alcohol and caffeine-containing foods and beverages (e.g., coffee, tea, chocolate) at least 4 hours before bedtime. Caffeine can interfere with sleep. Both caffeine and alcohol act as diuretics, creating the need to void during sleep time.
- If a bedtime snack is necessary, consume only light carbohydrates or a milk drink. Heavy or spicy foods can cause gastrointestinal upsets that disturb sleep.

MEDICATIONS
- Use sleeping medications only as a last resort. Use over-the-counter medications sparingly because many contain antihistamines that cause daytime drowsiness.
- Take analgesics before bedtime to relieve aches and pains.
- Consult with your health care provider about adjusting other medications that may cause insomnia.

BOX 45–5   Reducing Environmental Distractions in Hospitals

- Close window curtains if street lights shine through.
- Close curtains between clients in semiprivate and larger rooms.
- Reduce or eliminate overhead lighting; provide a night-light at the bedside or in the bathroom.
- Use a flashlight to check drainage bags, etc., without turning on the overhead lights.
- Ensure a clear pathway around the bed to avoid bumping the bed and jarring the client during sleeping hours.
- Close the door of the client's room.
- Adhere to agency policy about times to turn off communal televisions or radios.
- Lower the ring tone of nearby telephones.
- Discontinue use of the paging system after a certain hour (e.g., 2100 hours) or reduce its volume.
- Keep required staff conversations at low levels; conduct nursing reports or other discussions in a separate area away from client rooms.
- Wear rubber-soled shoes.
- Ensure that all cart wheels are well oiled.
- Perform only essential noisy activities during sleeping hours.

---

quiet room usually separate from the parents' room, a light or warm blanket as appropriate, and a location away from open windows or drafts.

Environmental distractions such as environmental noises and staff communication noise are particularly troublesome for hospitalized clients. Environmental noises include the sound of paging systems, telephones, and call lights; doors closing; elevator chimes; furniture squeaking; and linen carts being wheeled through corridors. Staff communication is a major factor creating noise, particularly at staff change of shift.

To create a restful environment, the nurse needs to reduce environmental distractions, reduce sleep interruptions, ensure a safe environment, and provide a room temperature that is satisfactory to the client. Some interventions to reduce environmental distractions, especially noise, are listed in Box 45–5.

The environment must also be safe so that the client can relax. People who are unaccustomed to narrow hospital beds may feel more secure with side rails.

Additional safety measures include

- Placing beds in low positions.
- Using night-lights.
- Placing call bells within easy reach.

Promoting Comfort and Relaxation

Comfort measures are essential to help the client fall asleep and stay asleep, especially if the effects of the person's illness interfere with sleep. A concerned, caring attitude, along with the following interventions, can significantly promote client comfort and sleep:

- Provide loose-fitting nightwear.
- Assist clients with hygienic routines.
- Make sure the bed linen is smooth, clean, and dry.
- Assist or encourage the client to void before bedtime.
- Offer to provide a back massage before sleep.

- Position dependent clients appropriately to aid muscle relaxation, and provide supportive devices to protect pressure areas.
- Schedule medications, especially diuretics, to prevent nocturnal awakenings.
- For clients who have pain, administer analgesics 30 minutes before sleep.
- Listen to the client's concerns and deal with problems as they arise.

People of any age, but especially elders, are unable to sleep well if they feel cold. Changes in circulation, metabolism, and body tissue density reduce the older person's ability to generate and conserve heat. To compound this problem, hospital gowns have short sleeves and are made of thin polyester. Bed sheets also are often made of polyester rather than a warm fabric, such as cotton flannel. The following interventions can be used to keep elders warm during sleep:

- Before the client goes to bed, warm the bed with prewarmed bath blankets.
- Use 100% cotton flannel sheets or apply thermal blankets between the sheet and bedspread.
- Encourage the client to wear own clothing, such as flannel nightgown or pajamas, socks, leg warmers, long underwear, sleeping cap (if scalp hair is sparse), or sweater, or use extra blankets.

Emotional stress obviously interferes with a person's ability to relax, rest, and sleep, and inability to sleep further aggravates feelings of tension. Sleep rarely occurs until a person is relaxed. Relaxation techniques can be encouraged as part of the nightly routine. Slow, deep breathing for a few minutes followed by slow, rhythmic contraction and relaxation of muscles can alleviate tension and induce calm. Imagery, meditation, and yoga can also be taught. These techniques are discussed in Chapter 19. ∞

Enhancing Sleep with Medications

Sleep medications often prescribed on a prn (as-needed) basis for clients include the sedative-hypnotics, which induce sleep, and antianxiety drugs or tranquilizers, which decrease anxiety and tension. When prn sleep medications are ordered in institutional settings, the nurse is responsible for making decisions with the client about when to administer them. These medications should be administered only with complete knowledge of their actions and effects and only when indicated.

Both nurses and clients need to be aware of the actions, effects, and risks of the specific medication prescribed. Although medications vary in their activity and effects, considerations include the following:

- Sedative-hypnotic medications produce a general central nervous system (CNS) depression and an unnatural sleep; REM or NREM sleep is altered to some extent and daytime drowsiness and a morning hangover effect may occur. Some of the new hypnotics, such as zolpidem (Ambien), do not alter REM sleep or produce rebound insomnia when discontinued.
- Antianxiety medications decrease levels of arousal by facilitating the action of neurons in the CNS that suppress responsiveness to stimulation. These medications are contraindicated

in pregnant women because of their associated risk of congenital anomalies, and in breast-feeding mothers because the medication is excreted in breast milk.

■ Sleep medications vary in their onset and duration of action and will impair waking function as long as they are chemically active. Some medication effects can last many hours beyond the time that the client's perception of daytime drowsiness and impaired psychomotor skills have disappeared. Clients need to be cautioned about such effects and about driving or handling machinery while the drug is in their system.

■ Sleep medications affect REM sleep more than NREM sleep. Clients need to be informed that one or two nights of increased dreaming (REM rebound) are usual after the drug is discontinued after long-term use.

■ Initial doses of medications should be low and increases added gradually, depending on the client's response. Elders, in particular, are susceptible to side effects because of their metabolic changes; they need to be closely monitored for changes in mental alertness and coordination. Clients need to be instructed to take the smallest effective dose and then only for a few nights or intermittently as required.

■ Regular use of any sleep medication can lead to tolerance over time (e.g., 4 to 6 weeks) and rebound insomnia. In some instances, this may lead clients to increase the dosage. Clients must be cautioned about developing a pattern of drug dependency.

■ Abrupt cessation of barbiturate sedative-hypnotics can create withdrawal symptoms such as restlessness, tremors, weakness, insomnia, increased heart rate, seizures, convulsions, and even death. Long-term users need to taper their medications under the supervision of a specialist.

About half of the clients who seek medical intervention for sleep problems are treated with sedative-hypnotics (Vitiello, 1999). Sometimes the prescription of hypnotics can be appropriate. For example, women with chronic difficulties maintaining

DRUG CAPSULE

zolpidem (Ambien)

THE CLIENT WITH MEDICATIONS THAT AFFECT SLEEP OR ALERTNESS

Zolpidem is used for the short-term management of insomnia. The medication is used to reduce sleep latency and awakenings, and to lengthen sleep durations. Unlike traditional benzodiazepine sedative-hypnotics, zolpidem does not reduce REM sleep durations or cause rebound insomnia when the drug is discontinued. At therapeutic doses, it causes little or no respiratory depression, and it has a low potential for abuse. Clients using it for short periods have not demonstrated tolerance, physical dependence, or withdrawal symptoms. It has a rapid onset of action and a half-life of 2.6 hours.

NURSING RESPONSIBILITIES

■ The drug has a rapid onset of action, so it should not be given until just prior to bedtime in order to minimize sedation while awake.

■ Clients should be monitored for side effects (e.g., daytime drowsiness and dizziness). Older clients and those with hepatic insufficiency should start with a lower dose (e.g., 5 mg).

CLIENT AND FAMILY TEACHING

■ Clients should be cautioned that zolpidem can intensify the actions of other CNS depressants and warned against combining zolpidem with alcohol and all other drugs that depress CNS function.

■ Clients should be cautioned not to take this medication until they are ready to go to bed because of its rapid onset of action.

modafinil (Provigil)

Modafinil has recently been approved by the FDA for the treatment of narcolepsy, excessive daytime sleepiness associated with obstructive sleep apnea, and shift work sleep disorder. Because the drug does not alter the function of the dopamine neurotransmitter system, modafinil lacks the addictive potential of traditional stimulants. It has a long half-life (approximately 15 hours) and thus can usually be administered only once a day (in the morning). It does not interfere with sleep at night.

NURSING RESPONSIBILITIES

■ Monitor the client for side effects, particularly if the client is elderly or has hepatic dysfunction. Side effects are rare and usually consist of headache, nausea, and nervousness.

■ If the client has obstructive sleep apnea, ensure that the client continues to use nasal CPAP.

CLIENT AND FAMILY TEACHING

■ Explain that modafinil is not a substitute for obtaining adequate amounts of sleep. Any client with the diagnosis of narcolepsy, obstructive sleep apnea, or shift work sleep disorder needs to obtain adequate amounts of sleep in addition to taking prescribed medications.

■ Caution clients with obstructive sleep apnea that is very important to continue using nasal CPAP and that modafinil is being prescribed only to reduce excessive daytime sleepiness and will not reduce the number of apneic episodes during sleep.

■ Modafinil may accelerate the metabolism of oral contraceptives, leading to lower plasma levels. Women using low-dose birth control pills may want to consider switching birth control methods or adding a second type of birth control.

Note: Prior to administering any medication, review all aspects with a current drug handbook or other reliable source.

TABLE 45–1 Selected Sedative-Hypnotic Medications Used for Insomnia

MEDICATION	HALF-LIFE
Chloral hydrate (Noctec)	7–10 hours
Eszopiclone (Lunesta)	6 hours
Ethchlorvynol (Placidyl)	10–20 hours
Flurazepam (Dalmane)	47–100 hours
Glutethimide (Doriden)	1–12 hours
Lorazepam (Ativan)	10–20 hours
Melatonin	1 hour
Temazepam (Restoril)	9–15 hours
Triazolam (Halcion)	1.5–5.5 hours
Zaleplon (Sonata)	1 hour
Zolpidem (Ambien)	2.6 hours

sleep or nonrestorative sleep associated with menopausal symptoms often benefit by the prescription of 10 mg of zolpidem, a low dose that was documented to be both safe and efficacious in this population. Hypnotics are not appropriate if clients have any symptoms suggestive of sleep-related breathing disorders, or decreased renal and/or hepatic function.

Table 45–1 presents some of the common medications used for enhancing sleep and the half-life of these medications. The half-life represents how long it takes for half of the medication to be metabolized and eliminated by the body; hence, those with shorter half-lives are less likely to cause residual drowsiness after administration, but may be less effective for the treatment of sleep maintenance insomnia.

Evaluating

Using data collected during care and the desired outcomes developed during the planning stage as a guide, the nurse judges whether client goals and outcomes have been achieved. Data collection may include (a) observations of the duration of the client's sleep, (b) questions about how the client feels on awakening, or (c) observations of the client's level of alertness during the day. Examples of client goals and related outcomes are shown in Identifying Nursing Diagnoses, Outcomes, and Interventions earlier in this chapter.

If the desired outcomes are not achieved, the nurse and client should explore the reasons, which may include answers to the following questions:

- Were etiologic factors correctly identified?
- Has the client's physical condition or medication therapy changed?
- Did the client comply with instructions about establishing a regular sleep–wake pattern?
- Did the client avoid ingesting caffeine?
- Did the client participate in stimulating daytime activities to avoid excessive daytime naps?
- Were all possible measures taken to provide a restful environment for the client?
- Were the comfort and relaxation measures effective?

NURSING CARE PLAN Sleep

ASSESSMENT DATA	NURSING DIAGNOSIS	DESIRED OUTCOMES*
Nursing Assessment Jack Harrison is a 36-year-old police officer assigned to a high-crime police precinct. One week ago he received a surface bullet wound to his arm. Today he arrives at the outpatient clinic to have the wound redressed. While speaking with the nurse, Mr. Harrison mentions that he has recently been promoted to the rank of detective and has assumed new responsibilities. He states that since his promotion, he has experienced increasing difficulty falling asleep and sometimes staying asleep. He expresses concern over the danger of his occupation and his desire to do well in his new position. He complains of waking up feeling tired and irritable.	*Insomnia* related to anxiety (as evidenced by difficulty falling and remaining asleep, fatigue, and irritability)	Sleep [0004] as evidenced by: - Sleeps through the night consistently - Feels rejuvenated after sleep - No dependence on sleep aids

Physical Examination

Height: 185.4 cm (6'2")
Weight: 85.7 kg (189 lb)
Temperature: 37.0°C (98.6°F)
Pulse: 80 BPM
Respirations: 18/minute
Blood pressure:
144/88 mm Hg

Diagnostic Data

CBC within normal range, x-ray left arm: evidence of superficial soft tissue injury

NURSING CARE PLAN Sleep *continued*

NURSING INTERVENTIONS*/SELECTED ACTIVITIES	RATIONALE
Sleep Enhancement [1850]	
Determine the client's sleep and activity pattern.	*The amount of sleep an individual needs varies with lifestyle, health, and age.*
Encourage Mr. Harrison to establish a bedtime routine to facilitate transition from wakefulness to sleep.	*Rituals and routines induce comfort, relaxation, and sleep.*
Encourage him to eliminate stressful situations before bedtime.	*Stress interferes with a person's ability to relax, rest, and sleep.*
Instruct Mr. Harrison and significant others about factors (e.g., physiologic, psychologic, lifestyle, frequent work shift changes, excessively long work hours, and other environmental factors) that contribute to sleep pattern disturbances.	*Knowledge of causative factors can enable the client to begin to control factors that inhibit sleep.*
Discuss with Mr. Harrison and his family comfort measures, sleep-promoting techniques, and lifestyle changes that can contribute to optimal sleep.	*Knowledge of factors that affect sleep enables the client to implement changes in lifestyle and prebedtime activities.*
Monitor bedtime food and beverage intake for items that facilitate or interfere with sleep.	*Milk and protein foods contain tryptophan, a precursor of serotonin, which is thought to induce and maintain sleep. Stimulants should be avoided because they inhibit sleep.*
Security Enhancement [5380]	
Discuss specific situations or individuals that threaten Mr. Harrison or his family.	*Fear is reduced when the reality of a situation is confronted in a safe environment. Awareness of factors that cause intensification of fears enhances control.*
Assist him to use coping responses that have been successful in the past.	*Feelings of safety and security increase when an individual identifies previously successful ways of dealing with anxiety-provoking or fearful situations.*
Anxiety Reduction [5820]	
Create an atmosphere to facilitate trust.	*Trust is an essential first step in the therapeutic relationship.*
Seek to understand Mr. Harrison's perspective of a stressful situation.	*Anxiety is a feeling aroused by a vague, nonspecific threat. Identifying the client's perspective will facilitate planning for the best approach to anxiety reduction.*
Encourage verbalization of feelings, perceptions, and fears.	*Open expression of feelings facilitates identification of specific emotions such as anger or helplessness, distorted perceptions, and unrealistic fears.*
Determine the client's decision-making ability.	*Maladaptive coping mechanisms are characterized by an inability to make decisions and choices.*

EVALUATION

Outcome met. Mr. Harrison acknowledges his insomnia is a somatic expression of his anxiety regarding job promotion and fear of failing. He states that talking with the police department counselor has been helpful. He is practicing relaxation techniques each night and sleeps an average of 7 hours a night. Mr. Harrison expresses a feeling of being rested upon awakening.

APPLYING CRITICAL THINKING

1. What further information would be helpful to obtain from Mr. Harrison about his sleep problem?
2. What suggestions can you make that may help him develop better sleep habits?

3. What are the most common problems that interfere with clients' ability to sleep?

See Critical Thinking Possibilities in Appendix A.

The NOC # for desired outcomes and the NIC # for nursing interventions are listed in brackets following the appropriate outcome or intervention. Outcomes, interventions, and activities selected are only a sample of those suggested by NOC and NIC and should be further individualized for each client.

CONCEPT MAP   **Sleep**

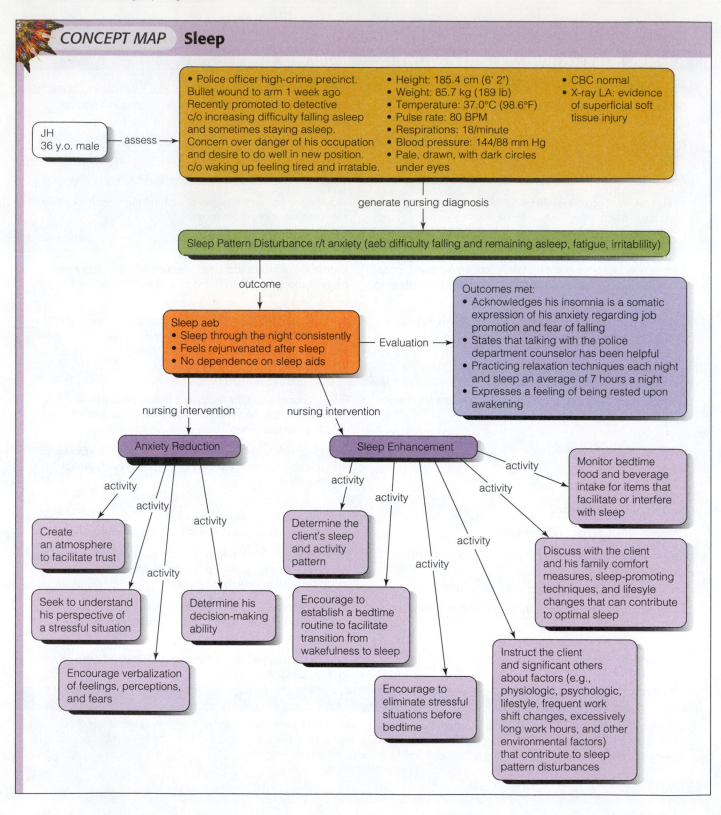

JH
36 y.o. male   → assess →

- Police officer high-crime precinct.
  Bullet wound to arm 1 week ago
  Recently promoted to detective
  c/o increasing difficulty falling asleep
  and sometimes staying asleep.
  Concern over danger of his occupation
  and desire to do well in new position.
  c/o waking up feeling tired and irratable.

- Height: 185.4 cm (6' 2")
- Weight: 85.7 kg (189 lb)
- Temperature: 37.0°C (98.6°F)
- Pulse rate: 80 BPM
- Respirations: 18/minute
- Blood pressure: 144/88 mm Hg
- Pale, drawn, with dark circles
  under eyes

- CBC normal
- X-ray LA: evidence
  of superficial soft
  tissue injury

↓ generate nursing diagnosis

Sleep Pattern Disturbance r/t anxiety (aeb difficulty falling and remaining asleep, fatigue, irritablility)

↓ outcome

Sleep aeb
- Sleep through the night consistently
- Feels rejunvenated after sleep
- No dependence on sleep aids

→ Evaluation →

Outcomes met:
- Acknowledges his insomnia is a somatic
  expression of his anxiety regarding job
  promotion and fear of falling
- States that talking with the police
  department counselor has been helpful
- Practicing relaxation techniques each night
  and sleep an average of 7 hours a night
- Expresses a feeling of being rested upon
  awakening

nursing intervention → **Anxiety Reduction**

nursing intervention → **Sleep Enhancement**

activity → Create
an atmosphere
to facilitate trust

activity → Seek to understand
his perspective of
a stressful situation

activity → Encourage verbalization
of feelings, perceptions,
and fears

activity → Determine his
decision-making
ability

activity → Determine the
client's sleep
and activity
pattern

activity → Encourage to
establish a bedtime
routine to facilitate
transition from
wakefulness to sleep

activity → Encourage to
eliminate stressful
situations before
bedtime

activity → Monitor bedtime
food and beverage
intake for items that
facilitate or interfere
with sleep

activity → Discuss with the client
and his family comfort
measures, sleep-promoting
techniques, and lifesyle
changes that can contribute
to optimal sleep

activity → Instruct the client
and significant others
about factors (e.g.,
physiologic, psychologic,
lifestyle, frequent work
shift changes, excessively
long work hours, and other
environmental factors)
that contribute to sleep
pattern disturbances

CHAPTER 45 **REVIEW**

CHAPTER HIGHLIGHTS

- Insufficient sleep is widespread among all age groups in this country. Approximately 50 million to 70 million Americans suffer from a chronic disorder of sleep and wakefulness that hinders daily functioning and adversely affects health. A 2006 report from the Institute of Medicine (IOM) states that sleep disorders and sleep deprivation are an unmet public health problem.
- Sleep is a naturally occurring altered state of consciousness in which a person's perception and reaction to the environment are decreased.
- Sleep is needed for optimal physiologic and psychologic functioning.
- The sleep cycle is controlled by specialized areas in the brain stem and is affected by the individual's circadian rhythm.
- During a normal night's sleep, an adult has four to six sleep cycles, each with NREM (quiet sleep) and REM (rapid-eye-movement) sleep.
- NREM (slow-wave) sleep consists of four stages, progressing from stage I, very light sleep, to stages III and IV, deep sleep. NREM sleep predominates during naps and nocturnal sleep periods.
- REM sleep recurs about every 90 minutes and is often associated with dreaming.

- The ratio of NREM to REM sleep varies with age.
- Many factors can affect sleep, including illness, environment, lifestyle, emotional stress, stimulants and alcohol, diet, smoking, motivation, and medications.
- Common sleep disorders include parasomnias (such as bruxism, nocturnal enuresis, sleeptalking, and somnambulism), insomnia, and sleep apnea.
- Assessment of a client's sleep includes obtaining a sleep history, obtaining a health history, and conducting a physical examination to detect signs suggestive of sleep apnea.
- Nursing responsibilities to help clients sleep include (a) teaching clients ways to enhance sleep, (b) supporting bedtime rituals, (c) creating a restful environment, (d) promoting comfort and relaxation, and (e) using prescribed sleep medications.
- Nonpharmacologic interventions to induce and maintain sleep are always the preferred interventions.

TEST YOUR KNOWLEDGE

1. A client is admitted for a sleep disorder. The nurse knows that the reticular activating system (RAS) is involved in the sleep–wake cycle. Which of the following letters indicates the location of the RAS?

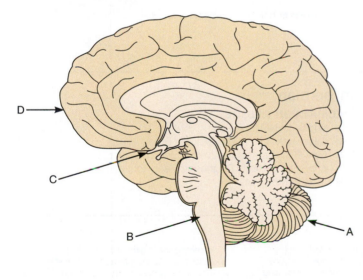

   1. A
   2. B
   3. C
   4. D

2. A client has a history of sleep apnea. The nurse should ask which of the following most appropriate questions?
   1. Do you have a history of cardiac irregularities?
   2. Do you have a history of any kind of nasal obstruction?
   3. Have you had chest pain with or without activity?
   4. Do you have difficulty with daytime sleepiness?

3. Because of significant concerns about financial problems a middle-aged client complains of difficulty sleeping. Which of the following would be an appropriate outcome for the nursing care plan? "By day 5, the client will:
   1. Sleep 8 to 10 hours per day."
   2. Report falling asleep within 20 to 30 minutes."
   3. Have a plan to pay all the bills."
   4. Decrease worrying about financial problems and will keep busy until bedtime."

4. A client reports to the nurse that she has been taking barbiturate sleeping pills every night for several months and now wishes to stop taking them. The nurse advises the client to:
   1. Take the last pill on a Friday night so disrupted sleep can be compensated on the weekend.
   2. Continue to take the pills since sleeping without them after such a long time will be difficult and perhaps impossible.
   3. Discontinue taking the pills.
   4. Continue taking the pills and discuss tapering the dose with the primary care provider.

5. During a well-child visit, a mother tells the nurse that her 4-year old daughter typically goes to bed at 10:30 PM and awakens each morning at 7 AM. She does not take a nap in the afternoon. Which of the following is the best response?
   1. Encourage the mother to consider putting her daughter to bed between 8 and 9 PM.
   2. Reassure the mother that it is normal for 4-year-olds to resist napping, but encourage her to insist that she rest quietly each afternoon.
   3. Recommend that her daughter be allowed to sleep later in the morning.
   4. Reassure her that her daughter's sleep pattern is normal and that she has outgrown her need for an afternoon nap.

6. A college student was referred to the campus health service because of difficulty staying awake in class. Of the following items, what should be included in the nurse's assessment? Select all that apply.
 1. Amount of sleep he usually obtains during the week and on weekends
 2. How much alcohol he usually consumes
 3. Onset and duration of symptoms
 4. Whether or not his classes are boring

7. During a yearly physical, a 52-year-old male client mentions that his wife frequently complains about his snoring. During the physical exam, the nurse notes that his neck size is 18 inches, his soft palate and uvula are reddened and swollen, and he is overweight. The most appropriate nursing intervention for this client is to:
 1. Recommend that he and his wife sleep in separate bedrooms so that his snoring does not disturb his wife.
 2. Refer him to a dietitian for a weight loss program.
 3. Caution him not to drink or take sleeping pills since they may make his snoring worse.
 4. Refer him to a sleep disorders center for evaluation and treatment of his symptoms.

8. A new nursing graduate's first job requires 12-hour night shifts. Which of the following strategies will make it easier for the graduate to sleep during the day and remain awake at night?
 1. Wear dark wrap-around sunglasses when driving home in the morning, and sleep in a darkened bedroom.
 2. Exercise on the way home to avoid having to stand around waiting for equipment at the gym.
 3. Drink several cups of strong coffee or 16 oz of caffeinated soda when beginning the shift.
 4. Try to stay in a brightly lit area when working at night.

9. The nurse is answering questions after a presentation on sleep at a local senior citizens center. A woman in her late 70s asks for an opinion about the advisability of allowing her husband to nap for 15 to 20 minutes each afternoon. The nurse's best response would be which of the following?
 1. "Taking an afternoon nap will interfere with his being able to sleep at night. If he's tired in the afternoon, see if you can interest him in some type of stimulating activity to keep him awake."
 2. "He shouldn't need to take an afternoon nap if he's getting enough sleep at night."
 3. "Unless your husband has trouble falling asleep at night, a brief afternoon nap is fine."
 4. "Encourage him to consume coffee or some other caffeinated beverage at lunch to prevent drowsiness in the afternoon."

10. During admission to a hospital unit, the client tells the nurse that her sleep tends to be very light and that it is difficult for her to get back to sleep if she's awakened at night. Which of the following interventions should the nurse implement? Select all that apply.
 1. Remind colleagues to keep their conversation in the halls to a minimum at night.
 2. Encourage the client's family members to bring in a radio to play soft music at night.
 3. Avoid scheduling medications and procedures including vital signs between 11 PM and 6 AM.
 4. Encourage the client to ask family members to bring in a fan to provide white noise.

See Answers to Test Your Knowledge in Appendix A. ∞

EXPLORE MEDIALINK www.prenhall.com/berman

DVD-ROM
- Audio Glossary
- NCLEX Review
- Video: Sleep and the Elderly

COMPANION WEBSITE
- Additional NCLEX Review
- Case Study: Client with Difficulty Falling Asleep
- Care Plan Activity: Client with a Sleep Disorder
- Application Activity: Diagnosing Sleep Apnea
- Links to Resources

READINGS AND REFERENCES

SUGGESTED READINGS
Griffiths, M. F., & Peerson, A. (2005). Risk factors for chronic insomnia following hospitalization. *Journal of Advanced Nursing, 49*, 245–253.
The researchers evaluated the sleep of 86 clients prior to elective cardiac and orthopedic procedures and 3 months after their discharge. Prior to surgery, 10% of the participants reported symptoms of insomnia (quite similar to the prevalence of insomnia in adults). Afterwards, 19% of the participants reported insomnia.
Lower, J., Bonsack, C., & Guion, J. (2003). Peace and quiet. *Nursing Management, 34*(4), 40A–40D.
The authors reviewed factors that make it difficult for clients to rest in hospitals and steps that are needed to help provide a healing
environment (e.g., uninterrupted sleep, massage, music). They describe their vision, implementation, and outcomes of providing quiet time between 2 and 4 PM for clients in two ICUs.
Tranmer, J. E., Minard, J. Fox, L. A., & Rebelo, L. (2003). The sleep of medical and surgical clients. *Clinical Nursing Research, 12*, 159–173.
The researchers surveyed 56 surgical clients and 54 medical clients about their sleep during a 3-day period. Surgical clients reported receiving more care during the night than medical clients, although the intensity of care decreased as the postop period lengthened. Medical clients were more likely than surgical clients to receive sedative or hypnotic medications. Most clients reported
receiving some type of analgesic at night and having their sleep interrupted at least once for vital signs, venipuncture, or dressing changes. Pain, noise, and environmental factors were frequency cited as causes of disturbed sleep.

RELATED RESEARCH
Carter, P. A., & Action, G. J. (2006). Personality and coping: Predictors of depression and sleep problems among caregivers of individuals who have cancer. *Journal of Gerontological Nursing, 32*(2), 45–53.
Dorsey, C. M., Lee, K. A., & Scharf, M. B. (2004). Effect of zolpidem on sleep in women with perimenopausal and postmenopausal insomnia: A 4-week, randomized, multicenter, double-blind, placebo-controlled study. *Clinical Therapeutics. 26*, 1578–1586.

Huth, M. M., Zink, K. A., & van Horn, N. R. (2005). The effects of massage therapy in improving outcomes for youth with cystic fibrosis: An evidence review. *Pediatric Nursing, 31,* 328–333.

McNamara, M. E., Burnham, D. C., Smith, C., & Carroll, D. L. (2003). The effects of back massage before diagnostic cardiac catheterization. *Alternative Therapies, 9*(1), 50–57.

Melancon, B., & Miller, L. H. (2005). Massage therapy versus traditional therapy for low back pain relief: Implications for holistic nursing practice. *Holistic Nursing Practice, 19*(3), 116–119.

Millman, R. P. (2005). Excessive sleepiness in adolescents and young adults: Causes, consequences, and treatment strategies. *Pediatrics, 115*(6), 1774–1786.

Mok, E., & Woo, C. P. (2004). The effects of slow stroke back massage on anxiety and shoulder pain in older stroke patients. *Complementary Therapy in Nursing and Midwifery, 10,* 209–216.

National Center on Sleep Disorders Research (n.d.). *2003 national sleep disorders research plan.* Retrieved July 4, 2006, from http://www.nhlbi.nih.gov/health/prof/sleep/res_plan/

Taras, H., & Potts-Datema, W. (2005). Sleep and student performance at school. *The Journal of School Health, 75*(7), 248–254.

REFERENCES

American Sleep Disorders Association. (2005). *The international classification of sleep disorders: Diagnostic and coding manual.* Lawrence, KS: Allen Press.

Arnold, E. (2004). Sorting out the 3 D's: Delirium, dementia, and depression. *Nursing, 34*(6), 36–42.

Colson, E. R., McCabe, L. K., Fox, K., Levenson, S., Colton, T., Lister, G., & Corwin, M. J. (2005). Barriers to following the back-to-sleep recommendations: Insights from focus groups with inner-city caregivers. *Ambulatory Pediatrics, 5*(6), 349–354.

Dochterman, J. M., & Bulechek, G. M. (Eds.). (2004). *Nursing interventions classification (NIC)* (4th ed.). St. Louis, MO: Mosby.

Gangwisch, J. E., Malaspina, D., Boden-Albala, B., & Heymsfield, S. B. (2005). Inadequate sleep as a risk factor for obesity: Analysis of the NHANES I. *Sleep, 28,* 1289–1296.

Institute of Medicine (IOM). (2006). *Sleep disorders and sleep deprivation: An unmet public health problem.* Washington, DC: Author.

Moorhead, S., Johnson, M., & Maas, M. (Eds.). (2004). *Nursing outcomes classification (NOC)* (3rd ed.). St. Louis, MO: Mosby.

NANDA International. (2007). *NANDA nursing diagnoses: Definitions and classification 2007–2008.* Philadelphia: Author.

National Sleep Foundation. (n.d.a). *A look at the school start times debate.* Retrieved June 29, 2006, from http://www.sleepfoundation.org/hottopics/index.php?secid=18&id=206

National Sleep Foundation. (n.d.b). *ABCs of ZZZZ—When you can't sleep.* Retrieved June 29, 2006, from http://www.sleepfoundation.org/sleeplibrary/index.php?secid=id=53

National Sleep Foundation. (n.d.c). *Aging gracefully and sleeping well.* Retrieved June 29, 2006, from http://www.sleepfoundation.org/hottopics/index.php?secid=12&id=225

National Sleep Foundation. (n.d.d). *Children's sleep habits.* Retrieved June 29, 2006, from http://www.sleepfoundation.org/hottopics/index.php?secid=11&id=39

National Sleep Foundation. (n.d.e). *Parents of teens: Recognize the signs and symptoms of sleep deprivation and sleep problems.* Retrieved July 2, 2006, from http://www.sleepfoundation.org/_content/hottopics/teensigns.pdf

National Sleep Foundation. (2005a). *Insomnia.* Retrieved June 29, 2006, from http://www.sleepfoundation.org/sleeptionary/index.php?id=19.

National Sleep Foundation. (2005b). *Insomnia symptoms.* Retrieved July 2, 2006, from http://www.sleepfoundation.org/sleeptionary/index.php?id=19&subsection=symptoms

National Sleep Foundation. (2006). National *Sleep Foundation 2006 Sleep in America poll highlights and key findings.* Retrieved July 4, 2006, from http://www.sleepfoundation.org/_content/hottopics/Highlights_facts_06.pdf

Orr, W. C. (2000). Editorial: Sleep and functional bowel disorders: Can bad bowels cause bad dreams? *American Journal of Gastroenterology, 95,* 1118–1121.

Robinson, S. B., Weitzel, T., & Henderson, L. (2005). The sh-h-h-h project. Nonpharmacological interventions. *Holistic Nursing Practice, 19*(6), 263–266.

Vitiello, M. V. (1999). Effective treatments for age-related sleep disturbances. *Geriatrics, 54,* 47–52.

SELECTED BIBLIOGRAPHY

Bephage, G. (2005). Promoting quality sleep in older people: The nursing care role. *British Journal of Nursing, 14*(4), 205–210.

Carlson, B. W., & Mascarella, J. J. (2005). Changes in sleep patterns in COPD. *American Journal of Nursing, 103*(12), 71–74.

Cmiel, C. A., Gasser, D. M., Oliphant, L. M., & Neveau, A. J. (2004). Noise control: A nursing team's approach to sleep promotion. *American Journal of Nursing, 104*(2), 40–48.

Cole, C., & Richards, K. C. (2006). Sleep in persons with dementia: Increasing quality of life by managing sleep disorders. *Journal of Gerontological Nursing, 32*(3), 48–53.

Dulak, S. B. (2005). Dangerous bedfellows. *RN, 68*(4), 33–37.

Hoffman, S. (2003). Sleep in older adults. *Geriatric Nursing, 24,* 210–216.

Honkus, V. L. (2003). Sleep deprivation in critical care units. *Critical Care Nursing Quarterly, 26*(3), 179–189.

Hughes, R. G., & Rogers, A. E. (2004). Are you tired? Sleep deprivation compromises nurses' health—and jeopardizes patients. *American Journal of Nursing, 104,* 36–37.

Joanna Briggs Institute. (2004). Strategies to manage sleep in residents of aged care facilities. *Best Practice. Evidence Based Practice Information Sheets for Health Professionals, 8*(3), 1–5.

Kennedy, M. (2004). Back to sleep. Many nurses don't follow the recommended sleep guidelines for infants. *American Journal of Nursing, 104*(6), 17.

Kreiger, A. C., & Redeker, N. S. (2002). Obstructive sleep apnea syndrome: Its relationship with hypertension. *Journal of Cardiovascular Nursing, 17,* 1–11.

Maindonald, E. (2005). Helping parents reduce the risk of SIDS. *Nursing, 35*(7), 50–53.

Mauk, K. L. (2005). Promoting sound sleep habits in older adults. *Nursing, 35*(2), 22,25.

McKibbin, C. L., Ancoli-Isreal, S., Dimsdale, J., Archuleta, C., von Kanel, R., Mills, P., et al. (2005). Sleep in spousal caregivers of people with Alzheimer's disease. *Sleep, 28,* 1245–1250.

Nagel, C. L., Markie, M. B., Richards, K. C., & Taylor, J. L. (2003). Sleep promotion in hospitalized elders. *Medsurg Nursing, 12*(5), 279–289.

Quillen, T. F. (2005). Sounding the alarm for narcolepsy. *Nursing, 35*(6), 74–75.

Rogers, A. E., & Dreher, H. M. (2002). Narcolepsy. *Nursing Clinics of North America, 37,* 1–18.

Smith, B. K. (2004). Test your stamina for workplace fatigue. *Nursing Management, 35*(10), 38–40.

Smyth, C. (2003). The Pittsburgh sleep quality index. *Medsurg Nursing, 12*(4), 261–262.

Thompson, D. G. (2005). Safe sleep practices for hospitalized infants. *Pediatric Nursing, 31*(5), 400–403.

Westley, C. (2004). Sleep: Geriatric self-learning module. *Medsurg Nursing, 13*(5), 291–295.

Williams, J. (2004). Gerontologic nurse practitioner care guidelines: Sleep in the elderly. *Geriatric Nursing, 25,* 310–312.

Yantis, M. A. (2002). Obstructive sleep apnea. *American Journal of Nursing, 102*(6), 83, 85.

Testing Your Understanding—Unit II
Fundamentals of Nursing: Concepts, Process, and Practice

 Pages 37–43
CHECKING YOUR COMPREHENSION

Choose the best answer for each of the following questions.

1. All of the following are neurotransmitters except
   a. dopamine.
   b. acetylcholine.
   c. chlorahydrine.
   d. noradrenaline.

2. The Research Notes section (p. 41) suggests that many mothers
   a. were not concerned for the safety of their children.
   b. know that SIDS occurs more commonly in African American infants.
   c. did not feel the advice from their healthcare provider was accurate.
   d. realized the study was too limited to make any generalizations regarding themes.

3. Sleep is characterized by all of the following EXCEPT:
   a. increased responsiveness to external stimuli.
   b. variable levels of consciousness.
   c. minimal physical activity.
   d. changes in the body's physiologic processes.

4. The primary function of Figure 45-1 is to
   a. compare and contrast time spent in REM and non-REM sleep.
   b. illustrate the four to six cycles of sleep of a healthy adult.
   c. illustrate the decrease of NREM within the sleep process.
   d. explain the limitations of REM 4.

Identify the following statements as true or false.

5. Toddlers and the elderly need the same amount of sleep.

6. Some members of Congress are trying to change the early start times of schooling for adolescents.

7. Sundown Syndrome is a sleep disorder most commonly associated with preschoolers.

Define each term as it is used in the chapter.

8. adversely

9. monotonous

10. stimuli

11. deterioration

Answer the following questions.

12. Explain what it means for a person to be in circadian synchronization.

13. Describe the differences between a "self-soother" and a "signaler."

14. As per the National Sleep Foundation, list which adults are more vulnerable for not getting enough sleep.

Discussion and Critical Thinking Questions

1. You are presented with a teenager who you feel may not be getting an adequate amount of sleep. What questions would you ask them and what suggestions would you make?

2. Evaluate Anatomy and Physiology Review: Reticular Activating System (p. 39). What is the overall main idea and the three most important supporting details in this visual?

Pages 43–48
CHECKING YOUR COMPREHENSION

Choose the best answer for each of the following questions.

1. Which of the following facts is not given regarding factors affecting sleep?
   a. The size of a bed may hinder sleep.
   b. Motivation can overcome the normal circadian drive to sleep.
   c. Dietary L-tryptophan, a compound found in milk, may induce sleep.
   d. Exercising late in the day may delay sleep.

2. Dreher's research model utilizing nonpharmacological interventions focused on
   a. training hospital staff regarding CNAs.
   b. teaching hospital patients the importance of sleep.
   c. promoting sleep for patients in hospitals.
   d. assessing the benefits and detriments of "sleep baskets."

3. Which statement is NOT true concerning narcolepsy?
   a. Fragmented sleep at night causes narcoleptics to sleep during the day.
   b. The onset of narcolepsy tends to occur between the ages of fifteen and thirty.
   c. GHB, the date rape drug, has been approved for the treatment of narcolepsy.
   d. People with narcolepsy do not have a normal sleep cycle.

4. By examining Box 45-4, one can learn that
   a. all parasomnias occur during REM sleep.
   b. sleeptalking and bruxism often occur simultaneously.
   c. periodic limb movements disorder often afflicts the elderly.
   d. somnambulism requires the sleepwalker to be woken and returned to bed.

Identify the following statements as true or false.

5. Narcolepsy is caused by a lack of hypocretin.

6. Many people who suffer from hypersomnia are found to have psychological problems which are the underlying cause of this condition.

7. Sleep apnea can be treated best by medication.

Define each term as it is used in the chapter.

8. subjective

9. albeit

10. malaise

11. benign

12. deleterious

Answer the following questions.

13. Explain the difference between chronic insomnia and chronic-intermittent insomnia.

14. Identify how environmental issues can affect a person's sleep.

15. List three drugs that promote and three drugs that hinder sleep.

Discussion and Critical Thinking Questions

1. Using the information in the text, explain the three sleep disturbances seen in children and what can be done in each circumstance.

2. Evaluate the implications of the study noted in "Research Note: Are Shortened Sleep Durations Contributing to the Growing Epidemic of Obesity?" and decide how these implications may vary a healthcare provider's treatment of a patient.

Pages 48–59
CHECKING YOUR COMPREHENSION

Choose the best answer for each of the following questions.

1. According to the text, when taking a patient's initial sleep history, it is important to ask all of the following questions EXCEPT:
   a. Do you take prescription medication?
   b. What size bed do you normally use?
   c. Has anyone told you that you thrash around while you sleep?
   d. Do you nap during the day?

2. Which of the following medications used for insomnia is less likely to cause residual drowsiness after administration?
   a. Temazepam
   b. Zaleplon
   c. Eszopiclone
   d. Zolpidem

3. The primary function of Box 45-5 (p. 52) is to
   a. identify how to reduce different environmental distractions in hospitals.
   b. compare different environmental distractions in hospitals.
   c. make connections between different environmental distractions in hospitals.
   d. show in order of importance how to reduce different environmental distractions in hospitals.

4. Which one of the following nursing interventions/selected activities was NOT included in the Nursing Care Plan for Jack Harrison?
   a. Teach Mr. Harrison the factors that contribute to sleep pattern disturbances.
   b. Suggest Mr. Harrison talk about his feeling and fears.
   c. Aid Mr. Harrison in figuring out how much sleep he needs to be productive and energetic in his daily life.
   d. Instruct Mr. Harrison when to ingest his sleep aid to ensure optimum sleep.

Identify the following statements as true or false.

5. Every nurse is able to investigate a complaint of excessive daytime sleepiness and sleep complaints lasting more than six months.

6. Often, the main cause of sleep apnea which is found during a physical exam is a deviated septum.

7. It is important to know a person's sleeping patterns before initiating the use of a sleeping aid.

Define each term as it is used in the chapter.

8. exacerbate

9. canthus

10. preclude

11. etiology

12. latency

13. explicit

Answer the following questions.

14. List the different tests that make up the polysomnography and describe what each one measures.

15. Explain what is meant by *sleep hygiene.*

Discussion and Critical Thinking Questions

1. Examine the four factors noted in the section "Client Teaching: Promoting Sleep" (p. 51). Discuss which activities that promote sleep would be the hardest to change and which would be the easiest to change.

2. This section includes one chart (Nursing Care Plan: Sleep) and one illustration (Concept Map: Sleep) that both focus on a patient, Jack Harrison, who has a dilemma pertaining to sleep. Discuss the similarities and the differences of these two visuals. Which one includes more information? Which one is easier for you to decipher? Was it necessary for the author to include both of them?

Chapter Review
END OF CHAPTER ANALYSIS

1. Which of the following would be the best strategy regarding the Chapter Highlights (p. 57)?
   a. Memorize the information before reading the chapter.
   b. Don't look at any of it until after reading the chapter.
   c. Skim it prior to reading the chapter to preview the information.
   d. Continually refer back to it during reading to ensure that you do not learn extraneous information.

2. After reading the chapter, you should be able to answer all of the following questions EXCEPT:
   a. What are the similarities and differences of REM and NREM sleep?
   b. What are the sleep enhancing medications that are specifically used for infants?
   c. What are the normal sleeping patterns and requirements for people of different ages?
   d. What may be some causes of excessive daytime sleepiness?

3. The chapter employs all of the following techniques to make it easier to understand EXCEPT:
   a. learning objectives.
   b. graphics and visuals.
   c. headings and subheadings.
   d. marginal annotations.

Group Projects

1. Keep a sleep journal for one week. Make copies of your journal for each member of your group. As a group, evaluate each group member's data and then generate a list of specific questions you would like to ask that person. Once these questions are answered by "the sleeper," create a sleep plan using the information in the chapter.

2. Many people in today's society are not aware that they may have difficulty sleeping when staying overnight in a hospital. As a group, write a letter with suggestions that may help patients optimize their sleep during their hospital stay.

3. Investigate the website of the National Sleep Foundation (http://www.sleepfoundation.org). After discussing what information on the website supports information from this chapter, decide what additional information from the website may be important for healthcare providers to learn about sleep.

Journal Ideas

1. Using the information presented in the chapter, reflect on the factors that may affect your own sleep and determine at least four changes that you can make to enhance the quality and quantity of your sleep.

2. After reviewing the recommendations in the chapter made to Jack Harrison, a 36-year-old police officer who had trouble sleeping, create a list of at least ten questions that you feel would be beneficial to ask him a month after beginning his new Sleep Plan.

Organizing Information

It is important to not only know a word's definition but also how it relates to the context of the text. Complete the following chart using the **Key Terms** noted on page 38.

Key Term	Definition	Connection to Content
biological rhythms (p. 38)	A daily cycle of activity observed in many living organisms controlled from inside the body.	Sleep is a complex biological rhythm which begins to develop by the 6th week of life.
electroencephalogram (p. 49)		
electromyogram (p. 49)		
electro-oculogram (p. 49)		
hypersomnia (p. 46)		
insomnia (p. 46)		
narcolepsy (p. 46)		
nocturnal emissions (p. 42)		
NREM sleep (p. 39)		
parasomnia (p. 48)		
polysomnography (p. 49)		
REM sleep (p. 39)		
sleep (p. 38)		
sleep apnea (p. 47)		
sleep architecture (p. 39)		
sleep hygiene (p. 51)		
somnology (p. 38)		

Unit III: Mathematics

From

Jeffrey Bennett

William Briggs

Using and Understanding Mathematics: A Quantitative Reasoning Approach

Fourth Edition

Chapter 1:
Mathematics and the Arts

An Introduction to Mathematics

Mathematics is defined as the study of the measurement, properties, and relationships of quantities and sets, using numbers and symbols. Mathematical significance can be found in almost every aspect of life so it makes sense that math has been taught since the times of Ancient Greece and Ancient Egypt.

There are many types of math that are commonly taught in today's schools, such as arithmetic, algebra, geometry, trigonometry, statistics, and calculus. In today's colleges there are also courses that explore such topics as math in art, math in nature, and math in sports. Most college students are required to take at least two math courses even if they are majoring in a discipline that is not related to mathematics. A degree in mathematics will prepare students for careers in the actuarial field, business and management, education, engineering, government, law enforcement, operation research, and statistics.

Strategies for Reading Mathematics Texts

When reading a math textbook, it is important to read the introduction, summaries, section headings, diagrams, and other illustrations in the chapter. It is necessary to look at the problems at the end of the chapter to understand what is expected of you and to decide if you are going to do the exercises as you learn each concept or if you are going to wait until you have completed the chapter. Take note of new terms and formulas. Review all of the examples that are given regarding newly learned computations. Solving problems is the most important part of learning mathematics, so be sure to carefully read through the problems and draw appropriate diagrams.

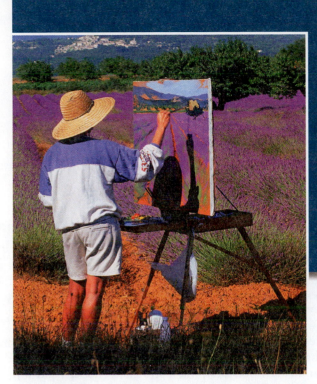

(Mathematics) seems to stand for all that is practical, poetry for all that is visionary, but in the kingdom of the imagination you will find them close akin, and they should go together as a precious heritage to every youth.

—Florence Milner,
School Review, 1898

Mathematics and the Arts

The connections between art and mathematics go deep into history. The ties are most evident in architecture: The Great Pyramids in Egypt, the Eiffel Tower in France, and modern-day skyscrapers all required mathematics in their design. But mathematics has contributed in equally profound ways to music, painting, and sculpture. In this chapter, we explore a few of the many connections between mathematics and the arts.

UNIT 11A Mathematics and Music

The roots of mathematics and music are entwined in antiquity. Pythagoras (c. 500 B.C.E.) claimed that "all nature consists of harmony arising out of number." He imagined that the planets circled the Earth on invisible heavenly spheres, obeying specific numeric laws and emitting the ethereal sounds known as the "music of the spheres." He therefore saw a direct connection between geometry and music. Over a thousand years later, the standard curriculum in medieval universities was the *quadrivium* (Latin for "crossroads"), consisting of arithmetic, geometry, music, and astronomy.

Sound and Music

Any vibrating object produces sound. The vibrations produce a **wave** (much like a water wave) that propagates through the surrounding air in all directions. When such a wave impinges on the ear, we perceive it as sound. Of course, some sounds, such as speech and screeching tires, do not qualify as music. Most musical sounds are made by vibrating strings (violins, cellos, guitars, and pianos), vibrating reeds (clarinets, oboes, and some organ pipes), or vibrating columns of air (other organ pipes, horns, and flutes).

One of the most basic qualities of sound is **pitch.** For example, a tuba has a "lower" pitch than a flute, and a violin has a "higher" pitch than a bass guitar. To understand pitch, find a taut string (a guitar string works best, but a stretched rubber band will do). When you pluck the string, it produces a sound with a certain pitch. Next, use your finger to hold the midpoint of the string in place, and pluck either half of the string. Note that a higher-pitched sound is produced, demonstrating an ancient musical principle discovered by the Greeks: *The shorter the string, the higher the pitch.*

It was many centuries before anyone understood why a shorter string creates a higher pitch, but we now know that it is due to a relationship between pitch and **frequency.** The frequency of a vibrating string is the rate at which it moves up and down. For example, a string that vibrates up and down 100 times each second (reaching the high point 100 times and the low point 100 times) has a frequency of 100 **cycles per second (cps).** The sound waves produced by the string vibrate with the same frequency as the string, and the relationship between pitch and frequency is quite simple: *The higher the frequency, the higher the pitch.*

The lowest possible frequency for a particular string, called its **fundamental frequency,** occurs when it vibrates up and down along its full length (Figure 11.1a).

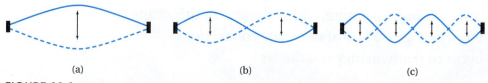

    (a)   (b)   (c)

FIGURE 11.1 A string vibrating up and down at (a) its fundamental frequency, (b) twice its fundamental frequency (waves half as long as those at the fundamental frequency), and (c) four times its fundamental frequency (waves 1/4 as long as those at the fundamental frequency).

Every string has its own fundamental frequency, which depends on characteristics including the length, density, and tension of the string. If you generate a wave that vibrates up and down along each half of the length of the string, the wave will have a frequency that is twice the fundamental frequency (Figure 11.1b). For example, if a string has a fundamental frequency of 100 cps, a wave that is half as long as the original wave has a frequency of 200 cps. Similarly, a wave one-quarter the length of the original wave has a frequency four times the fundamental frequency (Figure 11.1c). The same idea applies to other types of musical instruments, but the pitch is related to the frequency of vibration of a reed (for example, in a clarinet) or air column (for example, in an organ).

The relationship between pitch and frequency helps explain another discovery of the ancient Greeks: Pairs of notes sound particularly pleasing and natural together when one note is an **octave** higher than the other note. We now know that raising the pitch by an octave corresponds to a doubling of frequency. The piano keyboard (Figure 11.2) is helpful here. An octave is the interval between, say, middle C and the next higher C. For example, middle C has a frequency of 260 cps, the C above middle C has a frequency of 2×260 cps = 520 cps, and the next higher C has a frequency of 2×520 cps = 1040 cps. Similarly, the C below middle C has a frequency of about $\frac{1}{2} \times 260$ cps = 130 cps.

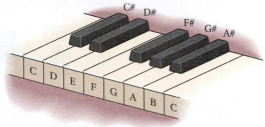

FIGURE 11.2 Piano keys.

Time out to think

The note middle A (above middle C) has a frequency of about 440 cps. What are the frequencies of the A notes an octave higher and an octave lower?

Scales

The musical tones that span an octave comprise a **scale.** The Greeks invented the 7-note (or diatonic) scale that corresponds to the white keys on the piano. In the 17th century, Johann Sebastian Bach adopted a 12-tone scale, which corresponds to both the white and the black keys on a modern piano. With Bach's music, the 12-tone scale spread throughout Europe, becoming a foundation of Western music. Many other scales are possible. For example, 3-tone scales are common in African music, scales with more than 12 tones occur in Asian music, and 19-tone scales are used in contemporary music.

On the 12-tone scale, the frequency separating each tone is called a **half-step,** corresponding to consecutive notes on the piano keyboard. For example, E and F are separated by a half-step, as are F and F# (read "F sharp"). In each half-step, the frequency increases by some *multiplicative* factor; let's call it f. The frequency of C is the frequency of B times the factor f, the frequency of C# is the frequency of C times the factor f, and so on. The frequencies of the notes across the entire scale are related as follows:

$$C \xrightarrow{f} C\# \xrightarrow{f} D \xrightarrow{f} D\# \xrightarrow{f} E \xrightarrow{f} F \xrightarrow{f} F\# \xrightarrow{f} G \xrightarrow{f} G\# \xrightarrow{f} A \xrightarrow{f} A\# \xrightarrow{f} B \xrightarrow{f} C$$

**By the Way**

Human speech consists of sounds with frequencies of 200 to 400 cycles per second. The range of a piano extends from about 27 to 4200 cycles per second. The maximum frequency audible to the human ear declines gradually with age, from about 20,000 cycles per second in children and young teenagers to about 12,000 cycles per second at age 50.

Because an octave corresponds to an increase in frequency by a factor of 2, the factor f must have the property

$$\underbrace{f \times f \times f \times f \times f \times f \times f \times f \times f \times f \times f \times f}_{12 \text{ times}} = f^{12} = 2$$

We therefore conclude that f is the *twelfth root* of two, or $f = \sqrt[12]{2} \approx 1.05946$.

We can now calculate the frequency of every note of a 12-tone scale. Starting from middle C, with its frequency of 260 cps, we multiply by $f = \sqrt[12]{2}$ to find that the frequency of C# is 260 cps $\times f \approx 275$ cps. Multiplying again by f gives the frequency of D as 275 cps $\times f \approx 292$ cps. Continuing in this way generates Table 11.1.

TABLE 11.1 Frequencies of Notes in the Octave Above Middle C

Note	Frequency (CPS)	Ratio to Frequency of Preceding Note	Ratio to Frequency of Middle C
C	260	$\sqrt[12]{2} \approx 1.05946$	$1.00000 = 1$
C#	275	$\sqrt[12]{2} \approx 1.05946$	1.05946
D (second)	292	$\sqrt[12]{2} \approx 1.05946$	1.12246
D#	309	$\sqrt[12]{2} \approx 1.05946$	1.18921
E (third)	328	$\sqrt[12]{2} \approx 1.05946$	$1.25992 \approx \frac{5}{4}$
F (fourth)	347	$\sqrt[12]{2} \approx 1.05946$	$1.33484 \approx \frac{4}{3}$
F#	368	$\sqrt[12]{2} \approx 1.05946$	1.41421
G (fifth)	390	$\sqrt[12]{2} \approx 1.05946$	$1.49831 \approx \frac{3}{2}$
G#	413	$\sqrt[12]{2} \approx 1.05946$	1.58740
A (sixth)	437	$\sqrt[12]{2} \approx 1.05946$	$1.68179 \approx \frac{5}{3}$
A#	463	$\sqrt[12]{2} \approx 1.05946$	1.78180
B (seventh)	491	$\sqrt[12]{2} \approx 1.05946$	1.88775
C (octave)	520	$\sqrt[12]{2} \approx 1.05946$	$2.00000 = 2$

By the Way

All entries in column 3 are the same because the same factor, $f \approx \sqrt[12]{2}$, separates every pair of notes. The parenthetical terms in column 1 are names used by musicians to describe intervals between the note shown and middle C.

Human speech is like a cracked kettle on which we tap crude rhythms for bears to dance to, while we long to make music that will melt the stars.

—Gustave Flaubert

Column 4 of Table 11.1 shows that a few tones have simple ratios of frequency to middle C. For example, the frequency of G is approximately $\frac{3}{2}$ times the frequency of middle C (musicians call this interval a *fifth*), and the frequency of F is approximately $\frac{4}{3}$ times the frequency of middle C (musicians call this interval a *fourth*). According to many musicians, the most pleasing combinations of notes, called **consonant tones,** are those whose frequencies have a simple ratio. Referring to consonant tones, the Chinese philosopher Confucius observed that small numbers are the source of perfection in music.

✳ EXAMPLE 1 *The Dilemma of Temperament*

Because the whole-number ratios in Table 11.1 are not exact, tuners of musical instruments have the problem of *temperament*, which can be demonstrated as follows. Start at middle C with a frequency of 260 cps. Using the whole-number ratios, find the frequency if you raise C by a sixth to A, raise A by a fourth to D, lower D by a fifth to G, and lower G by a fifth to C. Having returned to the same note, have you also returned to the same frequency?

SOLUTION According to Table 11.1, raising a note by a sixth increases its frequency by a factor of $\frac{5}{3}$. Thus, the frequency of A above middle C is $\frac{5}{3} \times 260$ cps $= 433.33$ cps. Raising this note by a fourth increases its frequency by $\frac{4}{3}$. Thus, D has a frequency of $\frac{4}{3} \times 433.33$ cps $= 577.77$ cps. Lowering D by a fifth (a factor of $\frac{2}{3}$) to G gives a frequency of $\frac{2}{3} \times 577.77 = 385.18$ cps. Finally, lowering G by another fifth (a factor of $\frac{2}{3}$) puts us back to middle C, with a frequency of $\frac{2}{3} \times 385.18$ cps $= 256.79$. Note that, by using whole-number ratios, we have not quite returned to the proper frequency of 260 cps for middle C. The problem is that the whole-number ratios are not exact. That is, $\frac{5}{3} \times \frac{4}{3} \times \frac{2}{3} \times \frac{2}{3} = \frac{80}{81}$ is close to, but not *exactly*, 1. **Now try Exercises 22–26.** ◄

Musical Scales as Exponential Growth

The increase in frequencies in a scale is just another example of exponential growth. Each successive frequency is $f \approx 1.05946$ times, or approximately 5.9% more than, the previous frequency. In other words, the frequencies increase at a fixed relative growth rate. Thus, we can use an exponential function (see Unit 9C) to find any frequency on the scale. Suppose we start at a frequency Q_0. Then the frequency Q of the note n half-steps higher is given by

$$Q = Q_0 \times 1.05946^n$$

✳ EXAMPLE 2 *Exponential Growth on Musical Scales*

Use the exponential growth law to find the frequency of the note a fifth above middle C, the note one octave and a fifth above middle C, and the note two octaves and a fifth above middle C.

SOLUTION We let the frequency of middle C be the initial value for the scale; that is, we set $Q_0 = 260$ cps. Table 11.1 shows that the note a fifth above middle C is G, which is seven half-steps above middle C. Thus, we let $n = 7$ in the exponential law and find that the frequency of G is

$$Q = Q_0 \times 1.05946^7 = 390 \text{ cps}$$

The note one octave and a fifth above middle C is $12 + 7 = 19$ half-steps above middle C. Letting $n = 19$, we find that the frequency of this note is

$$Q = Q_0 \times 1.05946^{19} = 779 \text{ cps}$$

The note two octaves and a fifth above middle C is $(2 \times 12) + 7 = 31$ half-steps above middle C. Letting $n = 31$, we find that the frequency of this note is

$$Q = Q_0 \times 1.05946^{31} = 1558 \text{ cps} \quad \textbf{Now try Exercises 27–29.} ◄$$

Of course, Beethoven's Eroica Symphony or Michelangelo's ceiling of the Sistine Chapel can be reduced to an adequate mathematical formula. There is, however, one little catch. The only person capable of making such an all-inclusive analysis must be able to feel the emotions that Beethoven and Michelangelo felt, to think in sound and paint as they did.

—J. MURRAY BARBOUR, MUSIC HISTORIAN

From Tones to Music

Although the simple frequencies of "pure" tones are the building blocks of music, the sounds of music are far richer and more complex. For example, a plucked violin string does much more than produce a single frequency. The vibration of the string is transferred through the bridge of the violin to its top, and the ribs transfer those vibrations to the back of the instrument. With the top and back of the violin in oscillation, the entire instrument acts as a resonating chamber, which excites and amplifies the higher harmonics of the original tone.

Similar principles generate rich and complex sounds in all instruments. On the left, Figure 11.3 shows a typical sound wave that might be produced by an instrument. It isn't a simple wave like those pictured in Figure 11.1. Instead, it consists of a combination of simple waves that are the harmonics of the fundamental. In fact, the complex wave is the *sum* of the three simple waves shown on the right in Figure 11.3. The fact that a musical sound can be expressed as a sum of simple harmonics is surely the deepest connection between mathematics and music. The French mathematician Jean Baptiste Joseph Fourier first enunciated this principle in about 1810. It was one of the most profound discoveries in mathematics.

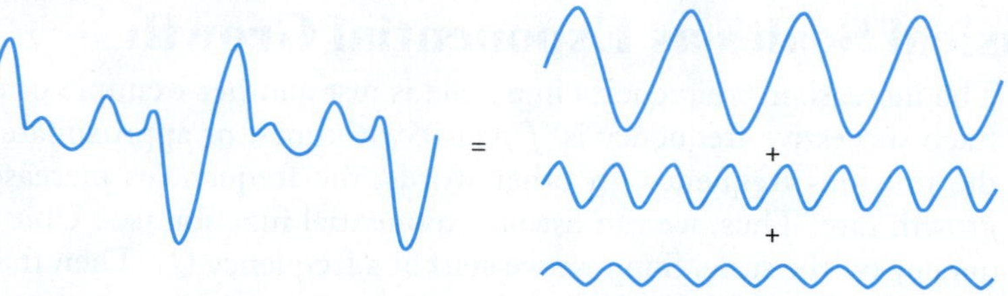

Stradivarius was essentially a craftsman of science, one with considerable, demonstrable knowledge of mathematics and acoustical physics.

—Thomas Levenson,
Measure for Measure:
A Musical History of
Science, pp. 207–208

FIGURE 11.3 The complex sound wave on the left is the sum of the three simple waves on the right.

Although mathematics helps in understanding music, many mysteries remain. For example, in about 1700, an Italian craftsman known as Stradivarius made what are still considered to be the finest violins and cellos ever produced. Despite years of study by mathematicians and scientists, no one has succeeded in reproducing the unique sounds of a Stradivarius instrument.

The Digital Age

When we talk about sound waves and imagine music to consist of waves, we are working with the **analog** picture of music. Until the early 1980s, nearly all musical recordings (phonograph cylinders, records, and tape recordings) were based on the analog picture of music. Storing music in the analog mode requires storing analogs of sound waves. For example, on records, the grooves in the vinyl surface are etched with the shape of the original musical sound wave. If you have listened to analog recordings, you know that this shape can easily become distorted or damaged.

Most recent musical recordings use a **digital** picture of music. A computer takes the analog version of a piece of music and chops it into very short time intervals (fractions of a second). The time intervals are used much like bins in a histogram. For each time interval, the computer measures the frequencies of the sound waves and records them numerically. This process, called *digitizing*, transforms the music into a list of numbers. The list can then be saved on a storage device such as a compact disc (CD) or downloaded as a digital music file. Inside a playback device such as a CD player or iPod, a computer uses a reverse process to convert the numbers back into sound waves so that they can be heard. As long as the time intervals are short enough, the music sounds smooth and authentic, with no evidence of digitizing.

Digital technology provides easy and endless ways to "process" music. Through techniques of **digital signal processing,** the sounds of a musical recording can be modified with computers. For example, extraneous sounds (background noises or "hiss") can be detected and removed. Changing the music by amplifying certain frequencies or attenuating others also is possible. Moreover, once digital music can be modified, it is a short step to creating music. Instruments called **synthesizers** can create and imitate a tremendous variety of sounds digitally without strings, brass tubes, or reeds. In the digital age, the dividing line between mathematics and music all but vanishes.

EXERCISES 11A

QUICK QUIZ

Choose the best answer to each of the following questions. Explain your reasoning with one or more complete sentences.

1. Musical sounds are generally produced by

   a. one object hitting another.

   b. objects that vibrate.

   c. objects that are being stretched to greater length.

2. If a string is vibrating up and down with a frequency of 100 cycles per second, the middle of the string is at its high point

   a. 100 times per second.

   b. 50 times per second.

   c. once every 100 seconds.

3. To make a sound with a higher pitch, you need to make a string vibrate with a

   a. higher frequency.

   b. lower frequency.

   c. higher maximum height.

4. The frequency of the lowest pitch you can hear from a particular string is the string's

   a. cycles per second.

   b. octave.

   c. fundamental frequency.

5. When you raise the pitch of a sound by an octave, the frequency of the sound

   a. doubles.

   b. goes up by a factor of 4.

   c. goes up by a factor of 8.

6. On a 12-tone scale, the frequency of each note is higher than that of the previous note by a factor of

   a. 2.

   b. 12.

   c. $\sqrt[12]{2}$.

7. The last entry in Table 11.1 shows that a frequency of 520 cps represents a note of C. What note has a frequency closest to $520 \times 1.5 = 780$ cps?

   a. D#

   b. E

   c. G

8. Suppose you made a graph by plotting notes in half-steps along the horizontal axis and the frequencies of these notes on the vertical axis. The general shape of this graph would be the same as that of a graph showing

   a. a linearly growing population.

   b. an exponentially growing population.

   c. a logistically growing population.

9. All musical sounds have a wave pattern that can be represented as

   a. a very simple constant-frequency wave.

   b. the sum of one or more individual constant-frequency waves.

   c. a series of half-step waves.

10. If you could look at the underlying computer code, you would find that the music stored on a CD or iPod was represented by

    a. lists of numbers.

    b. pictures of different-shaped waves.

    c. notes of a 12-step scale.

REVIEW QUESTIONS

11. What is pitch? How is it related to the frequency of a musical note?

12. Define *fundamental frequency*, *first harmonic*, and *octave*. Why are these concepts important in music?

13. What is a 12-tone scale? How are the frequencies of the notes on a 12-tone scale related to one another?

14. Explain how the notes of the scale are generated by exponential growth.

15. How do the wave forms of real musical sounds differ from the wave forms of simple tones? How are they related?

16. What is the difference between an analog and a digital recording of music? What are the advantages of digital recording?

DOES IT MAKE SENSE?

Decide whether each of the following statements makes sense (or is clearly true) or does not make sense (or is clearly false). Explain your reasoning.

17. If I pluck this string more often, then it will have a higher pitch.

18. Jack made the length of the string one-fourth of its original length, and the pitch went up two octaves.

19. Exponential growth is found even in musical scales.

20. A piano has 88 keys, so it must have a range of about 7 octaves.

21. The scratch on Jill's U2 phonograph record can be removed by a digital filter.

BASIC SKILLS & CONCEPTS

22. **Octaves.** Starting with a tone having a frequency of 220 cycles per second, find the frequencies of the tones that are one, two, three, and four octaves higher.

23. **Octaves.** Starting with a tone having a frequency of 1760 cycles per second, find the frequencies of the tones that are one, two, three, and four octaves lower.

24. **Notes of a Scale.** Find the frequencies of the 12 notes of the scale that starts at the F above middle C; this F has a frequency of 347 cycles per second.

25. **Notes of a Scale.** Find the frequencies of the 12 notes of the scale that starts at the G above middle C; this G has a frequency of 328 cycles per second.

26. **The Dilemma of Temperament.** Start at middle A, with a frequency of 437 cps. Using the whole-number ratios in Table 11.1, find the frequency if you raise A by a fifth to E. What is the frequency if you raise E by a fifth to B? What is the frequency if you lower B by a sixth to D? What is the frequency if you lower D by a fourth to A? Having returned to the same note, have you also returned to the same frequency? Explain.

27. **Exponential Growth and Scales.** Starting at middle C, with a frequency of 260 cps, find the frequency of the following notes:

    a. seven half-steps above middle C

    b. a sixth (nine half-steps) above middle C

    c. an octave and a fifth (seven half-steps) above middle C

    d. 25 half-steps above middle C

    e. three octaves and three half-steps above middle C

28. **Exponential Growth and Scales.** Starting at middle G, with a frequency of 390 cps, find the frequency of the following notes:

    a. six half-steps above middle G

    b. a third (four half-steps) above middle G

    c. an octave and a fourth (five half-steps) above middle G

    d. 25 half-steps above middle G

    e. two octaves and two half-steps above middle G

29. **Exponential Decay and Scales.** What is the frequency of the note seven half-steps *below* middle A (which has a frequency of 437 cps)? ten half-steps *below* middle A?

FURTHER APPLICATIONS

30. **Circle of Fifths.** The circle of fifths is generated by starting at a particular musical note and stepping upward by intervals of a fifth (seven half-steps). For example, starting at middle C, a circle of fifths includes the notes $C \rightarrow G \rightarrow D' \rightarrow A' \rightarrow E'' \rightarrow B'' \rightarrow \ldots$, where each ($'$) denotes a higher octave. Eventually the circle comes back to C several octaves higher.

    a. Show that the frequency of a tone increases by a factor of $2^{7/12} = 1.498$ if it is raised by a fifth. (Hint: Recall that each half-step corresponds to an increase in frequency by a factor of $f = \sqrt[12]{2}$.)

    b. By what factor does the frequency of a tone increase if it is raised by two fifths?

    c. Starting with middle C, at a frequency of 260 cycles per second, find the frequencies of the other notes in the circle of fifths.

    d. How many fifths are required for the circle of fifths to return to a C? How many octaves are covered by a complete circle of fifths?

    e. What is the ratio of the frequencies of the C at the beginning of the circle and the C at the end of the circle?

31. **Circle of Fourths.** A circle of *fourths* is generated by starting at any note and stepping upward by intervals of a fourth (five half-steps). By what factor is the frequency of a tone increased if it is raised by a fourth? How many fourths are required to complete the entire circle of fourths? How many octaves are covered in a complete circle of fourths?

32. **Rhythm and Mathematics.** In this unit, we focused on musical sounds, but rhythm and mathematics are also closely related. For example, in "4/4 time," there are four *quarter notes* in a measure. If two quarter notes have the duration of a *half note*, how many half notes are in one measure? If two *eighth notes* have the duration of a quarter note, how many eighth notes are in one measure? If two *sixteenth notes* have the duration of an eighth note, how many sixteenth notes are in one measure?

WEB PROJECTS

Find useful links for Web Projects on the text Web site: www.aw.com/bennett-briggs

33. **Mathematics and Music.** Many Web sites are devoted to connections between music and mathematics. Visit one such site and study a connection in some depth. Write a one- to two-page essay that describes this connection between mathematics and music.

34. **Internet Music.** Many Web sites make music available digitally. Some of these Web sites have come under attack for violating copyright laws. Find one such Web site. Describe how it works both from a user's standpoint and from a commercial standpoint. Do you think the site's use of music is legal? Is it ethical? Defend your opinions.

35. **Mathematics and Composers.** Many musical composers, both classical and modern, have used mathematics in their compositions. Research the life of one such composer. Write a one- to two-page essay discussing the role of mathematics in the composer's life and music.

IN THE NEWS

36. **Numbers and Music.** Look carefully at cassette or CD liner notes, music catalogs, or other materials related to musical products. Find as many different uses of numbers as possible in these materials, and explain how the numbers are related to the music.

37. **Digital Music.** The ease with which digital music can be copied has increased the importance of the copyright issue, especially with respect to music available on the Web. Find a recent article on issues of copying digital music. Discuss the article and its conclusions.

UNIT 11B Perspective and Symmetry

We now turn our attention to connections between mathematics and the visual arts, such as painting, sculpture, and architecture. At least three aspects of the visual arts relate directly to mathematics: *perspective*, *symmetry*, and *proportion*. In this unit, we will see how Renaissance mathematicians and artists discovered perspective and then we will explore the idea of symmetry. We'll save *proportion* for Unit 11C.

Perspective

People of all cultures have used geometrical ideas and patterns in their artwork. The ancient Greeks developed strong ties between the arts and mathematics because both endeavors were central to their view of the world. Much of the Greek outlook was lost during the Middle Ages, but the Renaissance brought at least two new developments that made mathematics an essential tool of artists. First, there was a renewed interest in natural scenes, which led to a need to paint with realism. Second, many of the artists of the day also worked as engineers and architects.

The desire to paint landscapes with three-dimensional realism brought Renaissance painters face to face with the matter of perspective. In their attempts to capture depth and volume on a two-dimensional canvas, these artists made a science of painting. The painters Brunelleschi (1377–1446) and Alberti (1404–1472) are generally credited with developing, in about 1430, a system of perspective that involved geometrical thinking. Alberti's principle that a painting "is a section of a projection" lies at the heart of drawing with perspective.

Suppose you want to paint a simple view looking down a hallway with a checker-board tile floor. Figure 11.4 shows a *side view* of the artist's eye, the canvas, and the

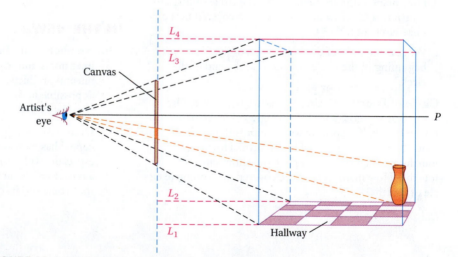

FIGURE 11.4 Side view of a hallway, showing perspectives.

hallway. Note the four lines labeled L_1, L_2, L_3, and L_4. The two side walls of the hallway intersect the floor and the ceiling along these four lines. These lines are important because they are parallel to each other in the scene and perpendicular to the canvas (or the plane containing the canvas).

Let's now look at the scene as the artist sees and paints it. The artist looks down the hallway with the point of view shown in Figure 11.5.

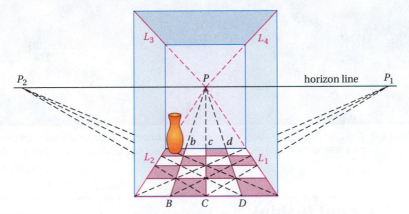

FIGURE 11.5 An artist's view of the hallway from Figure 11.4, showing perspectives. Adapted from M. Kline, *Mathematics in Western Culture.*

The lines L_1, L_2, L_3, and L_4, which are parallel in the actual scene, are not parallel in the painting. In fact, they all meet at a single point, labeled P, which is called the **principal vanishing point.** Thus, we have the first principle of perspective discovered by the Renaissance painters:

> *All lines that are parallel in the real scene and perpendicular to the canvas must intersect at the principal vanishing point of the painting.*

Note that other lines that are parallel to lines L_1, L_2, L_3, and L_4, such as the lines going straight down the hallway along the floor tiles, also meet at the principal vanishing point. For example, the line connecting the points B and b intersects P, as do the line connecting C and c and the line connecting D and d.

What happens to lines that are parallel in the actual scene but not perpendicular to the canvas, such as the diagonal lines along the floor tiles? If you study Figure 11.5 carefully, you'll see that such lines intersect at their own vanishing points, all on the horizontal line passing through the principal vanishing point. This line is called the **horizon line.** For example, the right-slanting diagonals of the floor tiles are parallel in the actual scene. But, in the painting, these lines meet at the vanishing point labeled P_1 on the horizon line. Similarly, the left-slanting diagonals meet at a vanishing point called P_2 on the horizon line. In fact, all sets of lines that are mutually parallel in the real scene (except those parallel to the horizon line) must meet at their own vanishing point on the horizon line.   **Now try Exercises 25–30.** ◄◄

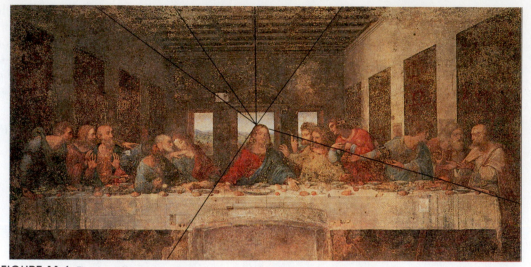

FIGURE 11.6 *The Last Supper*, by Leonardo da Vinci, shown with several lines that are parallel in the real scene and therefore converge at the principal vanishing point behind Christ.

Let no one who is not a mathematician read my works.

—LEONARDO DA VINCI

Time out to think

Imagine looking along a set of long parallel lines that stretches far into the distance, such as a set of train tracks or a set of telephone lines. The lines will appear to your eyes to get closer to each other as you look into the distance. If you were painting a picture of the scene, where would you put the principal vanishing point? Why?

Leonardo da Vinci (1452–1519) contributed greatly to the science of perspective. We can see da Vinci's mastery of perspective in many of his paintings. If you study *The Last Supper* (Figure 11.6), you will notice several parallel lines in the actual scene intersecting at the principal vanishing point of the painting, which is directly behind the central figure of Christ.

The German artist Albrecht Dürer (1471–1528) further developed the science of perspective. Near the end of his life, he wrote a popular book that stressed the use of geometry and encouraged artists to paint according to mathematical principles. Figure 11.7 is one of Dürer's woodcuts, showing an artist using his principles of perspective. A string from a point on the lute is attached to the wall at the point corresponding to the artist's eye. At the point where the string passes through the frame, a point is placed on the canvas. As the string is moved to different points on the lute, a drawing of the lute is created in perfect perspective on the canvas.

The artist Jan Vredeman de Vries (1527–1604) summarized much of the science of perspective in a book he published in 1604. Figure 11.8 shows a sketch from his book

FIGURE 11.7 Woodcut by Albrecht Dürer.

that illustrates how thoroughly perspective can be analyzed.

Time out to think

Identify some of the vanishing points in the sketch in Figure 11.8. What parallel lines from the real scene converge at each vanishing point?

Perspective drawing is sometimes abused deliberately. The painting *False Perspective* (Figure 11.9) by English artist William Hogarth (1697–1764) reminds us that perspective is essential in art. Note where the fishing line of the near man lands, and how the woman in the window appears to be light-

FIGURE 11.8 Sketch by Jan Vredeman de Vries.

ing the pipe of a man on a distant hill. The familiar work of Maurits C. Escher (1898–1972) also confounds us with its use and abuse of perspective. His drawing *Belvedere* (Figure 11.10) illustrates good use of perspective, yet the pillars of the structure are cleverly drawn to show impossible positions.

FIGURE 11.9 *False Perspective*, by William Hogarth.

FIGURE 11.10 *Belvedere*, by M. C. Escher.

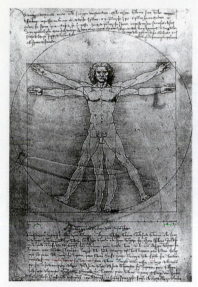

FIGURE 11.11 Leonardo da Vinci's sketch showing the symmetry of the human body.

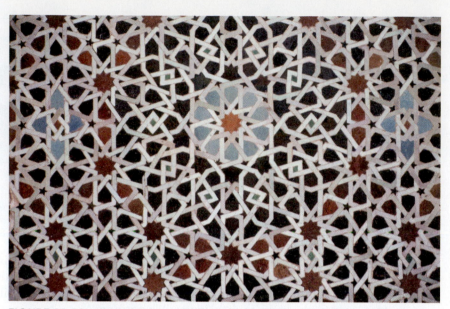

FIGURE 11.12 This Islamic tiling shows many elaborate symmetries. It is located in the Medersa Attarine, a 14th-century school of Muslim theology in Fez, Morocco.

Symmetry

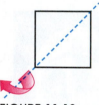

FIGURE 11.13

FIGURE 11.14
Reflection symmetry.

FIGURE 11.15
Rotation symmetry.

The term *symmetry* has many meanings. Sometimes it refers to a kind of balance. For example, *The Last Supper* (see Figure 11.6) is symmetrical because the disciples are grouped in four groups of three, with two groups on either side of the central figure of Christ. A human body is symmetrical because a vertical line drawn through the head and navel divides the body into two (nearly) identical parts (Figure 11.11).

Symmetry can also refer to repetition of patterns. Native American pottery is often decorated with simple borders that use repeating patterns. Similar symmetries are found in African, Muslim, and Moorish art such as that shown in Figure 11.12.

In mathematics, *symmetry* is a property of an object that remains unchanged under certain operations. For example, a circle still looks the same if it is rotated about its center. A square still looks the same if it is flipped across one of its diagonals (Figure 11.13). There are many such mathematical symmetries, often quite subtle. However, three symmetries are easy to identify:

- **Reflection symmetry:** An object remains unchanged when reflected across a straight line. For example, the letter A has reflection symmetry about a vertical line, while the letter H has reflection symmetry about a vertical and a horizontal line (Figure 11.14).

- **Rotation symmetry:** An object remains unchanged when rotated through some angle about a point. For example, the letters O and S have rotation symmetry because they are unchanged when rotated 180° (Figure 11.15).

- **Translation symmetry:** A pattern remains the same when shifted, say to the right or left. The pattern . . . XXX . . . (with the X's continuing in both directions) has translation symmetry because it still looks the same if we shift it to the left or to the right (Figure 11.16). (In mathematics and physics, *translating* an object means moving it in a straight line, without rotating it.)

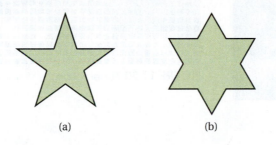

FIGURE 11.16 Translation symmetry.

✳EXAMPLE 1 *Finding Symmetries*

Identify the types of symmetry in each star in Figure 11.17.

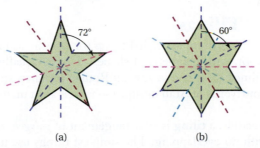

(a)　　　　　(b)

FIGURE 11.17

SOLUTION

a. The five-pointed star has five lines about which it can be flipped (reflected) without changing its appearance, so it has five reflection symmetries (Figure 11.18a). Because it has five vertices that all look the same, it can be rotated by $\frac{1}{5}$ of a full circle, or $360°/5 = 72°$, and it still looks the same. Similarly, its appearance remains unchanged if it is rotated by $2 \times 72° = 144°$, $3 \times 72° = 216°$, or $4 \times 72° = 288°$. Thus, this star has four rotational symmetries.

b. The six-pointed star has six reflection lines about which it can be flipped (reflected) without changing its appearance, so it has six reflection symmetries (Figure 11.18b). Because of its six vertices, it has rotation symmetry when rotated by $\frac{1}{6}$ of a full circle, or $360°/6 = 60°$. It also has symmetry if rotated by $2 \times 60° = 120°$, $3 \times 60° = 180°$, $4 \times 60° = 240°$, or $5 \times 60° = 300°$. Thus, this star has five rotational symmetries.

(a)　　　　　(b)

FIGURE 11.18 Each line represents a reflection symmetry. Rotation symmetries require rotation by multiples of the indicated angles.

Now try Exercises 31–37. ◄◄

FIGURE 11.19 *The Vision of the Empyrean,* by Gustave Dore.

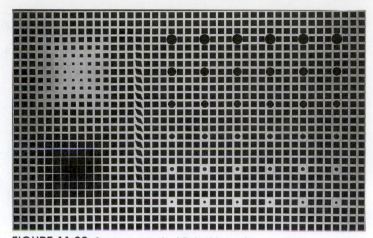

FIGURE 11.20 *Supernovae,* by Victor Vasarely.

FIGURE 11.21 A "Persian rug," generated on a computer by Anne Burns.

Symmetry in Art

Gustave Dore's (1832–1883) engraving *The Vision of the Empyrean* offers a dramatic illustration of rotation symmetry (Figure 11.19). This grand image of the cosmos can be rotated by many different angles and, at least on a large scale, appears much the same.

Sometimes, it is the *departures* from symmetry that make art effective. The 20th-century work *Supernovae* (Figure 11.20), by the Hungarian painter Victor Vasarely (1908–1997), might have started as a symmetric arrangement of circles and squares, but the gradual deviations from that pattern make a powerful visual effect.

Given the strong ties between mathematics and art, you may not be surprised that mathematical algorithms (recipes) can generate art on computers. Figure 11.21 shows an intricate Persian rug design generated on a computer by Anne Burns. The algorithm can be varied to give an endless array of patterns and symmetries.

Tilings

A form of art called *tilings* (or *tessellations*) involves covering a flat area, such as a floor, with geometrical shapes. Tilings usually have regular or symmetric patterns. Tilings are found in ancient Roman mosaics, stained glass windows, and the elaborate courtyards of Arab mosques—as well as in many modern kitchens and bathrooms.

More precisely, a **tiling** is an arrangement of *polygons* (see Unit 10A) that interlock perfectly with no overlapping. The simplest tilings use just one type of regular polygon. Figure 11.22 shows three such tilings made with equilateral triangles, squares, and regular hexagons, respectively. Note that there are no gaps or overlaps between the polygons in any of the three cases. In each case, the tiling is made by translating

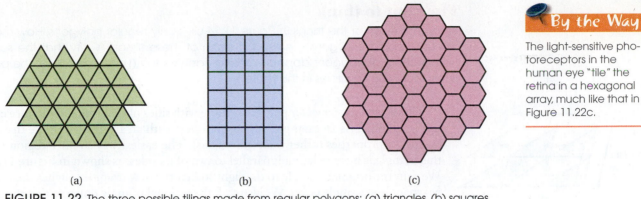

(a)   (b)   (c)

FIGURE 11.22 The three possible tilings made from regular polygons: (a) triangles, (b) squares, and (c) hexagons.

(shifting) the same basic polygon in various directions. Thus, these tilings have translation symmetry.

What happens if you try to make a tiling with, say, regular pentagons? If you try, you'll find that it simply does not work. The interior angles of a regular pentagon measure 108°. Thus, as Figure 11.23 shows, the angle that remains when three regular pentagons are placed next to each other is too small to fit another regular pentagon. In fact, a mathematical theorem states that tilings with a single regular polygon are possible only with equilateral triangles, squares, and hexagons (as in Figure 11.22).

Of course, more tilings are possible if we remove the restriction of using only a single type of regular polygon. For example, if we allow different regular polygons, but still require that the arrangement of polygons look the same around each vertex (intersection point), it is possible to make the eight different tiling patterns shown in Figure 11.24.

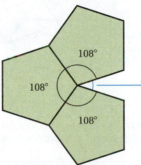

Angle = 360° − (3 × 108°) = 36°. This is too small for another pentagon to fit.

FIGURE 11.23 Regular pentagons cannot make a tiling.

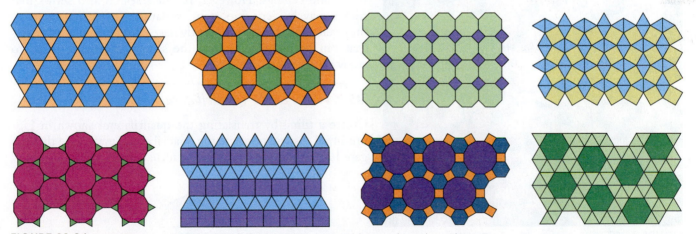

FIGURE 11.24 Eight tilings, each made by combining two or more types of regular polygons.

Time out to think

Verify that each of the tilings in Figure 11.24 uses only regular polygons. How many different regular polygons are used in each of these tilings? Verify that the same arrangement of polygons appears around each vertex. (Look carefully at the polygons; there are no circles in this figure.)

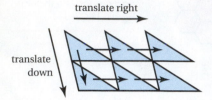

translate right

translate down

FIGURE 11.25 A tiling made by translating a triangle in two directions.

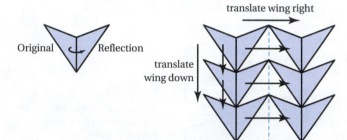

translate wing right

Original   Reflection

translate wing down

FIGURE 11.26 A tiling made by first reflecting a triangle to make a "wing," then translating the wing in two directions.

Tilings that use *irregular* polygons (those with sides of different lengths) are endless in number. As an example, suppose we start with an arbitrary triangle that has no special properties (other than three sides). The easiest way to tile a region with this triangle is by translating it parallel to two of its sides, as shown in Figure 11.25. We shift the original triangle to the right so that the new triangle touches the original triangle at a single point. We also shift the original triangle down so that the new triangle touches the original triangle at a single point. Then we repeat these right/left and up/down translations as many times as we like. The gaps created in this process are themselves triangles that interlock perfectly with the translated triangles to create a tiling.

Figure 11.26 shows another example. This time, we begin by reflecting an arbitrary triangle to produce a wing-shaped object, and then we translate this object up/down and right/left.

All of the tilings discussed so far are called *periodic tilings* because they have a pattern that is repeated throughout the tiling. In recent decades, mathematicians have explored tilings that are *aperiodic*, meaning that they do not have a pattern that repeats throughout the entire tiling. Figure 11.27 shows an aperiodic tiling created by British mathematician Roger Penrose. If you look at the center of the figure, there appears to be a fivefold symmetry (a rotational symmetry that you would find in a pentagon). However, if the figure were extended indefinitely in all directions, the same pattern would never be repeated.

Tilings can be beautiful and practical for such things as floors and ceilings. However, recent research also shows that tilings may be very important in nature. In particular, many molecules and crystals apparently have patterns and symmetries that can be understood with the same mathematics used to study tilings in art.

✳**EXAMPLE 2** *Quadrilateral Tiling*

Create a tiling by translating the quadrilateral shown in Figure 11.28. As you translate the quadrilateral, make sure that the gaps left behind have the same quadrilateral shape.

FIGURE 11.27 An aperiodic tiling by Roger Penrose.

FIGURE 11.28

SOLUTION We can find the solution by trial and error, translating the quadrilateral in different directions until we have correctly shaped gaps. Figure 11.29 shows the solution. Note that the translations are along the directions of the two diagonals of the quadrilateral. The gaps between the translated quadrilaterals are themselves quadrilaterals that interlock perfectly to complete the tiling.

Now try Exercises 38–43. ◄

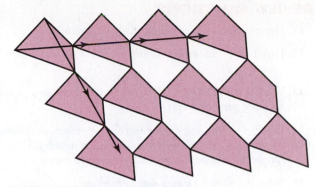

FIGURE 11.29 A quadrilateral tiling.

EXERCISES 11B

QUICK QUIZ

Choose the best answer to each of the following questions. Explain your reasoning with one or more complete sentences.

1. In a painting of train tracks that run perprndicular to the canvas, the principal vanishing point is

   a. the place in the real scene where the train tracks disappear from view.

   b. the place in the painting where the two rails meet.

   c. the place in the painting where the rails first appear to touch the sky.

2. *All* lines that are parallel in a real scene converge in a painting

   a. at the principal vanishing point.

   b. somewhere along the horizon line.

   c. somewhere along the top edge of the painting.

3. Study *The Last Supper* in Figure 11.6. Which of the following converge at the principal vanishing point?

   a. parallel beams in the ceiling

   b. lines connecting the heads of the disciples

   c. the vertical sides of the doors and windows

4. The symmetry in da Vinci's sketch of the human body in Figure 11.11 arises because

   a. he shows two sets of arms and legs.

   b. he has enclosed the bodies in a circle.

   c. the left and right sides of the sketch are nearly mirror images of each other.

5. The letter W has reflection symmetry along a line

   a. going diagonally through its middle.

   b. going horizontally through its middle.

   c. going vertically through its middle.

6. The letter Z has

   a. reflection symmetry.   b. rotation symmetry.

   c. translation symmetry.

7. A perfect circle has

   a. both reflection and rotation symmetry.

   b. reflection symmetry only.   c. rotation symmetry only.

8. Which of the following regular polygons *cannot* be used to make a tiling?

   a. equilateral triangles   b. regular hexagons

   c. regular octagons

9. Suppose you arrange regular pentagons so that they are as close together as possible on a flat floor. The pattern will not be a tiling because

   a. it will have gaps between some of the pentagons.

   b. regular pentagons lack any type of symmetry.

   c. tilings are possible only with three- and four-sided polygons.

10. A *periodic* tiling is one in which

    a. only regular polygons are used.

    b. only triangles are used.

    c. the same pattern repeats over and over.

REVIEW QUESTIONS

11. Describe the ideas of perspective and symmetry.

12. How is the principal vanishing point in a picture determined?

13. What is the horizon line? How is it important in a painting showing perspective?

14. Briefly describe and distinguish among reflection symmetry, rotation symmetry, and translation symmetry. Draw a simple picture that shows each type of symmetry.

15. What is a tiling? Draw a simple example.

16. Briefly explain why there are only three possible tiling patterns that consist of a single regular polygon. What are the three patterns?

17. Briefly explain why more tilings are possible if we remove the restriction of using regular polygons.

18. What is the difference between periodic and aperiodic tilings?

DOES IT MAKE SENSE?

Decide whether each of the following statements makes sense (or is clearly true) or does not make sense (or is clearly false). Explain your reasoning.

19. The principal vanishing point of the painting is so far away that it cannot be seen in the painting.

20. Sid does not need to use perspective in her ground-level painting of a flat desert because the desert is two-dimensional.

21. Jane wants near objects to look nearby and far objects to look far away in her painting, so she should use perspective.

22. Kenny likes symmetry, so he prefers the letter R to the letter O.

23. Susan found a sale on octagonal (eight-sided) floor tiles, so she bought them to tile her kitchen.(Assume she uses no other tiles on her floor.)

24. Frank always liked the symmetry of the Washington Monument (in Washington, D.C.).

BASIC SKILLS & CONCEPTS

25. **Vanishing Points.** Consider the simple drawing of a road and a telephone pole in Figure 11.30.

    a. Locate a vanishing point for the drawing. Is it the principal vanishing point?

    b. With proper perspective, draw three more telephone poles receding into the distance.

FIGURE 11.30

26. **Correct Perspective.** Consider the two boxes shown in Figure 11.31. Which one is drawn with proper perspective relative to a single vanishing point? Explain.

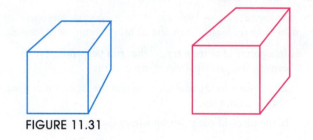

FIGURE 11.31

27. **Drawing with Perspective.** Make the square, circle, and triangle in Figure 11.32 into three-dimensional solid objects: a box, a cylinder, and a triangular prism, respectively. The given objects should be used as the front faces of the three-dimensional objects and all figures should be drawn with correct perspective relative to the given vanishing point P.

FIGURE 11.32

28. **Drawing MATH with Perspective.** Make the letters M, A, T, and H in Figure 11.33 into three-dimensional solid

letters. The given letters should be used as the front faces of three-dimensional letters as deep as the T is wide, and all letters should be drawn with correct perspective relative to the given vanishing point P.

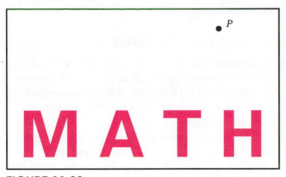

FIGURE 11.33

29. **Proportion and Perspective.** The drawing in Figure 11.34 shows two poles drawn with correct perspective relative to a single vanishing point. As you can check, the first pole is 2 centimeters tall in the drawing and the second pole is 2 centimeters away (measured base to base) with a height of 1.5 centimeters.

FIGURE 11.34

a. Draw two more vertical poles with correct perspective that are equally spaced along the baseline in the drawing. Assume the poles are of equal height in the real scene.

b. What are the heights of these two new poles in the drawing?

c. In the actual scene, would these four poles be equally spaced? Explain.

30. **Two Vanishing Points.** Figure 11.35 shows a road receding into the distance. In the direction of the arrow, draw a second road that intersects the first road. Be sure that the vanishing points of the two roads lie on the horizon line.

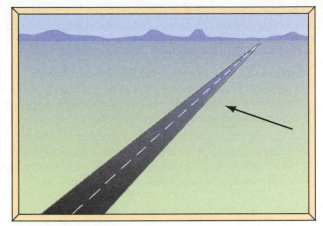

FIGURE 11.35

31. **Symmetry in Letters.** Find all of the capital letters of the alphabet that have

a. right/left reflection symmetry (such as A)

b. top/bottom reflection symmetry (such as H)

c. both right/left and top/bottom reflection symmetry

d. a rotational symmetry

32. **Star Symmetries.**

a. How many reflection symmetries does a four-pointed star have (Figure 11.36a)? How many rotational symmetries does a four-pointed star have?

b. How many reflection symmetries does a seven-pointed star have (Figure 11.36b)? How many rotational symmetries does a seven-pointed star have?

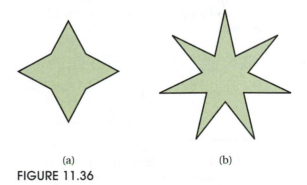

(a)   (b)
FIGURE 11.36

33. **Symmetries of Geometric Figures.**

a. Draw an equilateral triangle (all three sides have equal length). How many degrees can the triangle be rotated about its center so that it remains unchanged in appearance? (There are several correct answers.)

b. Draw a square (all four sides have equal length). How many degrees can the square be rotated about its center so that it remains unchanged in appearance? (There are several correct answers.)

c. Draw a regular pentagon (all five sides have equal length). How many degrees can the pentagon be rotated about its center so that it remains unchanged in appearance? (There are several correct answers.)

d. Can you see a pattern in parts a, b, and c? How many degrees can a regular *n*-gon be rotated about its center so that it remains unchanged in appearance? How many different angles answer this question for an *n*-gon?

Identifying Symmetries. Identify all of the symmetries in the figures of Exercises 34–37.

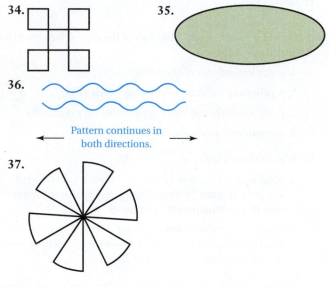

34.

35.

36.

Pattern continues in both directions.

37.

Tilings from Translating Triangles. In Exercises 38–39, make a tiling from each triangle using translations only, as in Figure 11.25.

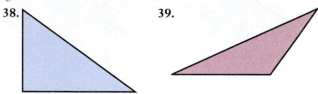

38.

39.

Tilings from Translating and Reflecting Triangles. For Exercises 40–41, make a tiling from the given triangle using translations and reflections, as in Figure 11.26.

40. The triangle in Exercise 38

41. The triangle in Exercise 39

Tilings from Quadrilaterals. In Exercises 42–43, make a tiling from the quadrilateral using translations, as in Figure 11.29.

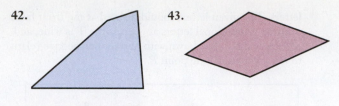

42.

43.

FURTHER APPLICATIONS

44. Desargues' Theorem. An early theorem of projective geometry, proved by French architect and engineer Girard Desargues (1593–1662), says that if two triangles (*ABC* and *abc* in Figure 11.37) are drawn so that the straight lines joining corresponding vertices (*Aa*, *Bb*, and *Cc*) all meet in a point *P* (corresponding to a vanishing point), then the corresponding sides (*AC* and *ac*, *AB* and *ab*, *BC* and *bc*), if extended, will meet in three points that all lie on the same line *L*. Draw two triangles of your own in such a way that the conditions of Desargues' theorem are satisfied. Verify that the conclusions of the theorem are true.

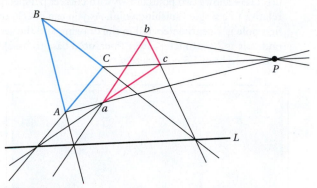

FIGURE 11.37

45. Why Quadrilateral Tilings Work. Consider the tiling with quadrilaterals shown in Figure 11.29. Look at any of the points at which four quadrilaterals meet in the tiling. Call such a point *P*. Given that the sum of the inside angles of any quadrilateral is 360°, show that the sum of the angles around the point *P* is also 360°, thus proving that the quadrilaterals interlock perfectly.

46. Tiling with a Rhombus. A rhombus is a quadrilateral in which all four sides have the same length and opposite sides are parallel. Show how a tiling can be made from a rhombus using translations only (as in Figure 11.25) and an initial reflection and then translations (as in Figure 11.26).

47. Project: Symmetry and Proportion in Art. Find one piece of pre-20th-century art and one piece of 20th-century or 21st-century art that you like. Use as many ideas from this unit as possible (involving perspective and symmetry) to write a two- to three-page analysis and comparison of these two pieces of art.

WEB PROJECTS

Find useful links for Web Projects on the text Web site:
www.aw.com/bennett-briggs

48. Art and Mathematics. Many Web sites are devoted to connections between art and mathematics. Visit one such site and study a connection in some depth. Write a one- to two-page essay that describes this connection between mathematics and art.

49. Art Museums. Many art museums have Web sites where you can explore their collections. Visit an art museum on the Web, and study its online collection. Describe a few pieces in which ideas of perspective or symmetry are important.

50. Escher. Look on the Web for art by M. C. Escher. Choose one of his works and write a short essay about his use of perspective in the piece.

51. Penrose Tilings. Many Web sites are devoted to Penrose tilings (aperiodic tilings). Visit one such site and learn more about the nature and uses of these tilings. Write a short essay describing your findings.

IN THE NEWS

52. Perspective in Life. Describe at least three ways in which the use of visual perspective affects your life.

53. Symmetry in Life. Find at least three objects from your daily life that exhibit some type of mathematical symmetry. Describe the symmetry in each case.

UNIT 11C Proportion and the Golden Ratio

In Unit 11B, we studied how mathematics enters into art through the ideas of symmetry and perspective. In this unit, we turn our attention to the third major mathematical idea involved with art: proportion.

The importance of proportion was expressed well by the astronomer Johannes Kepler (1571–1630):

> *Geometry has two great treasures: one is the theorem of Pythagoras; the other, the division of a line into extreme and mean ratio. The first we may compare to gold; the second we may name a precious jewel.*

Kepler's statement about *the division of a line into extreme and mean ratio* describes one of the oldest principles of proportion. It dates back to the time of Pythagoras (c. 500 B.C.E.), when scholars asked the following question: How can a line segment be divided into two pieces that have the most appeal and balance?

Although this was a question of beauty, there seemed to be general agreement on the answer. Suppose a line segment is divided into two pieces, as shown in Figure 11.38. We call the length of the long piece L and the length of the short piece 1.

The Greeks claimed that the most visually pleasing division of the line had the property that the ratio of the length of the long piece to the length of the short piece is the same as the ratio of the length of the entire line segment to the length of the long piece. That is,

$$\frac{L}{1} = \frac{L+1}{L}$$

This statement of proportion can be solved (see Exercise 29) to find that L has a special value, denoted by the Greek letter ϕ (phi, pronounced "fie" or "fee"), which is

$$\phi = \frac{1+\sqrt{5}}{2} = 1.61803\ldots$$

The senses delight in things duly proportioned.

—St. Thomas Aquinas (1225–1274)

L ————•—— 1

FIGURE 11.38

By the Way

The Greek letter ϕ is the first letter in the Greek spelling of Phydias, the name of a Greek sculptor who may have used the golden ratio in his work.

FIGURE 11.39

The number ϕ is more commonly called the **golden ratio** (or *golden section*); it is also sometimes called the *divine proportion*. Note that the golden ratio is an irrational number often approximated as 1.6, or $\frac{8}{5}$. Figure 11.39 shows that, for any line segment divided in two pieces according to the golden ratio, the ratio of the long piece to the short piece is

$$\frac{x}{y} = \frac{1.61803\ldots}{1} = \phi \approx \frac{8}{5}$$

✳**EXAMPLE 1** *Calculating a Golden Ratio*

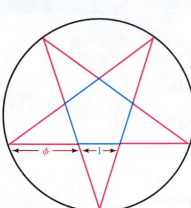

FIGURE 11.40

Suppose the line segment in Figure 11.40 is divided according to the golden ratio. If the length of the longer piece labeled x is 5 centimeters, how long is the entire line segment?

SOLUTION Because the line segment is divided in the golden ratio, we know that $x/y = \phi$. We can solve for y by multiplying both sides by y and dividing both sides by ϕ:

$$\frac{x}{y} = \phi \qquad \rightarrow \qquad y = \frac{x}{\phi}$$

Substituting $x = 5$ cm and the approximate value 1.6 for ϕ, we find

$$y = \frac{5 \text{ cm}}{\phi} \approx \frac{5 \text{ cm}}{1.6} \approx 3.1 \text{ cm}$$

The entire segment has a length of $x + y$, so its total length is approximately 5 cm + 3.1 cm = 8.1 cm. **Now try Exercises 21–22.** ◀◀

The Golden Ratio in Art History

Although the ancient Greeks struggled with the notion of irrational numbers, they embraced the golden ratio. For example, the *pentagram* (Figure 11.41) was the seal of the mystical Pythagorean Brotherhood. This five-pointed star inscribed in a circle produces a pentagon at the center. The golden ratio occurs in at least ten different ways in the pentagram. For example, if the length of each side of the pentagon is 1, then the length of each arm of the star is ϕ.

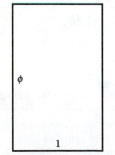

FIGURE 11.41 A pentagram.

....

Time out to think

Using a ruler, find at least one other place in the pentagram of Figure 11.41 where the ratio of the lengths of two line segments is the golden ratio.

From the golden ratio it is a short step to another famous Greek expression of proportion, the **golden rectangle**—a rectangle whose long side is ϕ times as long as its short side. A golden rectangle can be of any size, but its sides must have a ratio of $\phi \approx \frac{8}{5}$. Figure 11.42 shows a golden rectangle.

The golden rectangle had both practical and mystical importance to the Greeks. It became a cornerstone of their philosophy of *aesthetics*—the study of beauty. There is considerable speculation about the uses of the golden rectangle in art and architecture

FIGURE 11.42 A golden rectangle—the side lengths have a ratio $\phi \approx \frac{8}{5}$.

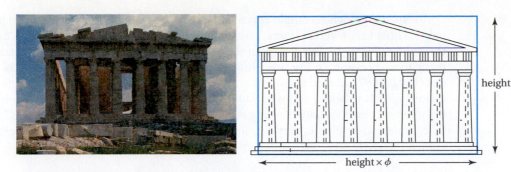

FIGURE 11.43 The proportions of the Parthenon closely match those of a golden rectangle.

in ancient times. For example, it is widely claimed that many of the great monuments of antiquity, such as the Pyramids in Egypt, were designed in accordance with the golden rectangle. And, whether by design or by chance, the proportions of the Parthenon (in Athens, Greece) match those of the golden rectangle very closely (Figure 11.43).

The golden rectangle also appears in many more recent works of art and architecture. The book *De Divina Proportione*, illustrated by Leonardo da Vinci in 1509, is filled with references to and uses of ϕ. Indeed, da Vinci's unfinished painting *St. Jerome* (Figure 11.44) places the central figure inside an imaginary golden rectangle. More recently, the French impressionist painter Georges Seurat is said to have used the golden ratio on every canvas. The abstract geometric paintings of the 20th-century Dutch painter Piet Mondrian (Figure 11.45) are filled with golden rectangles.

By the Way

The Parthenon was completed in about 430 B.C.E. as a temple to Athena Parthenos, the Warrior Maiden. It stands on the Acropolis (which means "the uppermost city"), about 500 feet above Athens.

FIGURE 11.44 *St. Jerome,* by Leonardo da Vinci, has the central figure positioned as though he were inside a golden rectangle.

Today, the golden rectangle appears in many everyday items. For example, photographs, note cards, cereal boxes, posters, and windows often have the proportions of the golden rectangle. But the question remains as to whether the golden rectangle is really more pleasing. In the late 19th century, the German psychologist Gustav Fechner (1801–1887) studied the question statistically. He showed several rectangles with various length to width ratios to hundreds of people and recorded their choices for the most and least visually pleasing rectangles. The results, given in Table 11.2, show that almost 75% of the participants chose rectangles that were very close to the golden rectangle.

TABLE 11.2   Fechner's Data

Length to Width Ratio	Most Pleasing Rectangle (Percentage Response)	Least Pleasing Rectangle (Percentage Response)
1.00	3.0	27.8
1.20	0.2	19.7
1.25	2.0	9.4
1.33	2.5	2.5
1.45	7.7	1.2
1.50	20.6	0.4
$\phi \approx 1.62$	35.0	0.0
1.75	20.0	0.8
2.00	7.5	2.5
2.50	1.5	35.7

Time out to think

Do you think that the golden rectangle is visually more pleasing than other rectangles? Explain.

✱EXAMPLE 2 *Household Golden Ratios*

The following household items were found to have the dimensions shown. Which item comes closest to having the proportions of the golden ratio?

- Standard sheet of paper: 8.5 in. × 11 in.
- 8 × 10 picture frame: 8 in. × 10 in.
- 35-mm slide: 35 mm × 23 mm

SOLUTION   The ratio of the sides of a standard sheet of paper is $11/8.5 = 1.29$, which is 20% less than the golden ratio. The ratio of the sides of a standard picture frame is $10/8 = 1.25$, which is 23% less than the golden ratio. The ratio of the sides of a 35-mm slide is $35/23 = 1.52$, which is 6% less than the golden ratio. Of the three objects, the 35-mm slide is closest to being a golden rectangle.

Now try Exercises 23–28. ◀◀

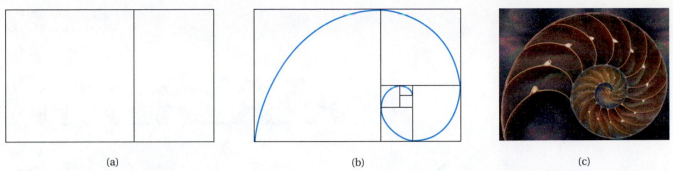

| (a) | (b) | (c) |

FIGURE 11.46 (a) A logarithmic spiral begins with a golden rectangle that is divided to make a square on the left. (b) The process is repeated in each successive golden rectangle, and a spiral is created by connecting the corners of all the squares. (c) A chambered nautilus shell looks much like a logarithmic spiral.

The Golden Ratio in Nature

The golden ratio appears to be common in the "artwork" of nature. One striking example is spirals created from golden rectangles. We begin by dividing a golden rectangle to make a square on its left side, as shown in Figure 11.46a. If you measure the sides of the remaining smaller rectangle to the right of the square, you'll see that it is a smaller golden rectangle.

We now repeat this splitting process on the second golden rectangle, this time making the square on the top (instead of the left) of the golden rectangle. This split makes a third, even smaller, golden rectangle. Continuing to split each new golden rectangle in this manner generates the result shown in Figure 11.46b. Now, we connect opposite corners of all the squares with a smooth curve. The result is a continuous curve called a **logarithmic spiral** (or *equiangular spiral*). This spiral very closely matches the spiral shape of the beautiful chambered nautilus shell (Figure 11.46c).

Another intriguing connection between the golden ratio and nature comes from a problem in population biology, first posed by a mathematician known as Fibonacci in 1202. Fibonacci's problem essentially asked the following question about the reproduction of rabbits.

> *Suppose that a pair of baby rabbits takes one month to mature into adults, then produces a new pair of baby rabbits the following month and each subsequent month. Further suppose that each newly born pair of rabbits matures and gives birth to additional pairs with the same reproductive pattern. If no rabbits die, how many pairs of rabbits are in the population at the beginning of each month?*

Figure 11.47 shows the solution to this problem for the first six months. Note that the number of pairs of rabbits at the beginning of each month forms a sequence that begins 1, 1, 2, 3, 5, 8. Fibonacci found that the numbers in this sequence continue to grow with the following pattern:

$$1, 1, 2, 3, 5, 8, 13, 21, 34, 55, \ldots$$

This sequence of numbers is known as the **Fibonacci sequence.**

If we let F_n denote the nth Fibonacci number, then we have $F_1 = 1$, $F_2 = 1$, $F_3 = 2$, $F_4 = 3$, and so forth. The most basic property of the Fibonacci sequence is that the next number in the sequence is the sum of the previous two numbers. For example, note that

$$F_3 = F_2 + F_1 = 1 + 1 = 2 \qquad \text{and} \qquad F_4 = F_3 + F_2 = 2 + 1 = 3$$

By the Way

Fibonacci, also known as Leonardo of Pisa, is credited with popularizing the use of Hindu-Arabic numerals in Europe. His book *Liber Abaci* (*Book of the Abacus*), published in 1202, explained their use and the importance of the number zero.

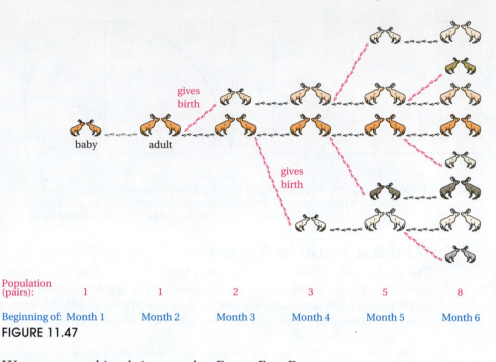

Population (pairs):	1	1	2	3	5	8
Beginning of:	Month 1	Month 2	Month 3	Month 4	Month 5	Month 6

FIGURE 11.47

We can express this rule in general as $F_{n+1} = F_n + F_{n-1}$.

Time out to think

Confirm that the above rule works for Fibonacci numbers F_3 through F_{10}. Use the rule to determine the eleventh Fibonacci number (F_{11}).

The connection between the Fibonacci numbers and the golden ratio becomes clear when we compute the ratios of successive Fibonacci numbers, as shown in Table 11.3. Note that, as we go further out in the sequence, the ratios of successive Fibonacci numbers get closer and closer to the golden ratio $\phi = 1.61803\ldots$.

TABLE 11.3 Ratios of Successive Fibonacci Numbers

$F_3/F_2 =$ $\quad$ $2/1 = 2.0$	$F_{11}/F_{10} =$ $\quad$ $89/55 = 1.618182$	
$F_4/F_3 =$ $\quad$ $3/2 = 1.5$	$F_{12}/F_{11} =$ $\quad$ $144/89 = 1.617978$	
$F_5/F_4 =$ $\quad$ $5/3 = 1.667$	$F_{13}/F_{12} =$ $\quad$ $233/144 = 1.618056$	
$F_6/F_5 =$ $\quad$ $8/5 = 1.600$	$F_{14}/F_{13} =$ $\quad$ $377/233 = 1.618026$	
$F_7/F_6 =$ $\quad$ $13/8 = 1.625$	$F_{15}/F_{14} =$ $\quad$ $610/377 = 1.618037$	
$F_8/F_7 =$ $21/13 = 1.6154$	$F_{16}/F_{15} =$ $\quad$ $987/610 = 1.618033$	
$F_9/F_8 = 34/21 = 1.61905$	$F_{17}/F_{16} =$ $\quad$ $1597/987 = 1.618034$	
$F_{10}/F_9 = 55/34 = 1.61765$	$F_{18}/F_{17} = 2584/1597 = 1.618034$	

There are many examples of the Fibonacci sequence in nature. The heads of sunflowers and daisies consist of a clockwise spiral superimposed on a counterclockwise spiral (both of which are logarithmic spirals), as shown in Figure 11.48. The number of individual florets in each of these intertwined spirals is a Fibonacci number—for example, 21 and 34 or 34 and 55. Biologists have also observed that the number of petals on many common flowers is a Fibonacci number (for example, irises have 3 petals, primroses have 5 petals, ragworts have 13 petals, and daisies have 34 petals). The arrangement of leaves on the stem of many plants also exhibits the Fibonacci sequence. And spiraling Fibonacci numbers can be identified on pine cones and pineapples.

(a)   (b)

FIGURE 11.48

EXERCISES 11C

QUICK QUIZ

Choose the best answer to each of the following questions. Explain your reasoning with one or more complete sentences.

1. The golden ratio is

a. exactly 1.6.

b. a perfect number discovered by Pythagoras.

c. $\dfrac{1 + \sqrt{5}}{2}$.

2. Which of the following is *not* a characteristic of the golden ratio?

a. It is an irrational number.

b. It is between 1 and 2.

c. It is the fourth number in the Fibonacci sequence.

3. If a one-foot line segment is divided according to the golden ratio, the two pieces

a. have equal length.

b. have lengths of roughly 2 inches and 10 inches.

c. have lengths of roughly 0.4 foot and 0.6 foot.

4. To make a golden rectangle, you should

a. inscribe a rectangle in a circle.

b. draw a rectangle so that the ratio of the long side to the short side is the golden ratio.

c. draw a rectangle so that the ratio of the diagonal to the short side is the golden ratio.

5. Suppose you want a bay window to have the proportions of a golden rectangle. If the window is to be 10 feet high, approximately how wide should it be?

a. 5 feet   b. $6\frac{1}{4}$ feet   c. 12 feet

6. Why did the Greeks tend to build rectangular buildings with the proportions of golden rectangles?

a. They thought these buildings were the most visually pleasing.

b. They thought these buildings were structurally stronger.

c. They thought these buildings could be constructed at the lowest possible cost.

7. Suppose you start with a golden rectangle and cut a square out of it. The remaining piece of the golden rectangle will be

a. another golden rectangle.

b. another square.

c. a logarithmic spiral.

8. The rabbit model of Fibonacci is an example of

a. a linearly growing population.

b. an exponentially growing population.

c. a logistically growing population.

9. The 18th, 19th, and 20th numbers in the Fibonacci sequence are, respectively, 2584, 4181, and 6765. The 21st number is

a. 2584×4181.   b. $4181 + 6765$.   c. 6765×1.6.

10. In what way does the golden ratio appear in the Fibonacci sequence?

a. It is the ratio between all pairs of successive Fibonacci numbers.

b. The ratio of successive Fibonacci numbers gets ever closer to the golden ratio as the numbers get higher.

c. It is the ratio of the last Fibonacci number to the first one.

REVIEW QUESTIONS

11. Explain the golden ratio in terms of proportions of line segments.

12. How is a golden rectangle formed?

13. What evidence suggests that the golden ratio and golden rectangle hold particular beauty?

14. What is a logarithmic spiral? How is it formed from a golden rectangle?

15. What is the Fibonacci sequence?

16. What is the connection between the Fibonacci sequence and the golden ratio? Give some examples of the Fibonacci sequence in nature.

DOES IT MAKE SENSE?

Decide whether each of the following statements makes sense (or is clearly true) or does not make sense (or is clearly false). Explain your reasoning.

17. Maria cut her 4-foot walking stick into two 2-foot sticks in keeping with the golden ratio.

18. Dan attributes his love of dominoes to the fact that dominoes are golden rectangles.

19. The circular pattern in the floor is attractive because it exhibits the golden ratio.

20. Each year, Juliet's age is another Fibonacci number.

BASIC SKILLS & CONCEPTS

21. **Golden Ratio.** Draw a line segment 6 inches long. Now subdivide it according to the golden ratio. Verify your work by computing the ratio of the whole segment length to the long segment length and the ratio of the long segment length to the short segment length.

22. **Golden Ratio.** A line is subdivided according to the golden ratio, with the smaller piece having a length of 5 meters. What is the length of the entire line?

23. **Golden Rectangles.** Measure the sides of each rectangle in Figure 11.49, and compute the ratio of the long side to the short side for each rectangle. Which ones are golden rectangles?

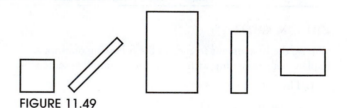

FIGURE 11.49

Dimensions of Golden Rectangles. Exercises 24–27 give the length of one side of a golden rectangle. Find the length of the other side. Notice that the other side could be either longer or shorter than the given side. Use the approximation $\phi \approx 1.62$ for your work.

24. 2.7 inches

25. 5.8 meters

26. 12.6 kilometers

27. 0.66 centimeter

28. **Everyday Golden Rectangles.** Find at least three everyday objects with rectangular shapes (for example, billboards, cereal boxes, windows). In each case, measure the side lengths and calculate the ratio. Are any of these objects golden rectangles? Explain.

FURTHER APPLICATIONS

29. **Finding ϕ.** The property that defines the golden ratio is

$$\frac{L}{1} = \frac{L+1}{L}$$

   a. Show that, if we multiply both sides by L and rearrange, this equation becomes

$$L^2 - L - 1 = 0$$

   Confirm that substituting the value of ϕ for L satisfies this equation.

   b. The quadratic formula states that, for any equation of the form $ax^2 + bx + c = 0$, the solutions are given by

$$x = \frac{-b + \sqrt{b^2 - 4ac}}{2a}$$

   and

$$x = \frac{-b - \sqrt{b^2 - 4ac}}{2a}$$

   Use the quadratic formula to solve for L in the formula for the golden ratio. Show that one of the roots is ϕ.

30. **Properties of ϕ.**

   a. Enter $\phi = \left(1 + \sqrt{5}\right)/2$ into your calculator. Show that $1/\phi = \phi - 1$.

   b. Now compute ϕ^2. How is this number related to ϕ?

31. **Logarithmic Spirals.** Draw a rectangle that is 10 centimeters on a side. Follow the procedure described in the text for subdividing the rectangle until you can draw a logarithmic spiral. Do all work carefully, and show your measurements with your work.

32. **The Lucas Sequence.** A sequence called the *Lucas sequence* is closely related to the Fibonacci sequence. The Lucas sequence begins with the numbers $L_1 = 1$ and $L_2 = 3$ and then uses the same relation $L_{n+1} = L_n + L_{n-1}$ to generate $L_3, L_4, \ldots$.

   a. Generate the first ten Lucas numbers.

   b. Compute the ratio of successive Lucas numbers L_2/L_1, L_3/L_2, L_4/L_3, and so on. Can you determine if these ratios approach a single number? What number is it?

33. **Graphing Fechner's Data.** Consider Gustav Fechner's data shown in Table 11.2. Make a histogram that displays the responses for both the most pleasing and the least pleasing rectangle proportions.

34. **Project: The Golden Navel.** An old theory claims that, on average, the ratio of the height of a person to the height of his/her navel is the golden ratio. Collect "navel ratio data" from as many people as possible. Graph the ratios in a histogram, find the average ratio over your entire sample, and discuss the outcome. Do your data support the theory?

35. **Project: Mozart and the Golden Ratio.** In a paper called "The Golden Section and the Piano Sonatas of Mozart" (*Mathematics Magazine*, Vol. 68, No. 4, 1995), John Putz gives the lengths (in measures) of the first part (*a*) and the second part (*b*) of the movements of the 19 Mozart piano sonatas. Some of the data are given below.

a = length of first part	b = length of second part
38	62
28	46
56	102
56	88
24	36
77	113
40	69
46	60
15	18
39	63
53	67

   a. The ratio of the length of the whole movement to the length of the longer segment is $(a + b)/b$. Add a third column to the table and compute this ratio for the given data.

   b. Make a histogram of the ratios that you computed in part a (choosing an appropriate bin size). Comment on how well they are approximated by ϕ.

   c. Read the article by John Putz. Do you believe that Mozart composed with the golden ratio in mind?

36. **Project: Debunking the Golden Ratio.** Find the article "Misconceptions about the Golden Ratio" by George Markowsky (*College Mathematics Journal*, Vol. 23, No. 1, 1992). Choose at least one of the misconceptions that Markowsky discusses, summarize it, and then explain whether you find his argument convincing. Discuss your opinion of whether the golden ratio has been consciously used by artists and architects in their work.

WEB PROJECTS

Find useful links for Web Projects on the text Web site:
www.aw.com/bennett-briggs

37. **Golden Controversies.** Many Web sites are devoted to the controversy concerning the role of the golden ratio in art. Find a specific argument on one side of this controversy and summarize it in a one- to two-page essay.

38. **Fibonacci Numbers.** Learn more about Fibonacci numbers and possible occurrences of the Fibonacci sequence in nature. Write a short essay about one aspect of Fibonacci numbers that you find interesting.

IN THE NEWS

39. **Proportion in Life.** Describe at least three ways in which the use of visual proportion affects your life.

40. **The Golden Ratio.** Find a recent picture of a new building or architectural design. Study the picture and decide whether the golden ratio is involved in any way.

CHAPTER 11 SUMMARY

UNIT	KEY TERMS	KEY IDEAS AND SKILLS
11A	sound wave pitch frequency harmonic octave musical scale digital recording	**Understand** how a plucked string produces sound. **Measure** frequency in cycles per second, and find harmonics of the frequency. **Understand** the musical scale and the ratios of frequencies among musical notes. **Understand** how the frequencies of a scale exhibit exponential growth. **Explain** the difference between analog and digital representations of music.

11B	perspective
	vanishing point
	horizon line
	symmetry
	   reflection
	   rotation
	   translation
		Understand the use of perspective in painting.
		Find symmetries in paintings and tilings.
		Create tilings with regular or irregular polygons.

11C	proportion golden ratio golden rectangle Fibonacci sequence	**The golden ratio:** $$\phi = \frac{1 + \sqrt{5}}{2} = 1.61803\ldots$$ **The Fibonacci sequence:** 1, 1, 2, 3, 5, 8, 13, 21, 34, 55, ... **Understand** claimed uses of the golden ratio in both art and nature.

Testing Your Understanding—Unit III

Using and Understanding Mathematics:
A Quantitative Reasoning Approach
Chapter 11: Mathematics and the Arts

Pages 71–79
CHECKING YOUR COMPREHENSION

Choose the best answer for each of the following questions.

1. To explain the concept of pitch, the authors use
   a. an illustration of a piano.
   b. a hands-on approach using a rubber band.
   c. a visual of fundamental frequency.
   d. a quote from Pythagoras.

2. Which of the following is not a half-step?
   a. B → C
   b. F# → G
   c. E → E#
   d. G# → A

3. Digital signal processing can do all of the following EXCEPT:
   a. modify music with computers.
   b. store music in an analog mode using a synthesizer.
   c. change the music by amplifying frequencies.
   d. remove background noises from recordings.

Identify the following statements as true or false.

4. Confucius would agree that both D# and G are constant notes.

5. CDs are etched with the shape of the original sound waves of the music they contain.

6. Each violin string when plucked produces more than a single frequency.

Answer each of the following questions.

7. Explain the main problem with temperament.

8. How does the 12-tone scale differ from the 7-tone scale?

9. Explain the inverse relationship between wave and frequency.

Define each term as it is used in the chapter.

10. entwined

11. propagates

12. exponential

13. oscillation

14. resonating

Discussion and Critical Thinking Questions

1. Discuss the incorrect information in the text regarding Pythagoras' belief. Why do you think the author would support one of Pythagoras' beliefs when we know that some of his other theories have been proven to be false?

2. After referring to Table 11.1, decide which of the following pairs of notes would sound agreeable. If you have access to a piano, play the notes and check your answers.

Pairs	Agreeable	Disagreeable
C & F		
G & A		
F# & D#		

Pages 80–93
CHECKING YOUR COMPREHENSION

Choose the best answer for each of the following questions.

1. Figure 11.4 and Figure 11.5 are the same except
   a. the principle vanishing point divides into P1 and P2 in Figure 11.5.
   b. in Figure 11.4 lines L1 and L4 are parallel.
   c. the vase in Figure 11.5 is in the opposite corner.
   d. Figure 11.5 shows the front view of the hallway.

2. Which of the following figures represents true reflective symmetry?
   a. Figure 11.21
   b. Figure 11.20
   c. Figure 11.27
   d. Figure 11.6

3. After reading the text, a reader can infer that
   a. all perception has symmetry.
   b. all shapes can be tiled using either periodic or aperiodic tiling.
   c. all artists understand perception.
   d. all shapes with horizontal lines can be tiled with rotating symmetry.

Identify the following statements as true or false.

4. Mutually parallel lines meet at opposite vanishing points.

5. Albrecht Durer and Jan Vredeman de Vries both believe the same concepts regarding perspective.

6. All upper case letters in the alphabet have either reflection or rotation symmetry.

Answer each of the following questions.

7. Why does the author write that Escher abused perspective?

8. Explain why pentagons by themselves cannot be used to make a tiling.

9. Explain why vanishing points are sometimes off of an artist's canvas.

Define each term as it is used in the chapter.

10. perpendicular

11. endeavors

12. realism

13. confounds

Discussion and Critical Thinking Questions

1. The text notes two situations in False Perspective by William Hogarth (Figure 11.9) that are falsely represented. As a group, find at least three other items in the painting that seem to abuse perspective.

2. During the Renaissance why were artists so interested by perspective? If they did not pay proper attention to perspective how would their painting have been affected?

Pages 93–102
CHECKING YOUR COMPREHENSION

Choose the best answer for each of the following questions.

1. What piece of information never changes when calculating a golden ratio?
   a. y
   b. φ
   c. x
   d. L

2. According to the text, it would be an abnormality to find a common flower with 11 petals because
   a. 11 is a multiple of φ.
   b. 11 is not a Fibonacci number.
   c. logarithmic spirals are always even.
   d. the Fibonacci sequence has shifted over the last few centuries.

3. To create a logarithmic spiral, which of the following must be performed?
   a. A straight line must be drawn to connect the square's corners.
   b. A golden rectangle must first be created.
   c. The golden ratio must be used to determine the Fibonacci numbers.
   d. An 8.5 inch x 11 inch rectangle must be drawn.

Identify the following statements as true or false.

4. Artists used golden rectangles to ensure their subjects were positioned in the middle of the canvas.

5. Two squares are produced when a golden rectangle is divided down the middle.

6. The divine proportion is an irrational number that is often approximated as 1.6 or 8/5.

Answer each of the following questions.

7. Explain why Markowsky agreed or disagreed with Fechner's statistical analysis of people's preferences regarding the golden rectangle.

8. How is it possible to determine the 18th number in the Fibonacci sequence without using the formula?

9. How is St. Thomas Acquinas' quote supported in the text?

Define each term as it is used in the chapter.

10. speculation

11. antiquity

12. abstract

13. mystical

Discussion and Critical Thinking Question

1. Discuss your thoughts regarding the idea of a one-sized rectangle being more pleasing to the eye than rectangles of other sizes and explain why this should or should not be the basis for mathematical formulae and beliefs.

Chapter Review
END OF CHAPTER ANALYSIS

Choose the best answer for each of the following questions.

1. The authors utilize all of the following to assist readers in understanding various concepts throughout the chapter EXCEPT:
   a. historical information.
   a. chapter summary.
   a. pie charts and bar graphs.
   a. paintings and illustrations.

2. After reading the chapter you should be able to answer all of the following questions EXCEPT:
   a. How many horizontal lines are in common paintings?
   a. What is translation symmetry?
   a. How many arms of a pentagon are equal to φ?
   a. What are the components of a complex sound wave?

2. The questions at the end of each section in the text should be initially answered
   a. prior to reading the text.
   a. after reading the text.
   a. when prompted by the text.
   a. as a review prior to a test.

Group Projects

1. Conduct your own survey using the length to width ratio found in Table 11.2. Discuss whether your findings agree or disagree with Fechner's findings.

2. As a group, create two similar pictures, one using correct perspective and one that subtly abuses perspective. Show them to your classmates and see if they can determine which takes liberties regarding perspective.

Journal Ideas

1. Based on what you have learned in the chapter, create one example of aperiodic tiling and explain in detail what makes it aperiodic.

2. The authors of the text refer to various quotes throughout the chapter. Choose one quote and write how it is explained and supported in the text.

Organizing Information

Mathematics books often contain many visuals, illustrations, and formulae to support information. To ensure comprehension of these concepts, it is important to be able to know the visual and well as verbal representation of each concept. Using the table below, choose five concepts taught in the chapter, create a visual representation (picture or formula), and then explain the concept in your own words.

Concept	Visual Representation	Explanation
1. Fundamental frequency		This is when a string gets to its lowest possible location when it's vibrating up and down.
2.		
3.		
4.		
5.		

Unit IV: History

From

Mark C. Carnes and John A. Garraty

The American Nation: A History of the United States

Thirteenth Edition

Volume One • To 1877

Chapter 2:
American Society in the Making

An Introduction to American History

American history examines history in terms of the development and growth of the United States. This field addresses history from social, economic, political, and religious accounts to better understand and appreciate a global perspective. Early American history focuses on the creation of a nation and the exploration of a new frontier. Most recent American history studies the changes our young nation has gone through as a result of economic times and social climate.

American history is a requirement for most college students since it helps provide students with a better understanding of the world they live in today. There are career opportunities for historians in government services, law, teaching, business, advertising, broadcasting, and historical services.

Strategies for Reading History Texts

When reading a history book, it is important not to be distracted by facts and dates, although they are an important part of the text. It is initially important to understand why events occurred and how they relate to other historical events. Readings on history are generally dense with information so it is important to take your time and discern the main idea of each section and then delve deeper into the passages to note the supporting ideas used by the authors. Keep in mind as you read any historical text that history is interpretive, so although the information has been well researched and documented, it is subject to differing accounts of interpretation.

American Society in the Making

CONTENTS

★ Mission San Diego de Alcalá, the oldest mission church in California. Franciscan friars adapted Spanish conceptions to American building materials, chiefly adobe bricks cemented with wet clay. Because these materials could not bear much weight, the architects had to devise ingenious wall supports to create structures such as this mission church.

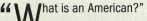

"What is an American?"

In 2006 a Purdue University survey asked this question of 1,500 U.S. citizens. More than 90 percent said that speaking and writing English well were important in defining American identity. Nearly as high a proportion equated American identity with a willingness to serve in the military and pledge allegiance to the nation. More than half reported that the "Christian faith" was also important in making someone an American, although nearly a third "strongly" disagreed.

But the roots of "American identity" extend deep into the past, before most inhabitants of what is now the United States spoke English or worshiped in Christian churches, before the United States even existed as a nation. Indeed the question, "What is an American?" was posed in 1762 by Hector St. John de Crèvecoeur, a French settler in New York. His answer was both perceptive and prophetic: "The American," he declared, was a "new race of man," a "promiscuous" blending of English, Scotch, Irish, French, Dutch, Germans, and Swedes. Freed from the traditions and constraints of Europe, Americans were a composite people "whose labours and posterity will one day cause great changes in the world."

But Crèvecoeur neglected the idea, outlined in the previous chapter, that American identity also emerged from the encounter of Indian, European, and African peoples. Other factors also explain the distinctiveness of American identity. Land in what is now the United States was astoundingly plentiful and, by European standards, greatly underutilized; the labor to farm it and extract its wealth was scarce. Europeans, too, discovered that their institutions were often ill-adapted to American conditions; this encouraged innovation. Religious enthusiasts and educational reformers also learned that they had more scope to realize their visions.

Factors as material as the landscape, as quantifiable as population patterns, as elusive as chance and calculation all shaped colonial social arrangements. Their cumulative impact did not at first produce anything like a uniform society. The "Americans" who evolved in what is now the United States were in many ways as different from each other as all were from their foreign cousins. The process by which these identities merged into an American nation remained incomplete. It was—and is—ongoing.

SETTLEMENT OF NEW FRANCE

France's colonial enterprise in North America progressed slowly after 1700. The main problem, as before, was the difficulty in persuading French people to occupy isolated settlements in remote American frontiers. But some did come. Military garrisons built and occupied forts along the shores of the Great Lakes and at strategic positions overlooking the Mississippi, Illinois, and other rivers. Solitary French traders, paddling canoes laden with metal tools, cloth, and alcohol, ventured deep into the wilderness in search of increasingly scarce animal pelts. Jesuit missionaries endeavored to plant Christianity among the Indians in the region of Lake Michigan and the Illinois River. Missionaries founded Detroit in 1701, Kaskaskia, south of Cahokia, in 1703, and Fort de Chartres in 1720.

Attempts to anchor New France with a colony at the mouth of the Mississippi were frustrated by the region's maze of swamps, marshes, and meandering waterways which, though ideal for hiding pirates, discouraged settlement. One French missionary, unable to locate the mouth of the Mississippi, complained that the "coast changes shape at every moment." In 1712 France chartered a private company to build a colony in the region. It laid out a town called New Orleans at the site of a short portage between the Mississippi River and Lake Pontchartrain. The company granted tracts of land to settlers and transported several thousand of them to Louisiana. Some established farms, planting indigo, tobacco, rice, and cotton; others acquired forest products, such as lumber, tar, and resin; still others traded for furs. The company established more settlements in the region, including one at Natchez, on a bluff above the Mississippi. But in 1729 the Natchez Indians wiped out this settlement and the company went bankrupt.

In 1731 the French government took control of Louisiana, with New Orleans as the administrative capital. Settlement lagged. The region was unsuited for farming, bemoaned one French official: "Now there is too much drought, now too much rain." By 1750 no more than 10,000 Europeans had colonized the region.

Few European women were among the immigrants to New France. In Louisiana, Frenchmen often married Indian women in Christian ceremonies, although the government tried to discourage the practice. Fur traders in the northern hinterlands also married Indians, whose knowledge of Indian languages, cultural practices, and tribal relations proved helpful for business—and essential for survival. Children of mixed-blood were frequently seen throughout New France.

As beaver and other game became scarce, traders went still farther west. Eventually they came upon tribes that had been driven from Pennsylvania and

★ In 1718, to strengthen its claim to Illinois, the French government removed the region from Canadian supervision and put it under the jurisdiction of the Company of the Indies. Later that year the company sent a military expedition from New Orleans to Illinois. It soon completed Fort de Chartres on the Mississippi River north of Kaskaskia. The log structure did not last long; in 1760 a stone structure, partially reconstructed above, was completed.

New York by the mighty Iroquois confederation. These Indians, fearful of the Iroquois, sought guns and ammunition. The traders complied, though not without misgivings. This escalation in armaments ensured that warfare among Indians would be more deadly, and that the isolated outposts of New France would be more vulnerable.

SOCIETY IN NEW MEXICO, TEXAS, AND CALIFORNIA

Once the Indians of the upper Mississippi acquired guns from French traders, the new weaponry quickly spread to the Indians of the Great Plains. Far earlier, the Apache and Comanche had become expert at riding European horses, which proliferated on the grasslands of the Great Plains. Now armed with light muskets, the Plains Indians became formidable foes; the Comanche were for several generations nearly invincible. Spanish raiders who had formerly seized Plains Indians for the slave trade now preyed upon less fearsome nomadic tribes, such as the Ute, who lived in the foothills of the Rockies.

The Comanche, always adept as buffalo hunters, found it even easier with guns. As the number and size of their hunting bands increased, the Comanche encroached on Apache territory. Soon Comanche warriors, occasionally assisted by French traders and soldiers, raided remote Spanish and Pueblo settlements in New Mexico and Texas. "We do not have a single gun," declared one Spanish missionary in

1719, "while we see the French giving hundreds of arms to Indians."

The new threat from marauding Indians and scheming Frenchmen prompted the Spanish to strengthen the *presidio* at Santa Fe and San Antonio and to build new missions in east Texas. In an effort to preempt future attacks, the Spanish also dispatched a military expedition into Nebraska. But Pawnee Indians and the French ambushed and routed the invaders; from now on, Spanish garrisons and their Pueblo allies mostly defended their towns and missions.

The ascendancy of the Plains Indians endangered all of the new frontier missions and discouraged further settlement by Hispanics. In 1759 a Spanish commander of a *presidio* complained that the Comanche were "so superior in firearms as well as in numbers that our destruction seems probable." Only San Antonio, with 600 Hispanic settlers, amounted to much.

★ **Spain's North American Frontier, c. 1800**

The trade in Indian slaves remained an enduring aspect of life along the sparsely populated northern rim of New Spain. Catholic missionaries usually prevented Spanish traders from enslaving Pueblo Indians, many of whom lived in mission towns and knew the rudiments of Catholicism. But no such arguments could protect the "wild" Indians such as the Ute of the foothills of the Rockies.

Because adult males resisted capture and incorporation into colonial society, most Indian slaves were women and children. In 1761 Father Pedro Serrano reported that at one New Mexican trade fair Indian maidens over the age of 10 were raped "in the sight of innumerable assemblies of barbarians and Catholics" before they were sold.

Indian slaves often had children by Hispanic fathers, who rarely acknowledged their paternity of such offspring. Known as *genizaros,* these children occupied the bottom rung of a social system largely based on the status of fathers. *Genizaros* learned Spanish and received training in Catholicism. In some towns, they comprised a third of the population. Females usually worked as household servants, males as indentured servants on ranches. Spanish officials, eager to increase the numbers of Spanish colonists, granted *genizaros* the right to own property. Many became ranchers and herders.

While the Comanche were imperiling the frontier of New Mexico and Texas, Spanish officials learned of a new threat in the 1760s: Britain and Russia were attempting to colonize the Northwest,

the region that now comprises Oregon and Washington. This threatened Spain's claims to California, a remote wilderness inhabited by some 300,000 Indians. As in New Mexico, Spain, having failed to attract Hispanic settlers, invited Franciscan missionaries to *create* "Spanish" settlers by converting the Indians to Catholicism and Hispanicizing their language and culture. This would not prove easy. The Indians of California belonged to over 300 tribes that spoke nearly 100 different languages.

In 1769 several score Jesuits and a detachment of Spanish soldiers established a *presidio* and mission in San Diego. Other missions followed at Monterey, Santa Barbara, and San Francisco; within several decades some twenty missions had been established in California.

The Jesuits monitored Indian life closely. They segregated all unmarried girls over the age of seven so as to prevent them from indulging in freer Indian sexual mores and to protect them from European rapists. The Jesuits also inculcated the discipline of work, overseeing the digging of irrigation ditches, the cultivation of crops, the tending of livestock, the manufacture of handicrafts, and the construction of churches, forts, and homes. The Indians received no wages, but instead were fed and cared for by the priests, whose first obligation was to God and the church. Because the California settlements were distant from New Spain, the missions survived chiefly by provisioning Spanish military garrisons.

Whatever success the Jesuits had in establishing the missions, however, was undone by disease. As had happened throughout the western hemisphere, the introduction of European pathogens among formerly isolated Indian populations resulted in catastrophic losses. European diseases hit all California Indians, not just those in the missions. By the close of the eighteenth century, Spain had failed in its effort to establish a strong Hispanic colony in California.

THE ENGLISH PREVAIL ON THE ATLANTIC SEABOARD

By the mid-eighteenth century, England had successfully addressed the chief problem that bedeviled the French and Spanish colonial efforts: a dearth of colonists. By then, European settlers, most of them English, had taken possession of much of the Atlantic seaboard. But this basic fact overlooks the important differences among the colonies. Each of the Middle Colonies had distinctive histories and settlement patterns. Even the New England colonies, though originally founded for similar religious purposes, soon diverged.

The southern parts of English North America comprised three regions: the Chesapeake Bay, consisting of "tidewater" Virginia and Maryland; the "low country" of the Carolinas (and eventually Georgia); and the "back country," a vast territory that extended from the "fall line" in the foothills of the Appalachians, where falls and rapids put an end to navigation on the tidal rivers, to the farthest point of western settlement. Not until well into the eighteenth century would the emergence of common features—export-oriented agricultural economies, a labor force in which black slaves figured prominently, the absence of towns of any size—prompt people to think of the "South" as a single region.

THE CHESAPEAKE COLONIES

When the English philosopher Thomas Hobbes wrote in 1651 that human life tended to be "nasty, brutish, and short," he might well have had in mind the royal colony of Virginia. Although the colony grew from about 1,300 to nearly 5,000 in the decade after the Crown took it over in 1624, the death rate remained appalling. Since more than 9,000 immigrants had entered the colony, nearly half the population died during that decade.

The climate helped make the Chesapeake area a death trap. "Hot and moist" is how Robert Beverly described the weather in *The History and Present State of Virginia* (1705), the dampness "occasioned by the abundance of low grounds, marshes, creeks, and rivers." Almost without exception newcomers underwent "seasoning," a period of illness that in its mildest form consisted of "two or three fits of a feaver and ague." Actually the relatively dry summers were the chief cause of the high death rate. During the summer the slower flow of the James River allowed relatively dense salt water to penetrate inland. This blocked the flow of polluted river water, which the colonists drank. The result was dysentery, the "bloody flux." If they survived the flux, and a great many did not, settlers still ran the seasonal risk of contracting a particularly virulent strain of malaria, which, though seldom fatal in itself, could so debilitate its victims that they often died of typhoid fever and other ailments.

Long after food shortages and Indian warfare had ceased to be serious problems, life in the Chesapeake remained precarious. Well into the 1700s a white male of 20 in Middlesex County, Virginia, could look forward only to about 25 more years of life. Across Chesapeake Bay, in Charles County, Maryland, life expectancy was even lower. The high death rate had important effects on family structure. Because relatively few people lived beyond their forties, more often than not children lost at least one of their parents before they reached maturity and in many instances both. Remarriage was a way of life. Apparently this situation did not cause drastic emotional problems for most people of the region. Men provided generously for their families in their wills, despite knowing that their wives would probably remarry quickly. Being brought up entirely by stepparents was so common that children tended to accept it almost as a matter of course.

Because of the persistent shortage of women in the Chesapeake region (men outnumbered women by three to two even in the early 1700s), widows easily found new husbands. Many men spent their entire lives alone or in the company of other men. Others married Indian women and became part of Indian society.

All Chesapeake settlers felt the psychological effects of their precarious and frustrating existence. Random mayhem and calculated violence posed a continuous threat to life and limb. Life was coarse at best and often as "brutish" as Hobbes had claimed, even allowing for the difficulties involved in carving out a community in the wilderness.

THE LURE OF LAND

Agriculture was the bulwark of life for the Chesapeake settlers and the rest of the colonial South; the tragic

MAINE
(Mass.)

VERMONT
(Claimed by N.H
& N.Y.)

NEW
HAMPSHIRE

MASSACHUSETTS

Salem
Boston
Cape Cod
Albany   Dedham   Plymouth
Providence
New
York   Hartford   CONN.
Newport
NEW   New Haven   RHODE
YORK   ISLAND

Lake Superior
Lake Huron
Lake Michigan
Lake Ontario
Lake Erie

St. Lawrence River
Connecticut R.
Hudson R.
Delaware R.
Susquehanna R.

PENNSYLVANIA   New
York   Long Island
Perth Amboy   EAST JERSEY
Philadelphia   Burlington
New Castle   WEST JERSEY

Wabash R.
Ohio R.

MARYLAND
Annapolis   DELAWARE

VIRGINIA   Chesapeake B.
Williamsburg
Jamestown

ATLANTIC
OCEAN

James R.
Roanoke R.

NORTH
CAROLINA
New Bern

Cape Fear R.

Pee Dee R.

SOUTH
CAROLINA

Savannah R.

Charleston

GEORGIA

Altamaha R.

Savannah

0   200 Kilometers
0   200 Miles

New England Colonies
Middle Colonies
Southern Colonies
★   Colonial Capitals

★ **English Colonies on the Atlantic Seaboard**

experiences of the Jamestown settlement revealed this quickly enough. Jamestown also suggested that a colony could not succeed unless its inhabitants were allowed to own their own land. The first colonists had agreed to work for seven years in return for a share of the profits. When their contracts expired there were few profits. To satisfy these settlers and to attract new capital, the London Company declared a "dividend" of land, its only asset. The surviving colonists each received 100 acres. Thereafter, as prospects continued poor, the company relied more and more on grants of land to attract both capital and labor. A number of wealthy Englishmen were given immense tracts, some running to several hundred thousand acres. Lesser persons willing to settle in Virginia received more modest grants. Whether dangled before a great tycoon, a country squire, or a poor farmer, the offer of land had the effect of encouraging immigration to the colony. This was a much-desired end, for without the labor to develop it the land was worthless.

Soon what was known as the **headright** system became entrenched in both Virginia and Maryland. Behind the system lay the eminently sound principle that land should be parceled out according to the availability of labor to cultivate it. For each "head" entering the colony authorities issued a "right" to take any 50 acres of unoccupied land. To "seat" a claim and receive title to the property, the holder of the headright had to mark out its boundaries, plant a crop, and construct some sort of habitation. This system was adopted in all the southern colonies and in Pennsylvania and New Jersey.

The first headrights were issued with no strings attached, but generally the grantor demanded a small annual payment called a *quitrent*. A quitrent was actually a tax that provided a way for the proprietors to derive incomes from their colonies. Quitrents were usually resented and difficult to collect.

The headright system encouraged landless Europeans to migrate to English America. More often than not, however, those most eager to come could not afford passage across the Atlantic. To bring such people to America, the **indentured servant** system was developed. Indenture resembled apprenticeship. In return for transportation indentured servants agreed to work for a stated period, usually about five years. During that time they were subject to strict control by the master and received no compensation beyond their keep. Indentured women were forbidden to marry and if they became pregnant (as many did in a land where men outnumbered women by seven to one) the time lost from work that resulted was added to their terms of service.

Servants lacked any incentive to work hard, whereas masters tended to "abuse their servantes . . .

Wessell Webling, His Indenture, 1622

with intollerable oppression." In this clash of wills the advantage lay with the master; servants lacked full political and civil rights, and masters could administer physical punishment and otherwise abuse them. An indenture, however, was a contract; servants could and did sue when planters failed to fulfill their parts of the bargain, and surviving court records suggest that they fared reasonably well when they did so.

Servants who completed their years of labor became free. Usually the former servant was entitled to an "outfit" (a suit of clothes, some farm tools, seed, and perhaps a gun). Custom varied from colony to colony. In the Carolinas and in Pennsylvania, for example, servants also received small grants of land from the colony when their service was completed.

The headrights issued when indentured servants entered the colonies went to whoever paid their passage, not to the servants. Thus the system gave a double reward to capital—land and labor for the price of the labor alone. Since well over half of the white settlers of the southern colonies came as indentured servants, the effect on the structure of southern society was enormous.

Most servants eventually became landowners, but with the passage of time their lot became harder. The best land belonged to the large planters, and as more land went into cultivation, crop prices fell. Many owners of small farms, former servants especially, slipped into dire poverty. Some were forced to become "squatters" on land along the fringes of settlement that no one had yet claimed. Squatting often led to trouble; eventually, when someone turned up with a legal title to the land, the squatters demanded "squatters' rights," the privilege of buying the land from the legal owner without paying for the improvements the squatters had made upon it. This led to lawsuits and sometimes to violence.

In the 1670s conflicts between Virginians who owned choice land and former servants on the outer edge of settlement brought the colony to the brink of class warfare. The costs of meeting the region's ever-growing need for labor with indentured servants were becoming prohibitive. Some other solution was needed.

"SOLVING" THE LABOR SHORTAGE: SLAVERY

Probably the first African blacks brought to English North America arrived on a Dutch ship and were sold at Jamestown in 1619. Early records are vague and incomplete, so it is not possible to say whether these Africans were treated as slaves or freed after a period

★ The Cape Coast Castle, on the slave coast of western Africa, looking out on the Atlantic Ocean. One of a dozen such forts operated by Britain, Spain, or the Netherlands, this castle held hundreds of African captives. Captains of slaving ships paid about 6 ounces of gold or 200 gallons of rum for each slave. The price was lower if the captains wanted to deal directly with African chieftains, but this required long, dangerous trips inland.

of years as were indentured servants. What is certain is that by about 1640 *some* blacks were slaves (a few, with equal certainty, were free) and that by the 1660s local statutes had firmly established the institution in Virginia and Maryland.

Slavery soon spread throughout the colonies. As early as 1626 there were eleven slaves in New Netherland, and when the English conquered that colony in 1664 there were 700 slaves in a population of about 8,000. The Massachusetts Body of Liberties of 1641—strange title—provided that "there shall never be any bond-slavery . . . amongst us; unlesse it be lawful captives taken in just warrs [i.e., Indians] and such strangers as willingly sell themselves, or *are solde* to us." However, relatively few blacks were imported until late in the seventeenth century, even in the southern colonies. In 1650 there were only 300 blacks in Virginia and as late as 1670 no more than 2,000.

White servants were much more highly prized. The African, after all, was almost entirely alien to both the European and the American ways of life. In a country starved for capital, the cost of slaves—roughly five times that of indentured servants—was another disadvantage. In 1664 the governor of Maryland informed Lord Baltimore that local planters would use more "neigros" "if our purses would endure it." As long as white servants were available, few planters acquired slaves.

In the 1670s the flow of indentured servants slackened, the result of improving economic conditions in England and the competition of other colonies for servants. At the same time, the formation of the Royal African Company (1672) made slaves more readily available. By 1700, nearly 30,000 slaves lived in the English colonies.

PROSPERITY IN A PIPE: TOBACCO

Labor and land made agriculture possible, but it was necessary to find a market for American crops in the Old World if the colonists were to enjoy anything but the crudest sort of existence. They could not begin to manufacture all the articles they required; to obtain from England such items as plows and muskets and books and chinaware, they had to have cash crops, what their English creditors called "merchantable commodities." Here, at least, fortune favored the Chesapeake.

The founders of Virginia tried to produce all sorts of things that were needed in the old country:

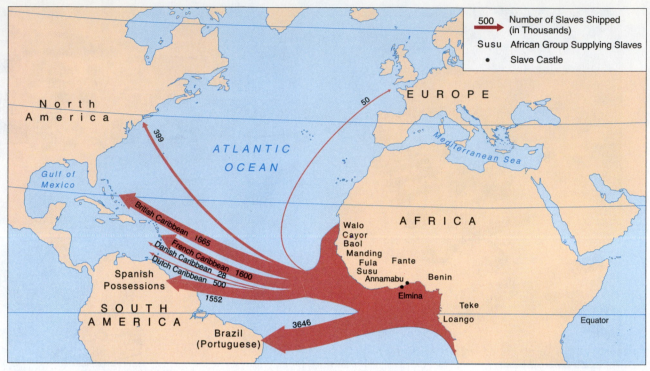

★ **African Slave Trade, 1451–1870**

DOCUMENT

James I, "A Counterblaste to Tobacco"

grapes and silk in particular, indigo, cotton, oranges, olives, sugar, and many other plants. But it was tobacco, unwanted, even strongly opposed at first, which became for farmers on both sides of Chesapeake Bay "their darling."

Tobacco was unknown in Europe until Spanish explorers brought it back from the West Indies. It was not common in England until the time of Sir Walter Raleigh. Then it quickly proved irresistible to thousands of devotees. At first the London Company discouraged its colonists from growing tobacco. Since it clearly contained some habit-forming drug, many people opposed its use. King James I wrote a pamphlet attacking the weed, in which, among other things, he anticipated the findings of modern cancer researchers by saying that smoking was a "vile and stinking" habit "dangerous to the Lungs." But English smokers and partakers of snuff ignored their king, and the Virginians ignored their company. By 1617 a pound of tobacco was worth more than 5 shillings in London. Company and Crown then changed their tune, granting the colonists a monopoly and encouraging them in every way.

Unlike wheat, which required expensive plows and oxen to clear the land and prepare the soil, tobacco plants could be set on semicleared land and cultivated with a simple hoe. Although tobacco required lots of human labor, a single laborer working two or three acres could produce as much as 1,200 pounds of cured tobacco, which, in a good year, yielded a profit of more than 200 percent. This being the case, production in America leaped from 2,500 pounds in 1616 to nearly 30 million pounds in the late seventeenth century, or roughly 400 pounds of tobacco for every man, woman, and child in the Chesapeake colonies.

The tidewater region was blessed with many navigable rivers, and the planters spread along their banks, giving the Chesapeake a shabby, helter-skelter character of rough habitations and growing tobacco, mostly planted in stump-littered fields, surrounded by fallow land and thickets interspersed with dense forest. There were no towns and almost no roads. English ships made their way up the rivers from farm to farm, gathering the tobacco at each planter's wharf. The vessels also served as general stores of a sort where planters could exchange tobacco for everything from cloth, shoes, tools, salt, and nails to such exotic items as tea, coffee, chocolate, and spices.

However, the tremendous increase in the production of tobacco caused the price to plummet in the late seventeenth century. This did not stop the expansion of the colonies, but it did alter the structure of their society. Small farmers found it more difficult to make a decent living. At the same time men with capital and individuals with political influence were amassing large tracts of land. If well-managed, a big

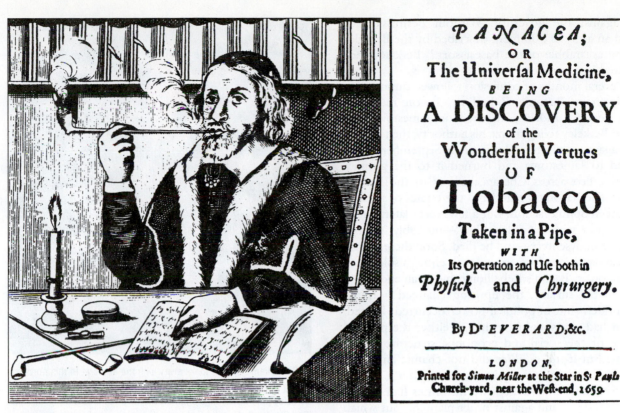

★ Tobacco companies advertised their product as far back as the seventeenth century. This 1659 advertisement lauds tobacco as a medical "panacea."

plantation gave its owner important competitive advantages over the small farmer. Tobacco was notorious for the speed with which it exhausted the fertility of the soil. Growers with a lot of land could shift frequently to new fields within their holdings, allowing the old fields to lie fallow and thus maintain high yields, but the only option that small farmers had when their land gave out was to move to unsettled land on the frontier. To do that in the 1670s was to risk trouble with properly indignant Indians. It might also violate colonial laws designed to slow westward migration and limit tobacco production. Neither was about to stop settlement.

BACON'S REBELLION

Chesapeake settlers showed little respect for constituted authority, partly because most people lived on isolated plantations and partly because the London authorities were usually ignorant of their needs. The first Virginians often ignored directives of the London Company, while early Marylanders regularly disputed the right of the Calverts' agents to direct the affairs of the proprietorship. The most serious challenge took place in Virginia in 1676. Planters in the outlying counties heartily disliked the officials in

Jamestown who ran the colony. The royal governor, Sir William Berkeley, and his "Green Spring" faction (the organization took its name from the governor's plantation) had ruled Virginia for more than 30 years. Outsiders resented the way Berkeley and his henchmen used their offices to line their pockets. They also resented their social pretensions, for Green Springers made no effort to conceal their opinion, which had considerable basis in fact, that western planters were a crude and vulgar lot.

Early in 1676 planters on the western edge of settlement, always looking for excuses to grab land by doing away with the Indians who owned it, asked Berkeley to authorize an expedition against Indians who had been attacking nearby plantations. Berkeley refused. The planters then took matters into their own hands. Their leader, Nathaniel Bacon, was (and remains today) a controversial figure. His foes described him as extremely ambitious and possessed "of a most imperious and dangerous hidden Pride of heart." But even his sharpest critics conceded that he was "of an inviting aspect and powerful elocution" and well qualified "to lead a giddy and unthinking multitude."

When Berkeley refused to authorize him to attack the Indians, Bacon promptly showed himself only too willing to lead that multitude not only against Indians but against the governor. Without permission he raised an army of 500 men, described by the Berkeley faction as "rabble of the basest sort." Berkeley then declared him a traitor.

Several months of confusion followed during what is known as **Bacon's Rebellion**. Bacon murdered some peaceful Indians, marched on Jamestown and forced Berkeley to legitimize his authority, then headed west again to kill more Indians. In September he returned to Jamestown and burned it to the ground. Berkeley fled across Chesapeake Bay to the Eastern Shore. The Baconites plundered the estates of some of the Green Spring faction. But a few weeks later, Bacon came down with a "violent flux"—probably it was a bad case of dysentery—and he died. Soon thereafter an English naval squadron arrived with enough soldiers to restore order. Bacon's Rebellion came to an end.

On the surface, the uprising changed nothing. No sudden shift in political power occurred. Indeed, Bacon had not sought to change either the political system or the social and economic structure of the colony. But if the *rebellion* did not change anything, nothing was ever again quite the same after it ended. With seeming impartiality, the Baconites had warred against Indians and against other planters. But which was the real enemy? Surely the Baconite and Green Springer factions had no differences that could not be compromised. And their common interest extended beyond the question of how to deal with Indians. Both wanted cheap labor.

In the quarter-century following Bacon's Rebellion the Chesapeake region thus became committed to black slavery. And slave ownership resulted in large differences in the wealth and lifestyles of growers of tobacco. The few who succeeded in accumulating twenty or more slaves and enough land to keep them occupied grew richer. The majority either grew poorer or at best had to struggle to hold their own.

More important, however, Bacon's Rebellion sealed an implicit contract between the inhabitants of the "great houses" and those who lived in more modest lodgings: Southern whites might differ greatly in wealth and influence, but they stood as one and forever behind the principle that Africans must have neither. This was the basis—the price—of the harmony and prosperity achieved by those who survived "seasoning" in the Chesapeake colonies.

THE CAROLINAS

The English and, after 1700, the Scots-Irish settlers of the tidewater parts of the Carolinas turned to agriculture as enthusiastically as had their Chesapeake neighbors. In substantial sections of what became North Carolina, tobacco flourished. In South Car-

★ Sir William Berkeley looks every inch the autocrat in this portrait, a copy of one painted by Sir Peter Lely. After Bacon's death, Berkeley took his revenge and had twenty three rebels hanged. Said King Charles II: "The old fool has killed more people in that naked country than I have done for the murder of my father."

olina, after two decades in which furs and cereals were the chief products, Madagascar rice was introduced in the low-lying coastal areas in 1696. It quickly proved its worth as a cash crop. By 1700 almost 100,000 pounds were being exported annually; by the eve of the Revolution rice exports from South Carolina and Georgia exceeded 65 million pounds a year.

Rice culture required water for flooding the fields. At first freshwater swamps were adapted to the crop, but by the middle of the eighteenth century the chief rice fields lay along the tidal rivers and inlets. Dikes and floodgates allowed fresh water to flow across the fields with the rising tide; when the tide fell, the gates closed automatically to keep the water in. The process was reversed when it was necessary to drain the land. Then the water ran out as the tide ebbed, and the pressure of the next flood pushed the gates shut.

In the 1740s another cash crop, indigo, was introduced in South Carolina by Eliza Lucas, a plantation owner. Indigo did not compete with rice either for land or labor. It prospered on high ground and needed care in seasons when the slaves were not busy in the rice paddies. The British were delighted to have a new source of indigo because the blue dye was important in their woolens industry. Parliament quickly placed a bounty—a bonus—on it to stimulate production.

Their tobacco, rice, and indigo, along with furs and forest products, meant that the southern colonies had no difficulty in obtaining manufactured articles from abroad. Planters dealt with agents in England and Scotland, called *factors,* who managed the sale of their crops, filled their orders for manufactures, and supplied them with credit. This was a great convenience but not necessarily an advantage, for it prevented the development of a diversified economy. Throughout the colonial era, while small-scale manufacturing developed rapidly in the North, it was stillborn in the South.

Reliance on European middlemen also retarded the development of urban life. Until the rise of Baltimore in the 1750s, Charleston was the only city of importance in the entire South. But despite its rich export trade, its fine harbor, and the easy availability of excellent lumber, Charleston's shipbuilding industry never remotely rivaled that of Boston, New York, or Philadelphia.

On the South Carolina rice plantations, slave labor predominated from the beginning, for free workers would not submit to its backbreaking and unhealthy regimen. The first quarter of the eighteenth century saw an enormous influx of Africans into all the southern colonies. By 1730 roughly three out of every ten people south of Pennsylvania were black,

and in South Carolina the blacks outnumbered the whites by two to one. "Carolina," remarked a newcomer in 1737, "looks more like a negro country than like a country settled by white people."

Given the existing race prejudice and the degrading impact of slavery, this demographic change had an enormous impact on life wherever African Americans were concentrated. In each colony regulations governing the behavior of blacks, both free and slave, increased in severity. The South Carolina Negro Act of 1740 denied slaves "freedom of movement, freedom of assembly, freedom to raise [their own] food, to earn money, to learn to read English." The blacks had no civil rights under any of these codes, and punishments were sickeningly severe. For minor offenses, whipping was common, for serious crimes, death by hanging or by being burned alive. Slaves were sometimes castrated for sexual offenses—even for lewd talk about white women—or for repeated attempts to escape.

Masters sought to acculturate the slaves in order to make them more efficient workers. A slave who could understand English was easier to order about; one who could handle farm tools or wait on tables was more useful than one who could not; a carpenter or a mason was more valuable still. But acculturation

★ Slaves on a South Carolina plantation, around 1790. Likely of Yoruba descent, they play west African instruments, such as the banjo, and also wear elaborate headgear, another Yoruba trait. But unlike their Yoruban contemporaries, who adorned faces and limbs with elaborate tattoos or scars, these slaves bear no evident body decorations. They are African, indisputably, but also American.

increased the slave's independence and mobility, and this posed problems. Most field hands seldom tried to escape; they expressed their dissatisfactions by pilferage and petty sabotage, by laziness, or by feigning stupidity. Most runaways were artisans who hoped to "pass" as free in a nearby town. It was one of the many paradoxes of slavery that the more valuable a slave became, the harder that slave was to control.

Few runaway slaves became rebels, however. Indeed, organized slave rebellions were rare, and while individual assaults by blacks on whites were common enough, personal violence was also common among whites, then and throughout American history. But the masters had sound reasons for fearing their slaves; the particular viciousness of the system lay in the fact that oppression bred resentment, which in turn produced still greater oppression.

What is superficially astonishing is that the whites grossly exaggerated the danger of slave revolts. They pictured the black as a kind of malevolent ogre, powerful, bestial, and lascivious, a cauldron of animal emotions that had to be restrained at any cost. Probably the characteristics they attributed to the blacks were really projections of their own passions. The most striking illustration was white fear that if blacks were free, they would breed with whites. Yet in practice, the interbreeding, which indeed took place, was almost exclusively the result of white men using their power as masters to have sexual relations with female slaves.

Thus the "peculiar institution" was fastened on America with economic, social, and psychic barbs. Ignorance and self-interest, lust for gold and for the flesh, primitive prejudices and complex social and legal ties, all combined to convince the whites that black slavery was not so much good as a fact of life. A few Quakers attacked the institution on the religious ground that all human beings are equal before God: "Christ dyed for all, both *Turks*, *Barbarians*, *Tartarians*, and *Ethyopians*." Yet some Quakers owned slaves, and even the majority who did not usually succumbed to color prejudice. Blackness was a defect, but it was no justification for enslavement, they argued. But the Quaker view attracted little attention anywhere—none in areas where slavery was important.

HOME AND FAMILY IN THE SOUTH

Life for all but the most affluent planters was by modern standards uncomfortable. Houses were mostly one- and two-room affairs, small, dark, and crowded. Furniture and utensils were sparse and crudely made. Chairs were rare; if a family possessed one it was reserved for the head of the house. People sat, slept, and ate on benches and planks. The typical dining table (the term itself was not in use) was made of two boards covered, if by anything, with a "board cloth." Toilets and plumbing of any kind were unknown; even chamber pots, which eliminated the nighttime trek to the privy, were beyond the reach of poorer families.

Clothes were equally crude and, since soap was expensive, rarely washed and therefore foul-smelling and often infested with vermin. Food was plentiful. Corn, served as bread, hominy, pancakes, and in various other forms, was the chief staple. But there was plenty of beef, pork, and game, usually boiled with various vegetables over an open fire.

White women (even indentured ones) rarely worked in the fields. Their responsibilities included tending to farm animals, making butter and cheese, pickling and preserving, spinning and sewing, and, of course, caring for children, which often involved orphans and stepchildren because of the fragility of life in the region. For exceptional women, the labor shortage created opportunities. Some managed large plantations; Eliza Lucas ran three in South Carolina for her absent father while still in her teens, and after the death of her husband, Charles Pinckney, she managed his extensive property holdings.

Southern children were not usually subjected to as strict discipline as were children in New England, but the difference was relative. Formal schooling for all but the rich was nonexistent; the rural character of society made the maintenance of schools prohibitively expensive. Whatever most children learned, they got from their parents or other relatives. A large percentage of Southerners were illiterate. As in other regions, children were put to some kind of useful work at an early age.

More well-to-do, "middling" planters had more comfortable lifestyles, but they still lived in relatively crowded quarters, having perhaps three rooms to house a family of four or five and a couple of servants. To sleep between sheets in a soft bed under blankets and quilts was luxury indeed in that world. Food in greater variety and abundance was another indication of a higher standard of living.

Until the early eighteenth century only a handful achieved real affluence. (The richest by far was Robert "King" Carter of Lancaster County, Virginia, who at the time of his death in 1732 owned 1,000 slaves and 300,000 acres.) Those fortunate few, masters of several plantations and many slaves, lived in solid, two-story houses of six or more rooms, furnished with English and other imported carpets, chairs, tables, wardrobes, chests, china, and silver. When the occasion warranted, the men wore fine broadcloth, the women the latest (or more likely the next-to-latest)

★ The harbor of Charleston, South Carolina, as depicted in the 1730s. Nearly a half dozen church steeples can be seen behind the commercial buildings along the bustling waterfront. Americans usually think of the 1600s as the great age of religion, but most colonial churches were founded after the 1740s.

fashions. Some even sent their children abroad for schooling. The founding of the College of William and Mary in Williamsburg, Virginia, in 1693 was an effort to provide the region with its own institution of higher learning, mainly in order to train clergymen. For decades, however, the College of William and Mary was not much more than a grammar school. Lawyers were relatively numerous, though rarely learned in the law. Doctors were so scarce that one sick planter wrote a letter to his brother in England describing his symptoms and asking him to consult a physician and let him know the diagnosis.

These large planters also held the commissions in the militia, the county judgeships, and the seats in the colonial legislatures. The control that these "leading families" exercised over their neighbors was not entirely unearned. They were, in general, responsible leaders. And they recognized the necessity of throwing open their houses and serving copious amounts of punch and rum to ordinary voters when election time rolled around. Such gatherings served to acknowledge the representative character of the system.

No matter what their station, southern families led relatively isolated lives. Churches, which might be expected to serve as centers of community life, were few and far between. By the middle of the eighteenth century the Anglican Church was the "established" religion, its ministers supported by public funds. The Virginia assembly had made attendance at Anglican services compulsory in 1619. In Maryland, Lord Baltimore's Toleration Act did not survive the settlement in the colony of large numbers of militant puritans. It was repealed in 1654, reenacted in 1657, then repealed again in 1692 when the Anglican Church was established.

For all its legal standing, the Anglican Church was not a powerful force in the South. Most of the ministers the Bishop of London sent to America were second-rate men who had been unable to obtain decent livings at home. If they had intellectual or spiritual ambitions when they arrived, their rural circumstances provided little opportunity to develop them. Most people had few opportunities to attend formal services. One result was that marriages tended to become civil rather than religious ceremonies.

Social events of any kind were great occasions. Births, marriages, and especially funerals called for much feasting; if there were neither heirs nor debts to satisfy, it was possible to "consume" the entire contents of a modest estate in celebrating the deceased's passing. (At one Maryland funeral the guests were provided with 55 gallons of an alcoholic concoction composed of brandy, cider, and sugar.)

Even the most successful planters were conserving types, not idle grandees chiefly concerned with conspicuous display. The vast, undeveloped country encouraged them to produce and then invest their savings in more production. William Byrd II (1674–1744), one of the richest men in Virginia, habitually rose before dawn. Besides his tobacco fields, he operated a sawmill and a grist mill, prospected for iron and coal, and engaged in the Indian trade.

GEORGIA AND THE BACK COUNTRY

West of the fall line of the many rivers that irrigated tidewater Chesapeake and Carolina lay the back country. This region included the Great Valley of Virginia, the Piedmont, and what became the final English colony, Georgia, founded by a group of London philanthropists in 1733. These men were concerned over the plight of honest persons imprisoned for debt, whom they intended to settle in the New World. (Many Europeans were still beguiled by the prospect of regenerating their society in the colonies. All told, about 50,000 British convicts were "transported" to America in the colonial period, partly to get rid of "undesirables," but partly for humane reasons.) The government, eager to create a buffer between South Carolina and the hostile Spanish in Florida, readily granted a charter (1732) to the group, whose members agreed to manage the colony without profit to themselves for a period of 21 years.

In 1733 their leader, James Oglethorpe, founded Savannah. Oglethorpe was a complicated person, vain, high-handed, and straitlaced, yet idealistic. He hoped to people the colony with sober and industrious yeoman farmers. Land grants were limited to 50 acres and made nontransferable. To ensure sobriety, rum and other "Spirits and Strong Waters" were banned. To guarantee that the colonists would have to work hard, the entry of "any Black . . . Negroe" was prohibited. Trade with Indians was to be strictly regulated in the interest of fair dealing.

Oglethorpe intended that silk, wine, and olive oil would be the main products—none of which, unfortunately, could be profitably produced in Georgia. His noble intentions came to naught. The settlers swiftly found ways to circumvent all restrictions. Rum flowed, slaves were imported, large land holdings amassed. Georgia developed an economy much like South Carolina's. In 1752 the founders, disillusioned, abandoned their responsibilities. Georgia then became a royal colony.

Now settlers penetrated the rest of the southern back country. So long as cheap land remained available closer to the coast and Indians along the frontier remained a threat, only the most daring and footloose hunters or fur traders lived far inland. But once settlement began, it came with a rush. Chief among those making the trek were Scots-Irish and German immigrants. By 1770 the back country contained about 250,000 settlers, 10 percent of the population of the colonies.

This internal migration did not proceed altogether peacefully. In 1771 frontiersmen in North Carolina calling themselves Regulators fought a pitched battle with 1,200 troops dispatched by the Carolina assembly, which was dominated by low-country interests. The Regulators were protesting their lack of representation in the assembly. They were crushed and their leaders executed. This was neither the last nor the bloodiest sectional conflict in American history.

PURITAN NEW ENGLAND

If survival in the Chesapeake required junking many European notions about social arrangements and submitting to the dictates of the wilderness, was this also true in Massachusetts and Connecticut? Ultimately it probably was, but at first puritan ideas certainly fought the New England reality to a draw.

Boston is located slightly more than 5° latitude north of Jamestown and almost 10° north of Charleston. Like other early New England towns and unlike these southern ones, Boston had a dependable water supply. The surrounding patchwork of forest, pond, dunes, and tide marsh was much more open than the malaria-infected terrain of the tidewater and low-country South. As a consequence New Englanders escaped "the agues and fevers" that beset settlers to the south, leaving them free to attend to their spiritual, economic, and social well-being. These differences alone made New England a much healthier habitat for settlers.

THE PURITAN FAMILY

New England's puritans were set apart from other English settlers by how much—and how long—they lived out of their baggage. The supplies the first arrivals brought with them eased their adjustment, as did the wherewithal of later, equally heavily laden arrivals. The puritans' baggage, however, included besides pots and pans, and saws and shovels, a plan for the proper ordering of society.

At the center of the plan was a covenant, or agreement, to ensure the upright behavior of all who took up residence. They sought to provide what John Winthrop described to the passengers on the *Arbella* as the imperative of human existence: "that every man might have need of other, and from hence they might be all knitt more nearly together in the Bond of brotherly affection."

The first and most important covenant governing puritan behavior was that binding family members. The family's authority was backed by the Fifth Commandment: "Honor thy father and thy mother, that thy days may be long upon the land." In a properly ordered puritan family, as elsewhere in the colonies, authority flowed downward. Sociologists describe such a family as nuclear and patriarchal; each household contained one family, and in it, the father was boss. His principal responsibilities consisted of providing for the physical welfare of the household, including any servants, and making sure they behaved properly. All economic dealings between the family and other parties were also transacted by him, even when the property involved had been owned by his wife prior to their marriage.

The Reverend John Cotton's outline of a woman's responsibilities clearly establishes her subordinate position: She should keep house, educate the children, and improve "what is got by the industry of the man." The poet Anne Bradstreet reduced the functions of a puritan woman to two: "loving Mother and obedient Wife." Colonial New England, and the southern colonies as well, did have their female blacksmiths, silversmiths, shipwrights, gunsmiths, and butchers as well as shopkeepers and teachers. Such early examples of domestic "liberation," however, were mostly widows and the wives of incapacitated husbands. Even so, most widows, especially young ones, quickly remarried.

Dealings with neighbors and relatives and involvement in church activities marked the outer limits of the social range of most puritan women. Care of the children was a full-time occupation when broods of twelve or fourteen were more common than those of one or two. Fewer children died in New England than in the Chesapeake or in Europe, though few families escaped a miscarriage or a child's death along the way. Childbearing and motherhood, therefore, commonly extended over three decades of a woman's life. Meanwhile, she also functioned as the chief operating officer of the household. Cooking, baking, sewing, and supervising servants, as well as mastering such arcane knowledge as the chemistry needed to make cheese from milk, bacon from pork, bread from grain, and beer from malt, all fell to her.

As puritan social standards required husbands to rule over wives, so parents ruled over children. The virtue most insistently impressed on New England children was obedience; refusal to submit to parental direction was disturbing in itself and for what it implied about the child's eternal condition. Cotton Mather's advice, "better whipt, than damned," graced many a New England rod taken up by a parent in anger, from there to be rapidly transferred to the afterparts of misbehaving offspring. But household chores kept children out of mischief. By age six or seven girls did sewing and helped with housework and boys were put to work outdoors. Older children might be sent to live with another family to work as servants or apprentices.

Such practices, particularly when set beside portraits of early New England families that depict toddlers as somber-faced miniature adults wearing clothes indistinguishable from those of their parents, may convey the impression that puritans hustled their young through childhood with as little love as possible. New Englanders harbored no illusions. "Innocent vipers" is how one minister described children,

★ New England children like David, Joanna, and Abigail Mason (painted by an unknown artist around 1670) were expected to emulate adults in their chores and their appearance. Nevertheless, diaries and letters indicate that children were cherished by their parents in a way closer to modern family love than what their European contemporaries experienced.

having fourteen of his own to submit as evidence. Anne Bradstreet, mother of eight, characterized one as harboring "a perverse will, a love of what's forbid / a serpent's sting in pleasing face lay hid." Yet for all their acceptance of the doctrine of infant damnation, puritan parents were not indifferent to the fate of their children. "I do hope," Cotton Mather confessed at the burial of one of the eight children he lost before the age of two, "that when my children are gone they are not lost; but carried unto the Heavenly Feast with Abraham." Another minister assigned children who died in infancy "the easiest room in hell."

Population growth reinforced puritan ideas about the family. When the outbreak of the English Civil War put an end to the Great Migration in the early 1640s, immigration declined sharply. Thereafter growth was chiefly due to the region's extraordinarily high birthrate (50 births for every 1,000 population, which is more than three times the rate today) and strikingly low mortality rate (about 20 per 1,000). This resulted in a population much more evenly distributed by age and sex than that in the South. The fact that most New England women married in their early twenties rather than their late teens suggests that the demand for women matched the supply. Demographic realities joined with puritan expectations to create a society of nuclear families distinct to the region.

VISIBLE PURITAN SAINTS AND OTHERS

When it came to religion, puritans believed that church membership ought to be the joint decision of a would-be member and those already in the church. Those seeking admission would tell the congregation why they believed that they had received God's grace. Obvious sinners and those ignorant of Christian doctrine were rejected out of hand. But what of pious and God-fearing applicants who lacked compelling evidence of salvation? In the late 1630s, with the Great Migration in full swing and new arrivals clamoring for admission to the churches, such "merit-mongers" were excluded, thereby limiting church membership to the community's "visible saints." A decade later, the Great Migration over and applications down, some of the saints began to have second thoughts.

By the early 1650s fewer than half of all New England adults were church members, and so exacting had the examination for membership become, particularly in churches where the minister and elders outdid each other in the ferocity of their questioning, that most young people refused to submit themselves to it. How these growing numbers of nonmembers could be compelled to attend church services was a problem ministers could not long defer. Meanwhile, the magistrates found it harder to defend the policy of not letting taxpayers vote because they were not church members. But what really forced reconsideration of the membership policy were the concerns of nonmember parents about the souls of their children, who could not be baptized.

At first the churches permitted baptism of the children of church members. Later, some biblical purists came out against infant baptism altogether, but most puritans approved this practice, which allowed them the hope that a child who died after receiving baptism might at least be spared Hell's hottest precincts. Since most of the first generation were church members, nearly all the second-generation New Englanders were baptized, whether they became church members or not. The problem began with the third generation, the offspring of parents who had been baptized but who did not become church members. By the mid-1650s it was clear that if nothing were done, a majority of the people would soon be living in a state of original sin. If that happened, how could the churches remain the dominant force in New England life?

Fortunately, a way out was at hand. In 1657 an assembly of Massachusetts and Connecticut ministers recommended a form of intermediate church membership that would permit the baptism of people who were not visible saints. Five years later, some 80 ministers and laymen met at Boston's First Church to hammer out what came to be called the **Half-Way Covenant**. It provided limited (halfway) membership for any applicant not known to be a sinner who was willing to accept the provisions of the church covenant. They and their children could be baptized, but the sacrament of communion and a voice in church decision making were reserved for full members.

The General Court of Massachusetts endorsed the recommendations of the Half-Way Synod and urged all the churches of the Commonwealth to adopt them. Two years later it quietly extended the right to vote to halfway church members.

Opponents of the Half-Way Covenant argued that it reflected a slackening of religious fervor. Michael Wigglesworth gave poetic voice to these views in "God's Controversy with New England" and "The Day of Doom," both written in 1662. Perry Miller, an authority on puritan New England, argued that the early 1660s marked the beginning of the decline, or "declension," of the puritan experiment. Some loss of religious intensity there may have been, but the rise in church memberships, the continuing prestige accorded ministers, and the lessening of the intrachurch squabbling after the 1660s suggest that the secularization of New England society had a long way to go.

DEMOCRACIES WITHOUT DEMOCRATS

Like the southern colonies, the New England colonies derived their authority from charters granted by the Crown or Parliament. Except for rare fits of meddling by London bureaucrats, they were largely left to their own devices where matters of purely local interest were concerned. This typically involved maintaining order by regulating how people behaved.

According to puritan theory, government was both a civil covenant, entered into by all who came within its jurisdiction, and the principal mechanism for policing the institutions on which the maintenance of the social order depended. When Massachusetts and Connecticut passed laws requiring church attendance, levying taxes for the support of the clergy, and banning Quakers from practicing their faith, they were acting as "shield of the churches." When they provided the death penalty both for adultery and for blaspheming a parent, they were defending the integrity of families. When they set the price a laborer might charge for his services or even the amount of gold braid that servants might wear on their jackets, they believed they were enforcing the puritan principle that people must accept their assigned stations in life. Puritan communities were, for a time, close-knit: murder, assault, and theft were rare. Disputes were adjudicated through an active court system.

But puritan civil authorities and ministers of the puritan (Congregational) church came under sharp attack from English Anglicans, Presbyterians, and Quakers. When the Massachusetts General Court hanged four stubborn Quakers who returned after being expelled from the colony, a royal order of 1662 forbade further executions.

Laws like these have prompted historians and Americans generally to characterize New England colonial legislation as socially repressive and personally invasive. Yet many of the laws remained in force through the colonial period without rousing much local opposition. Others, particularly those upholding religious discrimination or restricting economic activity, were repealed at the insistence of Parliament.

A healthy respect for the backsliding ways of humanity obliged New Englanders not to depend too much on provincial governments, whose jurisdiction extended over several thousand square miles. Almost of necessity, the primary responsibility for maintaining "Good Order and Peace" fell to the more than 500 towns of the region. These differed greatly in size and development. By the early eighteenth century, the largest—Boston, Newport, and Portsmouth—were on their way toward becoming urban centers. This was before "frontier" towns like Amherst, Kent, and Hanover had even been founded. Nonetheless, town life gave New England the distinctiveness it has still not wholly lost.

THE DOMINION OF NEW ENGLAND

The most serious threat to these arrangements occurred in the 1680s. Following the execution of Charles I in 1649, England was ruled by one man, the Lord Protector, Oliver Cromwell, a puritan. Cromwell's death in 1658 led to the restoration of the Stuart monarchy in the person of Charles II (1660–1685). During his reign and the abbreviated one of his brother, James II (1685–1688), the government sought to bring the colonies under effective royal control.

Massachusetts seemed in particular need of supervision. Accordingly, in 1684 its charter was annulled and the colony, along with all those north of Pennsylvania, became part of the Dominion of New England, governed by Edmund Andros.

Andros arrived in Boston in late 1686 with orders to make the northern colonies behave like colonies, not like sovereign powers. He set out to abolish popular assemblies, to change the land-grant system so as to provide the king with quitrents, and to enforce religious toleration, particularly of Anglicans. Andros, being a professional soldier and administrator, scoffed at those who resisted his authority. "Knoweing no other government than their owne," he said, they "think it best, and are wedded to . . . it."

Fortunately for New Englanders so wedded, the Dominion fell victim two years later to yet another political turnabout in England, the **Glorious Revolution**. In 1688 Parliament decided it had had enough of the Catholic-leaning Stuarts and sent James II packing. In his place it installed James's daughter Mary and her resolutely Protestant Dutch husband, William of Orange. When news of these events reached Boston in the spring of 1689, a force of more than a thousand colonists led by a contingent of ministers seized Andros and lodged him in jail. Two years later Massachusetts was made a royal colony that also included Plymouth and Maine. As in all such colonies the governor was appointed by the king. The new General Court was elected by property owners; church membership was no longer a requirement for voting.

SALEM BEWITCHED

In 1666, families living in the rural outback of the thriving town of Salem petitioned the General Court for the right to establish their own church. For political and economic reasons this was a questionable move, but in 1672 the General Court authorized the establishment of a separate parish. In so doing the Court put the 600-odd inhabitants of the village on their own politically as well.

Over the next 15 years three preachers came and went before, in 1689, one Samuel Parris became minister. Parris had spent 20 years in the Caribbean as a merchant and had taken up preaching only three years before coming to Salem. Accompanying him were his wife; a daughter, Betty; a niece, Abigail; and the family's West Indian slave, Tituba, who told fortunes and practiced magic on the side.

Parris proved as incapable of bringing peace to the feuding factions of Salem Village as had his predecessors. In January 1692 the church voted to dismiss him. At this point Betty and Abigail, now 9 and 11,

Ann Putnam's
Deposition
(1692)

along with Ann Putnam, a 12-year-old, started "uttering foolish, ridiculous speeches which neither they themselves nor any others could make sense of." A doctor diagnosed the girls' ravings as the work of the "Evil Hand" and declared them bewitched.

But who had done the bewitching? The first persons accused were three women whose unsavory reputations and frightening appearances made them likely candidates. Sarah Good, a pauper with a nasty tongue; Sarah Osborne, a bedridden widow; and the slave Tituba, who had brought suspicion on herself by volunteering to bake a "witch cake," made of rye meal and the girls' urine. The cake should be fed to a dog, Tituba said. If the girls were truly afflicted, the dog would show signs of bewitchment!

"Lookie There!"

The three women were brought before the local deputies to the General Court. As each was questioned, the girls went into contortions: "their arms, necks and backs turned this way and that way . . . their mouths stopped, their throats choked, their limbs wracked and tormented." Tituba, likely impressed by the powers ascribed to her, promptly confessed to being a witch. Sarah Good and Sarah Osborne each claimed to be innocent, although Sarah Good expressed doubts about Sarah Osborne. All three were sent to jail on suspicion of practicing witchcraft.

These proceedings triggered new accusations. By the end of April 1692, twenty four more people had been charged with practicing witchcraft. Officials in neighboring Andover, lacking their own "bewitched," called in the girls to help with their investigations. By May the hunt had extended to Maine and Boston and up the social ladder to some of the colony's most prominent citizens, including Lady Mary Phips, whose husband, William, had just been appointed governor.

By June, when Governor Phips convened a special court consisting of members of his council, more than 150 persons (Lady Phips no longer among them) stood formally charged with practicing witchcraft. In the next four months the court convicted twenty eight of them, most of them women. Five "confessed" and were spared; the rest were condemned to death. Several oth-

★ *Examination of a Witch.* A stern puritan patriarch adjusts his glasses to better examine a beautiful—and partially disrobed—young woman. Ostensibly, he is looking for the "witch's teats" with which she suckled "black dogs" and other creatures of the Devil. Completed in 1853 by T. H. Matteson, this painting subtly indicts puritan men as lecherous hypocrites. In fact, most accused witches were in their forties or fifties. The painting thus reveals more about the nineteenth-century reaction against puritanism than about the puritans themselves.

ers escaped. But nineteen persons were hanged. The husband of a convicted witch refused to enter a plea when charged with being a "wizard." He was executed by having stones piled on him until he suffocated.

Anyone who spoke in defense of the accused was in danger of being charged with witchcraft, but some brave souls challenged both the procedures and the findings of the court. Finally, at the urging of the leading ministers of the Commonwealth, Governor Phips adjourned the court and forbade any further executions.

No one involved in these gruesome proceedings escaped with reputation intact, but those whose reputations suffered most were the ministers. Among the clergy only Increase Mather deserves any credit. He persuaded Phips to halt the executions, arguing that "it were better that ten witches should escape, than that one innocent person should be condemned." The behavior of his son Cotton defies apology. It was not that Cotton Mather accepted the existence of witches—at the time everyone did, which incidentally suggests that Tituba was not the only person in Salem who practiced witchcraft—or even that Mather took such pride in being the resident expert on demonology. It was rather his vindictiveness. He even stood at the foot of the gallows bullying hesitant hangmen into doing "their duty."

The episode also highlights the anxieties puritan men felt toward women. Many puritans believed that Satan worked his will especially through the allure of female sexuality. Moreover, many of the accused witches were widows of high status or older women who owned property; some of the women, like Tituba, had mastered herbal medicine and other suspiciously potent healing arts. Such women, especially those who lived apart from the daily guidance of men, potentially subverted the patriarchal authorities of church and state. (For more on this topic, see Reviewing the Past, "The Crucible," pp. 72–73.)

HIGHER EDUCATION IN NEW ENGLAND

Along with the farmers and artisans who settled in New England with their families during the Great Migration came nearly 150 university-trained colonists. Nearly all had studied divinity. These men became the first ministers in Massachusetts and Connecticut, and a brisk "seller's market" existed for them. Larger churches began stockpiling candidates by hiring newly arrived Cambridge and Oxford graduates as assistants or teachers in anticipation of the retirement of their senior ministers. But New England puritans could not forever remain dependent on the graduates of English universities.

In 1636 the Massachusetts General Court appropriated £400 to found "a schoole or colledge." Two years later, just as the first freshmen gathered in Cambridge, John Harvard, a recent arrival who had died of tuberculosis, left the college £800 and his library. After a shaky start, during which students conducted a hunger strike against a sadistic and larcenous headmaster, Harvard settled into an annual pattern of admitting a dozen or so 14-year-old boys, stuffing their heads with four years of theology, logic, and mathematics, and then sending them out into the wider world of New England. In 1650 Harvard received from the General Court the charter under which it is still governed.

Immediately below Harvard on the educational ladder came the grammar schools, where boys spent seven years learning Latin and Greek "so far as they may be fitted for the Universitie." Boston founded the first—the Boston Latin School—in 1636. Massachusetts and Connecticut soon passed education acts, which required all towns of any size to establish such schools. New Englanders hoped, as the preamble to the Massachusetts law of 1647 stated, to thwart "that old deluder, Satan," whose "chief object was to keep men from the knowledge of the Scriptures," by ensuring "that Learning may not be buried in the graves of our forefathers." Not every New England town required to maintain a school actually did so. Those that did often paid their teachers poorly. Only the most dedicated Harvard graduates took up teaching as a career. Some parents kept their children at their chores rather than at school.

Yet the cumulative effect of the puritan community's educational institutions, the family and the church as well as the school, was impressive. A majority of men in mid-seventeenth-century New England could read and a somewhat smaller percentage could also write. By the middle of the eighteenth century, male literacy was almost universal. In Europe only Scotland and Sweden had achieved this happy state so early. Literacy among women also improved steadily, despite the almost total neglect of formal education for girls.

Spreading literacy created a thriving market for the printed word. Many of the first settlers brought impressive libraries with them, and large numbers of English books were imported throughout the colonial period. The first printing press in the English colonies was founded in Cambridge in 1638, and by 1700 Boston was producing an avalanche of printed matter. Most of these publications were reprints of sermons; ministers required only the smallest encouragement

Colonial Families: Adult and Child Reading

▶ *text continues on page 74*

Re-Viewing the Past

Winona Ryder stars in the 1996 movie based on Arthur Miller's 1953 play, *The Crucible,* an interpretation of the Salem witch trials of 1692. Ryder plays Abigail Williams, consumed with desire for John Proctor (Daniel Day-Lewis), a married man. Proctor has broken off their affair and reconciled with his wife, Elizabeth (Joan Allen). As the movie begins, Abigail and some other girls have sneaked into the woods with Tituba, a slave who practices black magic. They ask about their future husbands, and some beg her to cast a spell on their favorites. Abigail whispers something to Tituba, who recoils in horror. Abigail's dark eyes, glowing with fury, inform the movie audience of her message: She wants Elizabeth Proctor dead. Tituba slips into a trance and begins conjuring. Exhilarated by this illicit flouting of convention, and quivering with sexual energy, the girls throw off their clothes and dance wildly around a fire.

Then the minister happens onto the scene. The girls flee in terror. Some become hysterical. Later, when confronted by church elders Abigail blurts out that Tituba was a witch who was trying to steal their souls. Tituba initially denies the charges, but after being whipped she confesses. Pressed further, she names two other women as accomplices. At the mention of their names, Abigail's face contorts with pain and she moans; taking the cue, the other girls scream and writhe upon the floor. They supply the names of more witches. Alarmed by the enormity of Satan's plot, Massachusetts authorities initiate an investigation.

After one court session, Abigail saunters over to John, standing by the side of the church. When he asks what "mischief" she has been up to, Abigail averts her eyes demurely and then gives him a wicked grin. John smiles at this prodigy in the seductive arts. She responds with a kiss, her hand groping for his groin. He hesitates, but then roughly pushes her away. Her eyes blaze with hatred.

The girls' hysterics intensify. Eventually over 100 suspected witches, most of them women, are arrested. The Proctors themselves come under suspicion. Asked to recite the Ten Commandments, John omits the injunction against adultery; the magistrate looks at him searchingly. When Abigail accuses Elizabeth of being a witch, John lashes out at the girl.

"She is a whore," he declares in court. "I have known her, sir."

"He is lying," Abigail hisses. Suddenly her eyes widen, horror-stricken, and she screams that he, too, is in league with Satan. Her flawless histrionics again prevail: he is arrested.

During the trials, the magistrates look for physical evidence of satanic possession: unnatural flaps of skin or unusual warts—witch's teats—with which Satan's minions sap human souls. Family and neighbors, too, furnish evidence. Some cite occasions when the accused lost their tempers or stole livestock. But the main evidence is the behavior of the girls themselves, who squirm and howl, claiming that the spirits of the accused torment them. This "spectral" evidence unsettles the magistrates. Seeking stronger proof, they urge prisoners to confess. Those who do will be spared, for the act of confession signifies their break with Satan. Those who refuse must be hanged.

The Proctors are among those convicted and sentenced to death. (Because Elizabeth is pregnant, her execution is postponed.) When given the opportunity to save himself, John signs a confession. But inspired by his wife's quiet courage, he repudiates it, choosing to die with honor rather than live in shame. His noble death at the scaffold, and the deaths of others like him, cause the people of Massachusetts to end the witch hunt.

The Crucible warrants consideration apart from Ryder's remarkable performance. For one, the movie vividly recreates a puritan world inhabited by palpable spirits. Contemporary viewers may snicker at scenes of adults scanning the night sky for flying witches and evil birds, but the puritans believed in such things. They regarded comets, meteors, and lightning as signals from God. When Cotton Mather lost the pages of a lecture, he concluded that "Spectres, or Agents in the invisible World, were the Robbers."

Episodes and language taken directly from trial records, though sometimes altered, infuse the movie with verisimilitude. For example, the Proctors were in fact interrogated on their biblical knowledge. Whereas in the movie John falters by omitting the commandment against adultery, in history, the

★ Few portraits of single puritan women exist; their invisibility may help explain why some sought attention, perhaps by making witchcraft accusations. The young woman in this portrait became "visible" by becoming a mother.

fatal mistake was Elizabeth's. Asked to recite the Lord's Prayer, she substituted "hollowed be thy name" for "hallowed be thy name." The magistrates declared this to be a "depraving" act, for she had transformed the prayer into a curse—proof of satanic possession.

The movie's rendering of the girls' hysteria mostly corresponds with what we know from the historical record. A bewildered John Hale, a minister from Beverly, recorded that Abigail and her cousin were

> bitten and pinched by invisible agents. Their arms, necks and backs turned this way and that way, and returned back again, so as it was impossible for them to do of themselves. . . . Sometimes they were taken dumb, their mouths stopped, their throats choked, their limbs wracked and tormented so as might move an heart of stone. . . . with bowels of compassion for them.

Historians still puzzle over the girls' behavior. Probably they were seeking attention, or venting anxiety over their fate as women in a patriarchal society; certainly their choice of victims suggests that they were voicing parental enmity toward neighbors. The movie alludes to such issues, but mostly attributes the girls' hysteria to sexual frustration, a consequence of puritan repression.

Ryder's Abigail symbolizes adolescent sexuality: her lust for John (and corresponding hatred of Elizabeth) precipitates the witch hunt. In fact, the real Abigail did accuse Elizabeth of witchcraft. The trial record reports that when Elizabeth denied the charge, Abigail raised her hand as if to strike her, but instead touched Elizabeth's hood "very lightly" and cried out, "My fingers! My fingers—burned!" Then Abigail swooned to the floor. But if these few historical details provide some basis for Abigail's conjectured affair with Elizabeth's husband, others call it into question, the most telling being the gap in their ages: The real Abigail was 11 and Proctor, 60.

Whatever the merits of playwright Arthur Miller's speculation about Abigail and John, his larger questions have long intrigued historians: Were the puritans sexually repressive? If so, did young people assent to puritan strictures or rebel against them?

Such questions cannot be answered with certainty. Few puritans left written accounts of their illicit thoughts and sexual behavior. Social historians have approached the matter from a different angle. Nearly all marriages and births in colonial New England (and most other places) were recorded. Scholars have scoured such records to determine how many brides gave birth to babies within six months of marriage; such women almost certainly had engaged in premarital intercourse.

This data for about a dozen communities in puritan New England indicate an extraordinarily low rate of premarital intercourse, far below England's at the same time or New England's a century later. This confirms that young puritan couples were watched closely. Governor William Bradford of Plymouth Colony, commenting on the relative absence of premarital pregnancy, concluded that sinners there were "more discovered and seen and made public by due search,

★ Winona Ryder as a young puritan who accuses others of witchcraft.

inquisition and due punishment; for the churches look narrowly to their members, and the magistrates over all, more strictly than in other places." On the other hand, the low rate of premarital pregnancy might not signify puritan repression so much as young people's acceptance of puritan values.

When critics confronted Arthur Miller on his deviations from the historical record, and especially when they expressed skepticism over whether young Abigail Williams and the elderly John Proctor had an affair, Miller was unrepentant. "What's real?" he retorted. "We don't know what these people were like." Perhaps so, but one suspects that Winona Ryder's Abigail would have had a hard time of it in Salem in 1692. Could a bloom of such pungent and poisonous precocity have emerged through the stony soil of New England Puritanism, and if so, could it have survived the assiduous weeding of the puritans themselves?

QUESTIONS FOR DISCUSSION

- What factors, apart from those mentioned in this essay, could explain why puritan brides rarely had babies within six months of their marriage? Is this a good measure of premarital chastity?
- How did puritan courtship differ from modern courtship?

from their congregations to send off last Sunday's remarks to the local printer. But if ministers exercised a near monopoly of the printed word, they did not limit their output to religious topics. They also produced modest amounts of history, poetry, reports of scientific investigations, and treatises on political theory.

By the early eighteenth century the intellectual life of New England had taken on a character potentially at odds with the ideas of the first puritans. In the 1690s Harvard acquired a reputation for encouraging religious toleration. According to orthodox puritans, its graduates were unfit for the ministry and its professors were no longer interested in training young men for the clergy. In 1701 several Connecticut ministers, most of them Harvard graduates, founded a new "Collegiate School" designed to uphold the puritan values that Harvard seemed ready to abandon. The new college was named after its first English benefactor, Elihu Yale. It fulfilled its founders' hopes by sending more than half of its early graduates into the ministry. Nonetheless, as became all too clear at commencement ceremonies in 1722 when its president and six tutors announced themselves Anglicans, Yale quickly acquired purposes well beyond those assigned it by its creators.

The assumption that the clergy had the last word on learned matters, still operative at the time of the witchcraft episode, came under direct challenge in 1721. When a smallpox epidemic swept through Boston that summer, Cotton Mather, at the time the most prestigious clergyman in New England, recommended that the citizenry be inoculated. Instead of accepting Mather's authority, his heretofore silent critics seized on his support of the then-radical idea of inoculation to challenge both his motives and his professional credentials. They filled the unsigned contributor columns of New England's first newspaper, the *Boston Gazette,* and the *New England Courant,* which started in the midst of the inoculation controversy, with their views.

The *Courant* was published by James Franklin and his 16-year-old brother, Benjamin. The younger Franklin's "Silence Dogood" essays were particularly infuriating to members of the Boston intellectual establishment. Franklin described Harvard as an institution where rich and lazy "blockheads . . . learn little more than how to carry themselves handsomely . . . and from whence they return, after Abundance of Trouble, as Blockheads as ever, only more proud and conceited."

James Franklin was jailed in 1722 for criticizing the General Court, and shortly thereafter the *New England Courant* went out of business. Meanwhile, Ben had departed Boston for Philadelphia, where fame and fortune awaited him.

A MERCHANT'S WORLD

Prior experience (and the need to eat) turned the first New Englanders to farming. They grew barley (used to make beer), rye, oats, green vegetables, and also native crops such as potatoes, pumpkins, and, most important, Indian corn, or maize. Corn was easily cultivated. In the form of corn liquor, it was easy to store, to transport, and, in a pinch, to imbibe.

The colonists also had plenty of meat. They grazed cattle, sheep, and hogs on the common pastures or in the surrounding woodlands. Deer, along with turkey and other game birds, abounded. The Atlantic provided fish, especially cod, which was easily preserved by salting. In short, New Englanders ate an extremely nutritious diet. Abundant surpluses of firewood kept the winter cold from their doors. The combination contributed significantly to their good health and longevity.

But the shortness of the growing season, the rocky and often hilly terrain, and careless methods of cultivation, which exhausted the soil, meant that farmers did not produce large surpluses. Thus, while New Englanders could feed themselves without difficulty, they had relatively little to spare.

Winthrop's generation of puritans accepted this economic marginality. They were to fasten their attention upon the next world rather than the one they occupied on earth.

But later generations did not share the anticommercial bias of the early puritans. At the beginning of the eighteenth century a Boston minister told his congregation of another minister who reminded his flock that "the main end of planting this wilderness" was religion. A prominent member of the congregation could not contain his disagreement. "Sir," he cried out, "you are mistaken. You think you are preaching to the people of the Bay; our main end was to catch fish."

Fish, caught offshore from Cape Cod to Newfoundland, provided merchants with their opening into the world of transatlantic commerce. In 1643 five New England vessels set out with their holds packed with fish that they sold in Spain and the Canary Islands; they took payment in sherry and madeira, for which a market existed in England. One of these ships also had the dubious distinction of initiating New England into the business of trafficking in human beings when its captain took payment in African slaves, whom he subsequently sold in the West Indies. This was the start of the famous **triangular trade**. Only occasionally was the pattern truly triangular; more often, intermediate legs gave it a polygonal character. So long as their ships ended up with something that could be exchanged for English goods needed at

Colonial Products

Debating the Past

WERE PURITAN COMMUNITIES PEACEABLE?

A smooth, quiet river flows past this eighteenth-century puritan town. A church spire rises, treelike, from its center. The painting is a composition in harmony. In *The Scarlet Letter* (1850), however, Nathaniel Hawthorne shattered this placid image: Puritan towns, he suggested, were plagued with envy, intolerance, and hypocrisy. Hawthorne's harsh assessment, which many historians shared, persisted into the twentieth century. This view changed with Perry Miller (1933), whose elegant analysis of puritan sermons and writings amply demonstrated "the majesty and coherence of Puritan thinking." The rise of atheistic communism in the Soviet Union after World War II further contributed to an appreciation of the nation's puritan roots. Daniel Boorstin (1958) wrote approvingly of the strong families, religious faith, and democratic governance of puritan towns. During the 1960s a new generation of historians examined the issue. They had been influenced by Fernand Braudel, a French scholar. Braudel encouraged historians to reconstruct the "total history" of particular communities, rather like anthropologists. The publication of four such studies in 1970 reinvigorated colonial social history. John Demos discovered that families in Plymouth, Massachusetts, were beset with psychological conflicts; Philip Greven and Kenneth Lockridge found that Dedham and Andover, Massachusetts, lost cohesion rapidly; Paul Zuckerman, on the other hand, concluded that his puritan towns most nearly resembled "peaceable kingdoms." Other studies complicated the picture further: Paul Boyer and Stephen Nissenbaum (1974) contended that Salem was wracked with class and religious tensions, while other scholars found increasingly cohesive puritan communities. Which description was more characteristic of the puritan pattern? In recent decades, historians David Hackett Fischer (1989) and Alan Taylor (2001) insisted that the puritans should be examined not in towns such as this one but in relation to a much larger, even transatlantic, context.

Perry Miller, *Orthodoxy in Massachusetts* (1933) and *The New England Mind* (1939), Daniel Boorstin, *The Colonial Experience* (1958), John Demos, *A Little Commonwealth* (1970), Philip J. Greven, *Four Generations* (1970), Kenneth Lockridge, *A New England Town* (1970), Michael Zuckerman, *Peaceable Kingdoms* (1970), Paul Boyer and Stephen Nissenbaum, *Salem Possessed* (1974), David Hackett Fischer, *Albion's Seed* (1989), Alan Taylor, *American Colonies* (2001)

home, it did not matter what they started out with or how many things they bought and sold along the way.

So maritime trade and those who engaged in it became the driving force of the New England economy, important all out of proportion to the number of persons directly involved. Because those engaged congregated in Portsmouth, Salem, Boston, Newport, and New Haven, these towns soon differed greatly from towns in the interior. They were larger and faster growing, and a smaller percentage of their inhabitants was engaged in farming.

The largest and most thriving town was Boston, which by 1720 had become the commercial hub of the region. It had a population of more than 10,000; in the entire British Empire, only London and Bristol were larger. More than one-quarter of Boston's male adults had either invested in shipbuilding or were directly employed in maritime commerce. Ship captains and merchants held most of the public offices.

Beneath this emergent mercantile elite lived a stratum of artisans and small shopkeepers, and beneath these a substantial population of mariners, laborers, and "unattached" people with little or no property and still less political voice. In the 1670s, at least a dozen prostitutes plied their trade in Boston. By 1720 crime and poverty had become serious problems; public relief rolls frequently exceeded 200 souls, and dozens of criminals languished in the town jail. Boston bore little resemblance to what the first puritans had in mind when they planted their "Citty upon a Hill." But neither was it like any eighteenth-century European city. It stood there on Massachusetts Bay, midway between its puritan origins and its American future.

THE MIDDLE COLONIES: ECONOMIC BASIS

The Colonies to 1740

New York, New Jersey, Pennsylvania, and Delaware owe their collective name, the Middle Colonies, to geography. Sandwiched between New England and the Chesapeake region, they often receive only passing notice in accounts of colonial America. The lack of a distinctive institution, such as slavery or the town meeting, explains part of this neglect.

Actually, both institutions existed there. Black slaves made up about 10 percent of the population; indeed, one New York county in the 1740s had proportionally more blacks than large sections of Virginia. And eastern Long Island was settled by people from Connecticut who brought the town meeting system with them.

This quality of "in-betweenness" extended to other economic and social arrangements. Like

colonists elsewhere, most Middle Colonists became farmers. But where northern farmers concentrated on producing crops for local consumption and southerners for export, Middle Colony farmers did both. In addition to raising foodstuffs and keeping livestock, they grew wheat, which the thin soil and shorter growing season of New England did not permit but for which there existed an expanding market in the densely settled Caribbean sugar islands.

Social arrangements differed more in degree than in kind from those in other colonies. Unlike New England settlers, who clustered together in agricultural villages, families in the Hudson Valley of New York and in southeastern Pennsylvania lived on the land they cultivated, often as spatially dispersed as the tobacco planters of the Chesapeake. In contrast with Virginia and Maryland, however, substantial numbers congregated in the seaport centers of New York City and Philadelphia. They also settled interior towns like Albany, an important center of the fur trade on the upper Hudson, and Germantown, an "urban village" northwest of Philadelphia where many people were engaged in trades like weaving and tailoring and flour milling.

THE MIDDLE COLONIES: AN INTERMINGLING OF PEOPLES

The Middle Colonists also possessed traits that later would be seen as distinctly "American." Their ethnic and religious heterogeneity is a case in point. In the 1640s, when New Amsterdam was only a village, one visitor claimed to have heard 18 languages spoken there. Traveling through Pennsylvania a century later, the Swedish botanist Peter Kalm encountered "a very mixed company of different nations and religions." In addition to "Scots, English, Dutch, Germans, and Irish," he reported, "there were Roman Catholics, Presbyterians, Quakers, Methodists, Seventh Day men, Moravians, Anabaptists, and one Jew." In New York City one embattled English resident complained: "Our chiefest unhappiness here is too great a mixture of nations, & English the least part."

Scandinavian and Dutch settlers outnumbered the English in New Jersey and Delaware even after the English took over these colonies. William Penn's first success in attracting colonists was with German Quakers and other persecuted religious sects, among them Mennonites and Moravians from the Rhine Valley. The first substantial influx of immigrants into New York after it became a royal colony consisted of French Huguenots.

Early in the eighteenth century, hordes of Scots-Irish settlers from northern Ireland and Scotland de-

★ This painting is presumably of Lord Cornbury, the royal governor of New York and New Jersey in the early 1700s, in a dress. Why it was painted and by whom is unknown. Some regard the painting as proof that the eighteenth century tolerated a wide range of sexual behaviors. In *The Lord Cornbury Scandal* (1998), however, Patricia Bonomi views the painting as part of a plot to unseat a brusque and high-handed governor. Some of his enemies in the colonies dispatched letters to officials in London complaining of Cornbury's penchant for wearing women's clothing in public. Bonomi doubts that the charges were true.

scended on Pennsylvania. These colonists spoke English but felt little loyalty to the English government, which had treated them badly back home, and less to the Anglican Church, since most of them were Presbyterians. Large numbers of them followed the valleys of the Appalachians south into the back country of Virginia and the Carolinas.

Why so few English in the Middle Colonies? Here, again, timing provides the best answer. The English economy was booming. There seemed to be work for all. Migration to North America, while never drying up, slowed to a trickle. The result was colonies in which English settlers were a minority.

The intermingling of ethnic groups gave rise to many prejudices. Benjamin Franklin, though generally complimentary toward Pennsylvania's hard-work-

ing Germans, thought them clannish to a fault. The already cited French traveler Hector St. John de Crèvecoeur, while marveling at the adaptive qualities of "this promiscuous breed," complained that "the Irish . . . love to drink and to quarrel; they are litigious, and soon take to the gun, which is the ruin of everything." Yet by and large the various types managed to get along with each other successfully enough. Crèvecoeur attended a wedding in Pennsylvania where the groom's grandparents were English and Dutch and one of his uncles had married a Frenchwoman. The groom and his three brothers, Crèvecoeur added with some amazement, "now have four wives of different nations."

"THE BEST POOR MAN'S COUNTRY"

Ethnic differences seldom caused conflict in the Middle Colonies because they seldom limited opportunity. The promise of prosperity (promotional pamphlets proclaimed Pennsylvania "the best poor man's country in the world") had attracted all in the first place, and achieving prosperity was relatively easy, even for those who came with only a willingness to work. From its founding, Pennsylvania granted upward of 500 acres of land to families on arrival, provided they would pay the proprietor an annual quitrent. Similar arrangements existed in New Jersey and Delaware. Soon travelers in the Middle Colonies were being struck by "a pleasing uniformity of decent competence."

New York was something of an exception to this favorable economic situation. When the English took over New York, they extended the Dutch patroon system by creating 30 manorial estates covering about two million acres. But ordinary New Yorkers never lacked ways of becoming landowners. A hundred acres along the Hudson River could be bought in 1730 for what an unskilled laborer could earn in three months. Even tenants on the manorial estates could obtain long-term leases that had most of the advantages of ownership but did not require the investment of any capital. "One may think oneself to be a great lord," one frustrated "lord" of a New York manor wrote a colleague, "but it does not amount to much, as you well know."

Mixed farming offered the most commonly trod path to prosperity in the Middle Colonies, but not the only one. Inland communities offered comfortable livelihoods for artisans. Farmers always needed barrels, candles, rope, horseshoes and nails, and dozens of other articles in everyday use. Countless opportunities awaited the ambitious settler in the shops, yards, and offices of New York and Philadelphia. Unlike Boston, New York and Philadelphia profited from navigable rivers that penetrated deep into the back country. Although founded half a cen-

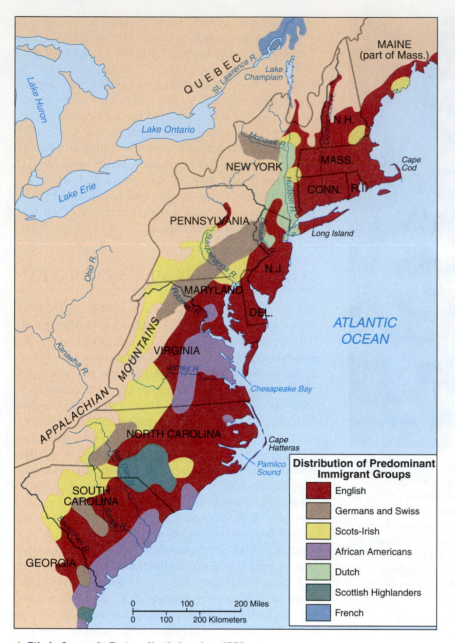

★ **Ethnic Groups in Eastern North America, 1750**

Distribution of Predominant Immigrant Groups

- English
- Germans and Swiss
- Scots-Irish
- African Americans
- Dutch
- Scottish Highlanders
- French

nation made it much more difficult for a skilled artisan to rise in the world.

THE POLITICS OF DIVERSITY

"Cannot more friendly and private courses be taken to set matters right in an infant province?" an exasperated William Penn asked the people of Pennsylvania in 1704. "For the love of God, me, and the poor country, be not so governmentish." However well-intentioned Penn's advice, however justified his annoyance, the Pennsylvanians ignored him. Instead, they and their fellows throughout the region constructed a political culture that diverged sharply from the patterns of New England and the South both in contentiousness and in the sophistication required of local politicians.

Superficially the governments of the Middle Colonies closely resembled those of earlier settlements. All had popularly elected representative assemblies, and most white male adults could vote. In Pennsylvania, where Penn had insisted that there be no religious test and where 50 acres constituted a freehold, something close to white universal manhood suffrage existed. In New York even non-property-holding white male residents voted in local elections, and rural tenants with lifetime leases enjoyed full voting rights.

In Pennsylvania and most of New York, representatives were elected by counties. In this they resembled Virginia and Maryland. But unlike the Southerners, voters did not tend to defer in politics to the landed gentry. In New York, in 1689, during the political vacuum following the abdication of King James II, Jacob Leisler, a disgruntled merchant and militia captain, seized control of the government. **Leisler's Rebellion** did not amount to much. He held power for less than two years before he was overthrown and sent to the gallows. Yet for two decades New York politics continued to be a struggle between the Leislerians, and other self-conscious "outs" who shared

tury after New York and Boston, Philadelphia grew more rapidly than either. In the 1750s, when its population reached 15,000, it passed Boston to become the largest city in English America.

Most Philadelphians who stuck to their business, particularly if it happened to be maritime commerce, did well for themselves. John Bringhurst, a merchant, began his career as a clerk. At his death in 1751 he left an estate of several thousand pounds. The city's "leather-apron" artisans often accumulated estates of more than £400, a substantial sum at the time. By way of contrast, in Boston after 1710, economic stag-

Leisler's dislike of English rule, and anti-Leislerians, who had in common only that they had opposed his takeover. Each group sought the support of a succession of ineffective governors, and the one that failed to get it invariably proceeded to make that poor man's tenure as miserable as possible.

New York lapsed into political tranquility during the governorship of Robert Hunter (1710–1719), but in the early 1730s conflict broke out over a claim for back salary by Governor William Cosby. When Lewis Morris, the chief justice of the supreme court, opposed Cosby's claim, the governor replaced him. Morris and his assembly allies responded by establishing the *New York Weekly Journal*. To edit the paper they hired an itinerant German printer, John Peter Zenger.

Governor Cosby might have tolerated the *Weekly Journal's* front-page lectures on the right of the people to criticize their rulers had the back pages not contained advertisements referring to his supporters as spaniels and to him as a monkey. After submitting to two months of "open and implacable malice against me," he shut down the paper, arrested Zenger, and charged him with seditious libel.

What began as a squalid salary dispute became one of the most celebrated tests of freedom of the press in the history of journalism. At the trial Zenger's attorney, James Hamilton, argued that the truth of his client's criticisms of Cosby constituted a proper defense against seditious libel. This reasoning (though contrary to English law at the time) persuaded the jury to acquit Zenger.

Politics in Pennsylvania turned on conflict between two interest groups, one clustered around the proprietor, the other around the assembly, which was controlled by a coalition of Quaker representatives from Philadelphia and the German-speaking Pennsylvania Dutch.

Neither the proprietary party nor the Quaker party qualifies as a political party in the modern sense of being organized and maintained for the purpose of winning elections. Nor can they be categorized as standing for "democratic" or "aristocratic" interests. But their existence guaranteed that the political leaders had to take popular opinion into account. Moreover, having once appealed to public opinion, they had to be prepared to defer to it. Success turned as much on knowing how to follow as on knowing how to lead.

The 1763 uprising of the "Paxton Boys" of western Pennsylvania put this policy to a full test. The uprising was triggered by eastern indifference to Indian attacks on the frontier—an indifference made possible by the fact that the east outnumbered the west in the assembly, 26 to 10. Fuming because they could obtain no help from Philadelphia against the Indians, a group of Scots-Irish from Lancaster county fell on a village of peaceful Conestoga Indians and murdered them in cold blood. Then these Paxton Boys marched on Philadelphia, several hundred strong.

Fortunately a delegation of burghers, headed by Benjamin Franklin, talked the Paxton Boys out of attacking the town by acknowledging the legitimacy of their grievances about representation and by promising to vote a bounty on Indian scalps! It was just such fancy footwork that established Franklin, the leader of the assembly party, as Pennsylvania's consummate politician. "Tell me, Mr. Franklin," a testy member of the proprietary party asked, "how is it that you are always with the majority?" Soon thereafter, the assembly sent Franklin to London to defend local interests against the British authorities, a situation in which he would definitely not be "with the majority."

BECOMING AMERICANS

In 1650, some 50,000 Europeans had come to North America. Most clung to the Atlantic coast, within easy reach of ships that could bring essential supplies, protection, and means of escape. Indians outnumbered Europeans by about 10 to 1; African slaves were still rare. French and Spanish colonization in what is now the United States was numerically even more inconsequential, with only about 1,000 Hispanics and even fewer Frenchmen. From the Appalachian Mountains to the Pacific, most Indians had probably never seen a European.

By 1750 the Atlantic seaboard was occupied by nearly a million European settlers, the great majority of English background, with perhaps a quarter of a million African slaves. The Indians had not been entirely removed: scores of Indian villages had been enveloped by English settlement. Tens of thousands more Indians had retreated into coastal swamplands or the foothills of the Appalachians. But east of the Appalachian Mountains, English-speaking peoples had become masters of the land.

During the 100 years after 1650, New Spain and New France had also grown; but far fewer than 20,000 Hispanic and French-speaking people lived in those colonies. In most places west of the Appalachians, Indians feared other tribes far more than European interlopers.

By 1750 an immense sea of English-speaking peoples and African slaves had flooded into the eastern portion of the continent. Soon, they would spill beyond the Appalachian Mountains. By sheer force of their numbers, American identity would be strongly associated with the English language. Most, too, were farmers, united by a seemingly inexhaustible craving

Milestones

1619	First Africans are sold in Virginia
1636	Puritans found Boston Latin School and Harvard College
1657	Half-Way Covenant leads to rise in puritan church memberships
1676	Western planters launch Bacon's Rebellion in Virginia
1684–1688	Edmund Andros rules Dominion of New England
1689	Leisler's Rebellion in New York seizes control of government
1692	Salem village holds witchcraft trials
1696	Virginia colonists found College of William and Mary
	Rice cultivation is introduced in South Carolina
1701	Connecticut ministers found Yale College
1733	George Oglethorpe leads settlement of Georgia

for land. But these enterprising immigrants also differed in fundamental ways. The cultures the immigrants brought with them varied according to the nationality, social status, and taste of the individual. The newcomers never lost their foreign heritage entirely, but they—and certainly their descendants—became something quite different from their relatives who remained in the Old World. They became what we call Americans.

But not right away.

★ SUPPLEMENTARY READING

Among general interpretations, D. J. Boorstin's *The Americans: The Colonial Experience* (1958), emphasizes the modern aspects of colonial society; Jon Butler's *Becoming America: The Revolution before 1776* (2000) similarly and more broadly emphasizes the rapid evolution of colonial society. Alan Kulikoff, *From British Peasants to Colonial American Farmers* (2000) underscores the importance of land in defining American life. Alan Taylor, *American Colonies* (2001), emphasizes the links between European and American societies.

On economic conditions, see John J. McCusker and Russell R. Menard, eds., *The Economy of British America, 1607–1789* (1991). For the economic growth of colonial New England, see Margaret Ellen Newell, *From Dependency to Independence* (1998). On the chronologically and geographically uneven development of slavery in America, consult Ira Berlin, *Generations of Captivity: A History of African-American Slaves* (2003) and *Many Thousands Gone* (1998). See also Philip D. Morgan, *Slave Counterpoint* (1998) and P. D. Curtin, *The Rise and Fall of the Plantation Complex* (1990). Alan Gallay, *The Indian Slave Trade* (2002) uncovers an issue that has long been overlooked.

On life in the colonial South, see T. W. Tate and David Ammerman, eds., *The Chesapeake in the Seventeenth Century* (1979), Allan Kulikoff, *Tobacco and Slaves* (1986), D. B. and A. H. Rutman, *A Place in Time* (1984), and Timothy H. Breen and Stephen Innes, *"Myne Owne Ground": Race and Freedom on Virginia's Eastern Shore* (1980).

Family and community life are surveyed in D. F. Hawke, *Everyday Life in Early America* (1988), and Edmund S. Mor-

gan, *The Puritan Family* (1966). The places of women and children are effectively presented in Laurel T. Ulrich, *Good Wives: Image and Reality in the Lives of Women in Northern New England* (1982), and Philip Greven, *The Protestant Temperament: Patterns of Child-Rearing, Religious Experience, and the Self in Early America* (1980). Richard Godbeer, *Sexual Revolution in Early America* (2002) corrects the stereotype of the puritans as sexually repressive.

The works of Perry Miller remain the starting point for any serious study of the cultural life of colonial New England. Among them, *Errand into the Wilderness* (1956) provides a good introduction. More recent studies, most of which modify Miller's judgments, include D. D. Hall, *Worlds of Wonder, Days of Judgment* (1989), and Patricia U. Bonomi, *Under the Cope of Heaven* (1986). Some recent scholarship contends that Puritan practices complemented economic development: for example, John Frederick Martin, *Profits in the Wilderness* (1991), Stephen Innes, *Creating the Commonwealth* (1995), and Mark A. Peterson, *The Price of Redemption* (1997).

Larry D. Gragg, *The Salem Witch Crisis* (1992) provides a narrative account. Paul Boyer and Stephen Nissenbaum, *Salem Possessed* (1974), argue that the episode grew out of tensions between different factions within the community. Mary Beth Norton, *In the Devil's Snare: The Salem Witchcraft Crisis of 1692* (2002), views the crisis as a response to fear of Indians. The subject is considered more generally in John Demos, *Entertaining Satan: Witchcraft and the Culture of Early New England* (1982). On women and witchcraft, see Elizabeth Reis, *Damned Women* (1997), Elaine G. Breslaw, *Tituba, Reluctant Witch of*

Salem (1996), and Carol F. Karlsen, *The Devil in the Shape of a Woman* (1987).

For an engaging overview of the ideology of gender authority in the seventeenth century, see Mary Beth Norton, *Founding Mothers and Fathers* (1996). On women and religion in New England, see also Susan Juster, *Disorderly Women* (1994). Karin Wolf, *Not All Wives* (2000), describes the range of women's activities in Philadelphia. For the role of women in Virginia, see Kathleen M. Brown, *Good Wives, Nasty Wenches and Anxious Patriarchs* (1996).

Educational and intellectual developments are treated in Bernard Bailyn, *Education in the Forming of American Soci-* ety (1960), and L. A. Cremin, *American Education: The Colonial Experience* (1970).

In recent years there has been a profusion of studies on the interrelationship between settlers and Indians: Jane T. Merritt, *At the Crossroads: Indians and Empire on a Mid-Atlantic Frontier* (2003), Richard White, *The Middle Ground* (1991), Daniel K. Richter, *Ordeal of the Longhouse* (1992), Daniel H. Usner, *Indians, Settlers, and Slaves in a Frontier Exchange Economy* (1992), Colin G. Calloway, *New Worlds for All: Indians, Europeans, and the Remaking of Early America* (1997), Karen O. Kupperman, *Indians and English* (2001), and James F. Brooks, *Captives and Cousins* (2002).

★ SUGGESTED WEB SITES

LVA Colonial Records Project—Index of Digital Facsimiles of Documents on Early Virginia
http://ajax.lva.lib.va.us/F/?func=file&file_name=find-b-clas27&local_base=CLAS27
This site contains reproductions of numerous documents.

DSL Archives: Slave Movement During the Eighteenth and Nineteenth Centuries (Wisconsin)
http://dpls.dacc.wisc.edu/slavedata/index.html
This site explores the slave ships and the slave trade that carried thousands of Africans to the New World.

Salem Witch Trials
http://etext.virginia.edu/salem/witchcraft/
This University of Virginia site offers an extensive archive of the 1692 trials as well as life in late seventeenth-century Massachusetts.

Salem Witchcraft Trials (1692)
http://www.law.umkc.edu/faculty/projects/ftrials/salem/salem.htm
Images, chronology, and court and official documents by Dr. Doug Linder of the University of Missouri–Kansas City Law School.

Benjamin Franklin
http://sln.fi.edu/franklin/rotten.html
This Franklin Institute site contains information and sources treating one of colonial America's most well-known figures.

Religion and the Founding of the American Republic
http://lcweb.loc.gov/exhibits/religion/religion.html
This Library of Congress site is an online exhibit about religion and the formation of the United States.

DoHistory
http://dohistory.org/
Focusing on the life of Martha Ballard, a late eighteenth-century New England woman, this site employs selections from her diary, excerpts from a book and film about her life, and other primary documents that enable students to conduct their own historical investigation.

Anglicans, Puritans, and Quakers in Colonial America
http://www.mun.ca/rels/ang/texts/ang1.html
This site provides information on the major religious movements in colonial America.

Testing Your Understanding—Unit IV

The American Nation: A History of the United States, 13th Edition
Volume One • To 1877
Chapter 2: American Society in the Making

Pages 110–117
CHECKING YOUR COMPREHENSION

Choose the best answer for each of the following questions.

1. Many men who immigrated to New France married Indian women because
   a. the men wanted to marry women who knew the land.
   b. the European women who immigrated to New France married native fur traders.
   c. only a limited number of European women immigrated to New France.
   d. they were forced by the remaining elders of the Natchez tribe.

2. All of the following are reasons Spain failed to establish a strong Hispanic colony in California EXCEPT:
   a. widespread disease killed many settlers.
   b. the genizaros were granted the right to own property.
   c. Britain and Russia were looking to colonize the Northwest.
   d. the missions in California were self-sustaining and far from New Spain.

3. The headright system was based on giving land on the basis of the
   a. availability of labor to work the land.
   b. wealth of the immigrant.
   c. importance of the family in Europe.
   d. ability to stake out the land and claim it properly.

4. In Virginia between 1624 and 1634, the main reason for the high death rate was
   a. the shortage of food and supplies.
   b. the relatively dry summers.
   c. a lack of suitable clothing.
   d. the war between the Englishmen and the Indians.

Identify the following statements as true or false.

5. In the early 1700's the Chesapeake Colonies were plagued by disease, such as malaria and typhoid fever.

6. The Jesuits tried to instill their values, morals, and religious beliefs on the Indians.

7. In the sixteenth century people began to think of the "South" as a single region.

8. The Comanche were against the use of guns because they believed that fighting should be civilized.

Answer each of the following questions.

9. Explain the genizaros and their place in society.

10. List the three regions of the southern part of English North America.

11. Describe each step of the indentured servant system.

12. Explain the impact that the high death rate had on family structure in the Chesapeake Colonies.

Define each term as it is used in the chapter.

13. garrisons

14. formidable

15. rudiments

16. inculcated

17. bedeviled

18. imperiling

Discussion and Critical Thinking Questions

1. Using the information in the chapter, compare and contrast life in the New England Colonies, Middle Colonies, and Southern Colonies. Explain which colony would lend itself to a better life.

2. Discuss The Massachusetts Body of Liberties of 1641 provision regarding slavery. What is this proclamation stating, and whose rights does it protect?

Pages 117–129
CHECKING YOUR COMPREHENSION

Choose the best answer for the following questions.

1. Initially, Company & Crown informed the colonists that
   a. they were to only grow tobacco on fully cleared land.
   b. smoking tobacco was an unhealthy practice.
   c. they opposed the growing of tobacco.
   d. they had to grow more wheat and less tobacco.

2. Which of the following events did not occur during Bacon's Rebellion?
   a. Peaceful Indians were murdered.
   b. Berkeley was taken captive as he fled across the Chesapeake Bay.
   c. Estates of the Green Spring faction were plundered.
   d. Jamestown was burned to the ground.

3. Which of the following would NOT be useful information when examining the affluence of families in the South?
   a. The presence of meat at their meals.
   b. The type of clothing worn by both the men and women in the families.
   c. The schooling of the children.
   d. The number of chairs in a family's house.

4. What do the authors infer regarding the gibberish spoken by Betty Parris, Abigail Parris, and Ann Putnam?
   a. The girls were faking it.
   b. The girls were taken over by Satan.
   c. The girls' fathers told them to do it for revenge.
   d. The girls were paid by Lady Mary Phips to act in that manner.

Identify the following statements as true or false.

5. After Bacon's Rebellion, the colonists joined together in their belief that Africans should not acquire wealth or influence.

6. The South Carolina Negro Act of 1740 allowed slaves to travel as long as they had documentation from their owners.

7. The Puritans believed that children were born damned and needed to be taught how to be good in order to get passage into heaven.

8. Charles II and James II caused the Glorious Rebellion, which brought the colonies under effective royal control.

Define each term as it is used in the chapter.

9. fallow
10. indignant
11. panacea
12. acculturate
13. lascivious
14. compulsory
15. beset
16. contingent

Answer each of the following questions.

17. Explain why it was so important for the colonists to have "merchantable commodities."

18. What effect did the tobacco crop have on the soil? What was one way the colonists were able to combat this problem?

19. Explain why the membership of the Puritan church decreased so rapidly, and what steps were taken to overcome this declining population.

Discussion and Critical Thinking Questions

1. Utilizing the information in this section, discuss the paradox noted regarding slavery.

2. Which two illustrations in this section depict the lifestyle of the times? What specific information explained in the text is shown in the two pictures you chose?

3. Discuss the gender roles in the different communities. What were the advantages and disadvantages of being male/female in the different locales?

Pages 129–139
CHECKING YOUR COMPREHENSION

Choose the best answer for each of the following questions.

1. Yale University was founded because
   a. Harvard's ideology was becoming too lenient.
   b. Elihu Yale felt unjustly uneducated.
   c. Anglicans took over the administration of Harvard in 1722.
   d. there was a need for a more conservative university.

2. Portsmouth, Salem, Boston, Newport, and New Haven differed from towns in the interior in all ways EXCEPT:
   a. they were larger.
   b. a smaller percent of their inhabitants farmed.
   c. they grew faster.
   d. a larger percent of the males were married.

3. The underlying cause of the 1763 uprising of the Paxton Boys was
   a. Ben Franklin's acknowledgement of their strife.
   b. the decline of Leisler's Rebellion.
   c. the West's dominance in the assembly.
   d. a salary dispute between Paxton and Hamilton.

4. According to the text, by 1750
   a. only European settlers occupied the Atlantic seaboard.
   b. there were no Indians east of the Appalachians.
   c. New Spain and New France had grown.
   d. African slaves were found west of the Appalachians.

Identify the following statements as true or false.

5. Benjamin Franklin's "Silence Dogood" essays were well received by those who read them.

6. It can be inferred from the text that Puritans in New England believed that heaven existed.

7. The farms in the Middle Colonies produced food for local consumption and for export.

8. It was easier for an artisan to accumulate more wealth living in Boston than New York.

Define each term as it is used in the chapter.

9. imbibe
10. dubious
11. quitrent
12. stagnation
13. itinerant
14. seditious

Answer each of the following questions.

15. Explain the concept of triangular trade.

16. Who was John Peter Zenger and why was he arrested?

17. What are the two reasons cited in the text explaining why Lord Cornburg was portrayed in a painting wearing a dress?

Discussion and Critical Thinking Questions

1. Using information from "Ethnic Groups in Eastern North America, 1750," explain the trend of the Scots-Irish immigrants and the Dutch immigrants.

2. What is the overall message the author is trying to convey in the text accompanying the illustration on page 133?

3. Compare and contrast the differences between the educational system in New England from the 1630's to the 1730's and our educational system today.

Chapter Review
END OF CHAPTER ANALYSIS

Choose the best answer for each of the following questions.

1. The chapter addresses all of the following areas EXCEPT:
   a. the crops planted in the colonies.
   b. the introduction of slavery into the colonies.
   c. the trial of John Peter Zenger.
   d. the importance of Leisler's Rebellion.

2. The chapter employs all of the following techniques to make the information easier to understand EXCEPT:
   a. section headings.
   b. marginal links.
   c. illustrations.
   d. highlighting.

3. Before you read the chapter, all of the following techniques would be useful EXCEPT:
   a. annotating the text.
   b. taking note of the words in bold and italics.
   c. turning the headings into questions.
   d. previewing the illustrations.

Group Projects

1. Using the list on page 110, write a 2–3 sentence summary of each concept noted. As a group, review each summary to ensure the necessary information is included.

2. Discuss the common threads among the different groups of immigrants that made the colonies their home.

Journal Ideas

1. Explore the question, "What is an American?" In your journal write what you feel makes someone an American. Try to include personal experiences about yourself and your family that illustrate what makes you an American.

2. After reading "Reviewing the Past" (pp. 130–131), reflect on the events in the movie *The Crucible*. Connect the information you learned in the chapter to what you have read in this section about this movie. Do you feel that the movie correctly portrays the climate of the time and the information about Salem and the Puritans in this chapter?

Organizing Information

Complete the outline using the information under the heading "The Chesapeake Colonies" (p. 114).

(1) The Chesapeake Colonies
  (a) English philosopher Thomas Hobbes (1651) "nasty, brutish, and short"
  (b) Colonies grew from _____ from 1624–1634
    (i) _____
    (ii) 9,000 immigrants entered during this time
      1. Nearly half died during this decade

(2) Climate = death trap
  (a) Described by Robert Beverly (1705) in "The History and _____ of Virginia"
  (b) Dry summers were a major problem
    (i) James River flowed slower, causing trouble

      1. _____

      2. _____

      3. _____

(3) Indian Warfare was also a major problem.
  (a) In 1700, males in _____ lived approximately 45 years.
  (b) In 1700, males in Maryland lived _____
    (i) This greatly affected the family structure in this area.

      1. _____

      2. _____

      3. _____

Unit V: Humanities and the Visual Arts

"Orientation"

by Daniel Orozco

"The Other Two"

by Edith Wharton

An Introduction to Literature

Literature is defined as the body of written work of a language, period, or culture. It is often noted as creative writing that is recognized for its artistic value. There are many types (or genres) of literature, such as poetry, prose fiction, drama, and essays.

Literature courses are required for most college students. Introductory courses often give students an overall view of literature, while upper-level literature courses usually focus on a particular author, time period, or genre. A degree in literature will prepare students to enter careers in such diverse fields as education, law, mass media, publishing, communications, and the arts.

Strategies for Reading Literature

When reading literature, it is necessary to pay particular attention to the message (or theme) the author is trying to convey about life, society, or human nature. There are often many literary devices that you need to recognize, identify, interpret, and analyze. The author's careful use of language may include such literary devices as metaphors, similes, rhyme, alliteration, and tone. Another important aspect of literature is to understand that behind every action is a reason, and it is often necessary to delve deep into the literature to reveal the author's intended meaning. Using a reflective journal (see Organizing Information at the end of this section) while you read may help you organize your thoughts about the story's action and characters. It will also allow you to make comments and ask questions while you read.

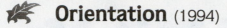 **Orientation** (1994)

Those are the offices and these are the cubicles. That's my cubicle there, and this is your cubicle. This is your phone. Never answer your phone. Let the Voicemail System answer it. This is your Voicemail System Manual. There are no personal phone calls allowed. We do, however, allow for emergencies. If you must make an emergency phone call, ask your supervisor first. If you can't find your supervisor, ask Phillip Spiers, who sits over there. He'll check with Clarissa Nicks, who sits over there. If you make an emergency phone call without asking, you may be let go.

These are your IN and OUT boxes. All the forms in your IN box must be logged in by the date shown in the upper left-hand corner, initialed by you in the upper right-hand corner, and distributed to the Processing Analyst whose name is numerically coded in the lower left-hand corner. The lower right-hand corner is left blank. Here's your Processing Analyst Numerical Code Index. And here's your Forms Processing Procedures Manual.

You must pace your work. What do I mean? I'm glad you asked that. We pace our work according to the eight-hour workday. If you have twelve hours of work in your IN box, for example, you must compress that work into the eight-hour day. If you have one hour of work in your IN box, you must expand that work to fill the eight hour day. That was a good question. Feel free to ask questions. Ask too many questions, however, and you may be let go.

That is our receptionist. She is a temp. We go through receptionists here. They quit with alarming frequency. Be polite and civil to the temps. Learn their names, and invite them to lunch occasionally. But don't get close to them, as it only makes it more difficult when they leave. And they always leave. You can be sure of that.

5 The men's room is over there. The women's room is over there. John LaFountaine, who sits over there, uses the women's room occasionally. He says it is accidental. We know better, but we let it pass. John LaFountaine is harmless, his forays into the forbidden territory of the women's room simply a benign thrill, a faint blip on the dull flat line of his life.

Russell Nash, who sits in the cubicle to your left, is in love with Amanda Pierce, who sits in the cubicle to your right. They ride the same bus together after work. For Amanda Pierce, it is just a tedious bus ride made less tedious by the idle nattering of Russell Nash. But for Russell Nash, it is the highlight of his day. It is the highlight of his life. Russell Nash has put on forty pounds, and grows fatter with each passing month, nibbling on chips and cookies while peeking glumly over the partitions at Amanda Pierce, and gorging himself at home on cold pizza and ice cream while watching adult videos on TV.

Amanda Pierce, in the cubicle to your right, has a six-year-old son named Jamie, who is autistic. Her cubicle is plastered from top to bottom with the boy's crayon artwork—sheet after sheet of precisely drawn concentric circles and ellipses, in black and yellow. She rotates them every other Friday. Be sure to comment on them. Amanda Pierce also has a husband, who is a lawyer. He subjects her to an escalating array of painful and humiliating sex games, to which Amanda Pierce reluctantly submits. She comes to work exhausted and freshly wounded each morning, wincing from the abrasions on her breasts, or the bruises on her abdomen, or the second-degree burns on the backs of her thighs.

But we're not supposed to know any of this. Do not let on. If you let on, you may be let go.

Amanda Pierce, who tolerates Russell Nash, is in love with Albert Bosch, whose office is over there. Albert Bosch, who only dimly registers Amanda Pierce's existence, has eyes only for Ellie Tapper, who sits over there. Ellie Tapper, who hates Albert Bosch, would walk through fire for Curtis Lance. But Curtis Lance hates Ellie Tapper. Isn't the world a funny place? Not in the ha-ha sense, of course.

Anika Bloom sits in that cubicle. Last year, while reviewing quarterly reports in a meeting 10
with Barry Hacker, Anika Bloom's left palm began to bleed. She fell into a trance, stared into
her hand, and told Barry Hacker when and how his wife would die. We laughed it off. She
was, after all, a new employee. But Barry Hacker's wife is dead. So unless you want to know
exactly when and how you'll die, never talk to Anika Bloom.

Cohn Heavey sits in that cubicle over there. He was new once, just like you. We warned
him about Anika Bloom. But at last year's Christmas Potluck, he felt sorry for her when he saw
that no one was talking to her. Cohn Heavey brought her a drink. He hasn't been himself since.
Cohn Heavey is doomed. There's nothing he can do about it, and we are powerless to help
him. Stay away from Cohn Heavey. Never give any of your work to him. If he asks to do something, tell him you have to check with me. If he asks again, tell him I haven't gotten back
to you.

This is the Fire Exit. There are several on this floor, and they are marked accordingly. We
have a Floor Evacuation Review every three months, and an Escape Route Quiz once a month.
We have our Biannual Fire Drill twice a year, and our Annual Earthquake Drill once a year.
These are precautions only. These things never happen.

For your information, we have a comprehensive health plan. Any catastrophic illness, any
unforeseen tragedy is completely covered. All dependents are completely covered. Larry
Bagdikian, who sits over there, has six daughters. If anything were to happen to any of his
girls, or to all of them, if all six were to simultaneously fall victim to illness or injury—stricken
with a hideous degenerative muscle disease or some rare toxic blood disorder, sprayed with
semiautomatic gunfire while on a class field trip, or attacked in their bunk beds by some
prowling nocturnal lunatic—if any of this were to pass, Larry's girls would all be taken care of.
Larry Bagdikian would not have to pay one dime. He would have nothing to worry about.

We also have a generous vacation and sick leave policy. We have an excellent disability in-
surance plan. We have a stable and profitable pension fund. We get group discounts for the
symphony, and block seating at the ballpark. We get commuter ticket books for the bridge. We
have Direct Deposit. We are all members of Costco.

This is our kitchenette. And this, this is our Mr. Coffee. We have a coffee pool, into which 15
we each pay two dollars a week for coffee, filters, sugar, and CoffeeMate. If you prefer Cremora
or half-and-half to CoffeeMate, there is a special pool for three dollars a week. If you prefer
Sweet'n Low to sugar, there is a special pool for two-fifty a week. We do not do decaf. You are
allowed to join the coffee pool of your choice, but you are not allowed to touch the Mr. Coffee.

This is the microwave oven. You are allowed to heat food in the microwave oven. You are
not, however, allowed to cook food in the microwave oven.

We get one hour for lunch. We also get one fifteen-minute break in the morning, and one
fifteen-minute break in the afternoon. Always take your breaks, if you skip a break, it is gone
forever. For your information, your break is a privilege, not a right. If you abuse the break policy, we are authorized to rescind your breaks. Lunch, however, is a right, not a privilege. If you
abuse the lunch policy, our hands will be tied, and we will be forced to look the other way. We
will not enjoy that.

This is the refrigerator. You may put your lunch in it. Barry Hacker, who sits over there,
steals food from this refrigerator. His petty theft is an outlet for his grief. Last New Year's Eve,
while kissing his wife, a blood vessel burst in her brain. Barry Hacker's wife was two months
pregnant at the time, and lingered in a coma for half a year before dying. It was a tragic loss for
Barry Hacker. He hasn't been himself since. Barry Hacker's wife was a beautiful woman. She
was also completely covered. Barry Hacker did not have to pay one dime. But his dead wife
haunts him. She haunts all of us. We have seen her, reflected in the monitors of our computers,
moving past our cubicles. We have seen the dim shadow of her face in our photocopies. She

pencils herself in in the receptionist's appointment book, with the notation: To see Barry Hacker. She has left messages in the receptionist's Voicemail box, messages garbled by the electronic chirrups and buzzes in the phone line, her voice echoing from an immense distance within the ambient hum. But the voice is hers. And beneath her voice, beneath the tidal whoosh of static and hiss, the gurgling and crying of a baby can be heard.

In any case, if you bring a lunch, put a little something extra in the bag for Barry Hacker. We have four Barrys in this office. Isn't that a coincidence?

20   This is Matthew Payne's office. He is our Unit Manager, and his door is always closed. We have never seen him, and you will never see him. But he is here. You can be sure of that. He is all around us.

This is the Custodian's Closet. You have no business in the Custodian's Closet.

And this, this is our Supplies Cabinet. If you need supplies, see Curtis Lance. He will log you in on the Supplies Cabinet Authorization Log, then give you a Supplies Authorization Slip. Present your pink copy of the Supplies Authorization Slip to Ellie Tapper. She will log you in on the Supplies Cabinet Key Log, then give you the key. Because the Supplies Cabinet is located outside the Unit Manager's office, you must be very quiet. Gather your supplies quietly. The Supplies Cabinet is divided into four sections. Section One contains letterhead stationery, blank paper and envelopes, memo and note pads, and so on. Section Two contains pens and pencils and typewriter and printer ribbons, and the like. In Section Three we have erasers, correction fluids, transparent tapes, glue sticks, et cetera. And in Section Four we have paper clips and push pins and scissors and razor blades. And here are the spare blades for the shredder. Do not touch the shredder, which is located over there. The shredder is of no concern to you.

Gwendolyn Stich sits in that office there. She is crazy about penguins, and collects penguin knickknacks: penguin posters and coffee mugs and stationery, penguin stuffed animals, penguin jewelry, penguin sweaters and T-shirts and socks. She has a pair of penguin fuzzy slippers she wears when working late at the office. She has a tape cassette of penguin sounds which she listens to for relaxation. Her favorite colors are black and white. She has personalized license plates that read PEN GWEN. Every morning, she passes through all the cubicles to wish each of us a good morning. She brings Danish on Wednesdays for Hump Day morning break, and doughnuts on Fridays for TGIF afternoon break. She organizes the Annual Christmas Potluck, and is in charge of the Birthday List. Gwendolyn Stich's door is always open to all of us. She will always lend an ear, and put in a good word for you; she will always give you a hand, or the shirt off her back, or a shoulder to cry on. Because her door is always open, she hides and cries in a stall in the women's room. And John LaFountaine—who, enthralled when a woman enters, sits quietly in his stall with his knees to his chest—John LaFountaine has heard her vomiting in there. We have come upon Gwendolyn Stich huddled in the stairwell, shivering in the updraft, sipping a Diet Mr. Pibb and hugging her knees. She does not let any of this interfere with her work. If it interfered with her work, she might have to be let go.

Kevin Howard sits in that cubicle over there. He is a serial killer, the one they call the Carpet Cutter, responsible for the mutilations across town. We're not supposed to know that, so do not let on. Don't worry. His compulsion inflicts itself on strangers only, and the routine established is elaborate and unwavering. The victim must be a white male, a young adult no older than thirty, heavyset, with dark hair and eyes, and the like. The victim must be chosen at random, before sunset, from a public place; the victim is followed home, and must put up a struggle; et cetera. The carnage inflicted is precise: the angle and direction of the incisions; the layering of skin and muscle tissue; the rearrangement of the visceral organs; and so on. Kevin Howard does not let any of this interfere with his work. He is, in fact, our fastest typist. He types as if he were on fire. He has a secret crush on Gwendolyn Stich, and leaves a red-foil-wrapped Hershey's Kiss on her desk every afternoon. But he hates Anika Bloom, and keeps well away from her. In his presence, she has uncontrollable fits of shaking and trembling. Her left palm does not stop bleeding.

25   In any case, when Kevin Howard gets caught, act surprised. Say that he seemed like a nice person, a bit of a loner, perhaps, but always quiet and polite.

This is the photocopier room. And this, this is our view. It faces southwest. West is down there, toward the water. North is back there. Because we are on the seventeenth floor, we are afforded a magnificent view. Isn't it beautiful? It overlooks the park, where the tops of those trees are. You can see a segment of the bay between those two buildings there. You can see the sun set in the gap between those two buildings over there. You can see this building reflected in the glass panels of that building across the way. There. See? That's you, waving. And look there. There's Anika Bloom in the kitchenette, waving back.

Enjoy this view while photocopying. If you have problems with the photocopier, see Russell Nash. If you have any questions, ask your supervisor. If you can't find your supervisor, ask Phillip Spiers. He sits over there. He'll check with Clarissa Nicks. She sits over there. If you can't find them, feel free to ask me. That's my cubicle. I sit in there.

Questions

1. What is the situation throughout this story? Who is talking? To whom is he talking? Does the listener have any chance to comment on the speaker's discourse?

2. In the first four paragraphs, is there anything unusual about the speaker's language? What does Orozco have the speaker say in paragraph 5 that alerts you to the unusual nature of the persons in the office?

3. Is there anything funny about the situations of fellow employees in the office? If not, how does one account for the fact that the story is comic? How do the speaker's controlled descriptions of the plights of the various office workers contribute to the story's comic tone?

4. Why is Kevin Howard the last one to be described by the speaker? Of what is Kevin guilty? What might the story be like if Kevin Howard had been mentioned first? Describe the comic technique of paragraph 25.

The Other Two

I

Waythorn, on the drawing-room hearth, waited for his wife to come down to dinner.

It was their first night under his own roof, and he was surprised at his thrill of boyish agitation. He was not so old, to be sure—his glass gave him little more than the five-and-thirty years to which his wife confessed—but he had fancied himself already in the temperate zone; yet here he was listening for her step with a tender sense of all it symbolised, with some old trail of verse about the garlanded nuptial door-posts floating through his enjoyment of the pleasant room and the good dinner just beyond it.

They had been hastily recalled from their honeymoon by the illness of Lily Haskett, the child of Mrs. Waythorn's first marriage. The little girl, at Waythorn's desire, had been transferred to his house on the day of her mother's wedding, and the doctor, on their arrival, broke the news that she was ill with typhoid, but declared that all the symptoms were favourable. Lily could show twelve years of unblemished health, and the case promised to be a light one. The nurse spoke as reassuringly, and after a moment of alarm Mrs. Waythorn had adjusted herself to the situation. She was very fond of Lily—her affection for the child had perhaps been her decisive charm in Waythorn's eyes—but she had the perfectly balanced nerves which her little girl had inherited, and no woman ever wasted less tissue in unproductive worry. Waythorn was therefore quite prepared to see her come in presently, a little late because of a last look at Lily, but as serene and well-appointed as if her good-night kiss had been laid on the brow of health. Her composure was restful to him; it acted as ballast to his somewhat unstable sensibilities. As he pictured her bending over the child's bed he thought how soothing her presence must be in illness; her very step would prognosticate recovery.

His own life had been a gray one, from temperament rather than circumstance, and he had been drawn to her by the unperturbed gaiety which kept her fresh and elastic at an age when most women's activities are growing either slack or febrile. He knew what was said about her; for, popular as she was, there had always been a faint undercurrent of detraction. When she had appeared in New York, nine or ten years earlier, as the pretty Mrs. Haskett whom Gus Varick had unearthed somewhere—was it in Pittsburg or Utica?—society, while promptly accepting her, had reserved the right to cast a doubt on its own indiscrimination. Enquiry, however, established her undoubted connection with a socially reigning family, and explained her recent divorce as the natural result of a runaway match at seventeen; and as nothing was known of Mr. Haskett it was easy to believe the worst of him.

Alice Haskett's remarriage with Gus Varick was a passport to the set whose recognition she coveted, and for a few years the Varicks were the most popular couple in town. Unfortunately the alliance was brief and stormy, and this time the husband had his champions. Still, even Varick's stanchest supporters admitted that he was not meant for matrimony, and Mrs. Varick's grievances were of a nature to bear the inspection of the New York courts. A New York divorce is in itself a diploma of virtue, and in the semi-widowhood of this second separation Mrs. Varick took on an air of sanctity, and was allowed to confide her wrongs to some of the most scrupulous ears in town. But when it was known that she was to marry Waythorn there was a momentary reaction. Her best friends would have preferred to see her remain in the rôle of the injured wife, which was as becoming to her as crape to a rosy complexion. True, a decent time had elapsed, and it was not even suggested that Waythorn had supplanted his predecessor. People shook their heads over him, however, and one grudging friend, to whom he affirmed that he took the step with his eyes open, replied oracularly: "Yes—and with your ears shut."

Waythorn could afford to smile at these innuendoes. In the Wall Street phrase, he had "discounted" them. He knew that society has not yet adapted itself to the consequences of divorce, and that till the adaptation takes place every woman who uses the freedom the law accords her must be her own social justification. Waythorn had an amused confidence in his wife's ability to justify herself. His expectations were fulfilled, and before the wedding took place Alice Varick's group had rallied openly to her support. She took it all imperturbably: she had a way of surmounting obstacles without seeming to be aware of them, and Waythorn looked back with wonder at the trivialities over which he had worn his nerves thin. He had the sense of having found refuge in a richer, warmer nature than his own, and his satisfaction, at the moment, was humourously summed up in the thought that his wife, when she had done all she could for Lily, would not be ashamed to come down and enjoy a good dinner.

The anticipation of such enjoyment was not, however, the sentiment expressed by Mrs. Waythorn's charming face when she presently joined him. Though she had put on her most engaging teagown she had neglected to assume the smile that went with it, and Waythorn thought he had never seen her look so nearly worried.

"What is it?" he asked. "Is anything wrong with Lily?"

"No; I've just been in and she's still sleeping." Mrs. Waythorn hesitated. "But something tiresome has happened."

He had taken her two hands, and now perceived that he was crushing a paper between them.

"This letter?"

"Yes—Mr. Haskett has written—I mean his lawyer has written."

Waythorn felt himself flush uncomfortably. He dropped his wife's hands.

"What about?"

"About seeing Lily. You know the courts—"

"Yes, yes," he interrupted nervously.

Nothing was known about Haskett in New York. He was vaguely supposed to have remained in the outer darkness from which his wife had been rescued, and Waythorn was one of the few who were aware that he had given up his business in Utica and followed her to New York in order to be near his little girl. In the days of his wooing, Waythorn had often met Lily on the doorstep, rosy and smiling, on her way "to see papa."

"I am so sorry," Mrs. Waythorn murmured.

He roused himself. "What does he want?"

"He wants to see her. You know she goes to him once a week."

"Well—he doesn't expect her to go to him now, does he?"

"No—he has heard of her illness; but he expects to come here."

"*Here?*"

Mrs. Waythorn reddened under his gaze. They looked away from each other.

"I'm afraid he has the right. . . . You'll see. . . ." She made a proffer of the letter.

Waythorn moved away with a gesture of refusal. He stood staring about the softly lighted room, which a moment before had seemed so full of bridal intimacy.

"I'm so sorry," she repeated. "If Lily could have been moved—"

"That's out of the question," he returned impatiently.

"I suppose so."

Her lip was beginning to tremble, and he felt himself a brute.

"He must come, of course," he said. "When is—his day?"

"I'm afraid—to-morrow."

"Very well. Send a note in the morning."

The butler entered to announce dinner.

Waythorn turned to his wife. "Come—you must be tired. It's beastly, but try to forget about it," he said, drawing her hand through his arm.

"You're so good, dear. I'll try," she whispered back.

Her face cleared at once, and as she looked at him across the flowers, between the rosy candle-shades, he saw her lips waver back into a smile.

"How pretty everything is!" she sighed luxuriously.

He turned to the butler. "The champagne at once, please. Mrs. Waythorn is tired."

In a moment or two their eyes met above the sparkling glasses. Her own were quite clear and untroubled: he saw that she had obeyed his injunction and forgotten.

II

Waythorn, the next morning, went down town earlier than usual. Haskett was not likely to come till the afternoon, but the instinct of flight drove him forth. He meant to stay away all day—he had thoughts of dining at his club. As his door closed behind him he reflected that before he opened it again it would have admitted another man who had as much right to enter it as himself, and the thought filled him with a physical repugnance.

He caught the "elevated" at the employees' hour, and found himself crushed between two layers of pendulous humanity. At Eighth Street the man facing him wriggled out, and another took his place. Waythorn glanced up and saw that it was Gus Varick. The men were so close together that it was impossible to ignore the smile of recognition on Varick's handsome overblown face. And after all—why not? They had always been on good terms, and Varick had been divorced before

Waythorn's attentions to his wife began. The two exchanged a word on the perennial grievance of the congested trains, and when a seat at their side was miraculously left empty the instinct of self-preservation made Waythorn slip into it after Varick.

The latter drew the stout man's breath of relief. "Lord—I was beginning to feel like a pressed flower." He leaned back, looking unconcernedly at Waythorn. "Sorry to hear that Sellers is knocked out again."

"Sellers?" echoed Waythorn, starting at his partner's name.

Varick looked surprised. "You didn't know he was laid up with the gout?"

"No, I've been away—I only got back last night." Waythorn felt himself reddening in anticipation of the other's smile.

"Ah—yes; to be sure. And Sellers's attack came on two days ago. I'm afraid he's pretty bad. Very awkward for me, as it happens, because he was just putting through a rather important thing for me."

"Ah?" Waythorn wondered vaguely since when Varick had been dealing in "important things." Hitherto he had dabbled only in the shallow pools of speculation, with which Waythorn's office did not usually concern itself.

It occurred to him that Varick might be talking at random, to relieve the strain of their propinquity. That strain was becoming momentarily more apparent to Waythorn, and when, at Cortlandt Street, he caught sight of an acquaintance and had a sudden vision of the picture he and Varick must present to an initiated eye, he jumped up with a muttered excuse.

"I hope you'll find Sellers better," said Varick civilly, and he stammered back: "If I can be of any use to you—" and let the departing crowd sweep him to the platform.

At his office he heard that Sellers was in fact ill with the gout, and would probably not be able to leave the house for some weeks.

"I'm sorry it should have happened so, Mr. Waythorn," the senior clerk said with affable significance. "Mr. Sellers was very much upset at the idea of giving you such a lot of extra work just now."

"Oh, that's no matter," said Waythorn hastily. He secretly welcomed the pressure of additional business, and was glad to think that, when the day's work was over, he would have to call at his partner's on the way home.

He was late for luncheon, and turned in at the nearest restaurant instead of going to his club. The place was full, and the waiter hurried him to the back of the room to capture the only vacant table. In the cloud of cigar-smoke Waythorn did not at once distinguish his neighbours: but presently, looking about him, he saw Varick seated a few feet off. This time, luckily, they were too far apart for conversation, and Varick, who faced another way, had probably not even seen him; but there was an irony in their renewed nearness.

Varick was said to be fond of good living, and as Waythorn sat despatching his hurried luncheon he looked across half enviously at the other's leisurely degustation of his meal. When Waythorn first saw him he had been helping himself with critical deliberation to a bit of Camembert at the ideal point of liquifaction, and now, the cheese removed, he was just pouring his *café double* from its little two-storied earthen pot. He poured slowly, his ruddy profile bent above the task, and one beringed white hand steadying the lid of the coffee-pot; then he stretched his other hand to the decanter of cognac at his elbow, filled a liqueur-glass, took a tentative sip, and poured the brandy into his coffee-cup.

Waythorn watched him in a kind of fascination. What was he thinking of—only of the flavour of the coffee and the liqueur? Had the morning's meeting left no more trace in his thoughts than on his face? Had his wife so completely passed out of his life that even this odd encounter with her present husband, within a week after her remarriage, was no more than an incident in his day? And as Waythorn mused, another idea struck him: had Haskett ever met Varick as Varick and he had just met? The recollection of Haskett perturbed him, and he rose and left the restaurant, taking a circuitous way out to escape the placid irony of Varick's nod.

It was after seven when Waythorn reached home. He thought the footman who opened the door looked at him oddly.

"How is Miss Lily?" he asked in haste.

"Doing very well, sir. A gentleman—"

"Tell Barlow to put off dinner for half an hour," Waythorn cut him off, hurrying upstairs.

He went straight to his room and dressed without seeing his wife. When he reached the drawing-room she was there, fresh and radiant. Lily's day had been good; the doctor was not coming back that evening.

At dinner Waythorn told her of Sellers's illness and of the resulting complications. She listened sympathetically, adjuring him not to let himself be over-worked, and asking vague feminine questions about the routine of his office. Then she gave him the chronicle of Lily's day; quoted the nurse and doctor, and told him who had called to inquire. He had never seen her more serene and unruffled. It struck him, with a curious pang, that she was very happy in being with him, so happy that she found a childish pleasure in rehearsing the trivial incidents of her day.

After dinner they went to the library, and the servant put the coffee and liqueurs on a low table before her and left the room. She looked singularly soft and girlish in her rosy pale dress, against the dark leather of one of his bachelor armchairs. A day earlier the contrast would have charmed him.

He turned away now, choosing a cigar with affected deliberation.

"Did Haskett come?" he asked, with his back to her.

"Oh yes—he came."

"You didn't see him, of course?"

She hesitated a moment. "I let the nurse see him."

That was all. There was nothing more to ask. He swung round toward her, applying a match to his cigar. Well, the thing was over for a week, at any rate. He would try not to think of it. She looked up at him, a trifle rosier than usual, with a smile in her eyes.

"Ready for your coffee, dear?"

He leaned against the mantelpiece, watching her as she lifted the coffee-pot. The lamplight struck a gleam from her bracelets and tipped her soft hair with brightness. How light and slender she was, and how each gesture flowed into the next! She seemed a creature all compact of harmonies. As the thought of Haskett receded, Waythorn felt himself yielding again to the joy of possessorship. They were his, those white hands with their flitting motions, his the light haze of hair, the lips and eyes. . . .

She set down the coffee-pot, and reaching for the decanter of cognac, measured off a liqueur-glass and poured it into his cup.

Waythorn uttered a sudden exclamation.

"What is the matter?" she said, startled.

"Nothing; only—I don't take cognac in my coffee."

"Oh, how stupid of me," she cried.

Their eyes met, and she blushed a sudden agonised red.

III

Ten days later, Mr. Sellers, still house-bound, asked Waythorn to call on his way down town.

The senior partner, with his swaddled foot propped up by the fire, greeted his associate with an air of embarrassment.

"I'm sorry, my dear fellow; I've got to ask you to do an awkward thing for me."

Waythorn waited, and the other went on, after a pause apparently given to the arrangement of his phrases: "The fact is, when I was knocked out I had just gone into a rather complicated piece of business for—Gus Varick."

"Well?" said Waythorn, with an attempt to put him at his ease.

"Well—it's this way: Varick came to me the day before my attack. He had evidently had an inside tip from somebody, and had made about a hundred thousand. He came to me for advice, and I suggested his going in with Vanderlyn."

"Oh, the deuce!" Waythorn exclaimed. He saw in a flash what had happened. The investment was an alluring one, but required negotiation. He listened quietly while Sellers put the case before him, and, the statement ended, he said: "You think I ought to see Varick?"

"I'm afraid I can't as yet. The doctor is obdurate. And this thing can't wait. I hate to ask you, but no one else in the office knows the ins and outs of it."

Waythorn stood silent. He did not care a farthing for the success of Varick's venture, but the honour of the office was to be considered, and he could hardly refuse to oblige his partner.

"Very well," he said, "I'll do it."

That afternoon, apprised by telephone, Varick called at the office. Waythorn, waiting in his private room, wondered what the others thought of it. The newspapers, at the time of Mrs. Waythorn's marriage, had acquainted their readers with every detail of her previous matrimonial ventures, and Waythorn could fancy the clerks smiling behind Varick's back as he was ushered in.

Varick bore himself admirably. He was easy without being undignified, and Waythorn was conscious of cutting a much less impressive figure. Varick had no experience of business, and the talk prolonged itself for nearly an hour while Waythorn set forth with scrupulous precision the details of the proposed transaction.

"I'm awfully obliged to you," Varick said as he rose. "The fact is I'm not used to having much money to look after, and I don't want to make an ass of myself—" He smiled, and Waythorn could not help noticing that there was something pleasant about his smile. "It feels uncommonly queer to have enough cash to pay one's bills. I'd have sold my soul for it a few years ago!"

Waythorn winced at the allusion. He had heard it rumoured that a lack of funds had been one of the determining causes of the Varick separation, but it did not occur to him that Varick's words were intentional. It seemed more likely that the desire to keep clear of embarrassing topics had fatally drawn him into one. Waythorn did not wish to be outdone in civility.

"We'll do the best we can for you," he said. "I think this is a good thing you're in."

"Oh, I'm sure it's immense. It's awfully good of you—" Varick broke off, embarrassed. "I suppose the thing's settled now—but if—"

"If anything happens before Sellers is about, I'll see you again," said Waythorn quietly. He was glad, in the end, to appear the more self-possessed of the two.

The course of Lily's illness ran smooth, and as the days passed Waythorn grew used to the idea of Haskett's weekly visit. The first time the day came round, he stayed out late, and questioned his wife as to the visit on his return. She replied at once that Haskett had merely seen the nurse downstairs, as the doctor did not wish any one in the child's sick-room till after the crisis.

The following week Waythorn was again conscious of the recurrence of the day, but had forgotten it by the time he came home to dinner. The crisis of the disease came a few days later, with a rapid decline of fever, and the little girl was pronounced out of danger. In the rejoicing which ensued the thought of Haskett passed out of Waythorn's mind, and one afternoon, letting himself into the house with a latch-key, he went straight to his library, without noticing a shabby hat and umbrella in the hall.

In the library he found a small effaced-looking man with a thinnish gray beard sitting on the edge of a chair. The stranger might have been a piano-tuner, or one of those mysteriously efficient persons who are summoned in emergencies to adjust some detail of the domestic machinery. He blinked at Waythorn through a pair of gold-rimmed spectacles and said mildly: "Mr. Waythorn, I presume? I am Lily's father."

Waythorn flushed. "Oh—" he stammered uncomfortably. He broke off, disliking to appear rude. Inwardly he was trying to adjust the actual Haskett to the image of him projected by his wife's reminiscences. Waythorn had been allowed to infer that Alice's first husband was a brute.

"I am sorry to intrude," said Haskett, with his over-the-counter politeness.

"Don't mention it," returned Waythorn, collecting himself. "I suppose the nurse has been told?"

"I presume so. I can wait," said Haskett. He had a resigned way of speaking, as though life had worn down his natural powers of resistance.

Waythorn stood on the threshold, nervously pulling off his gloves.

"I'm sorry you've been detained. I will send for the nurse," he said; and as he opened the door he added with an effort: "I'm glad we can give you a good report of Lily." He winced as the *we* slipped out, but Haskett seemed not to notice it.

"Thank you, Mr. Waythorn. It's been an anxious time for me."

"Ah, well, that's past. Soon she'll be able to go to you." Waythorn nodded and passed out.

In his own room he flung himself down with a groan. He hated the womanish sensibility which made him suffer so acutely from the grotesque chances of life. He had known when he married that his wife's former husbands were both living, and that amid the multiplied contacts of modern existence there were a thousand chances to one that he would run against one or the other, yet he found himself as much disturbed by his brief encounter with Haskett as though the law had not obligingly removed all difficulties in the way of their meeting.

Waythorn sprang up and began to pace the room nervously. He had not suffered half as much from his two meetings with Varick. It was Haskett's presence in his own house that made the situation so intolerable. He stood still, hearing steps in the passage.

"This way, please," he heard the nurse say. Haskett was being taken upstairs, then: not a corner of the house but was open to him. Waythorn dropped into another chair, staring vaguely ahead of him. On his dressing-table stood a photograph of Alice, taken when he had first known her. She was Alice Varick then—how fine and exquisite he had thought her! Those were Varick's pearls about her neck. At Waythorn's instance they had been returned before his marriage. Had Haskett ever given her any trinkets—and what had become of them, Waythorn wondered? He realised suddenly that he knew very little of Haskett's past or present situation; but from the man's appearance and manner of speech he could reconstruct with curious precision the surroundings of Alice's first marriage. And it startled him to think that she had, in the background of her life, a phase of existence so different from anything with which he had connected her. Varick, whatever his faults, was a gentleman, in the conventional, traditional sense of the term: the sense which at that moment seemed, oddly enough, to have most meaning to Waythorn. He and Varick had the same social habits, spoke the same language, understood the same allusions. But this other man . . . it was grotesquely uppermost in Waythorn's mind that Haskett had worn a made-up tie attached with an elastic. Why should that ridiculous detail symbolise the whole man? Waythorn was exasperated by his own paltriness, but the fact of the tie expanded, forced itself on him, became as it were the key to Alice's past. He could see her, as Mrs. Haskett, sitting in a "front parlour" furnished in plush, with a pianola, and a copy of "Ben Hur" on the centre-table. He could see her going to the theatre with Haskett—or perhaps even to a "Church Sociable"—she in a "picture hat" and Haskett in a black frock-coat, a little creased, with the made-up tie on an elastic. On the way home they would stop and look at the illuminated shop-windows, lingering over the photographs of New York actresses. On Sunday afternoons Haskett would take her for a walk, pushing Lily ahead of them in a white enamelled perambulator, and Waythorn had a vision of the people they would stop and talk to. He could fancy how pretty Alice must have looked, in a dress adroitly constructed from the hints of New York fashion-paper, and how she must have looked down on the other women, chafing at her life, and secretly feeling that she belonged in a bigger place.

For the moment his foremost thought was one of wonder at the way in which she had shed the phase of existence which her marriage with Haskett implied. It was as if her whole aspect, every gesture, every inflection, every allusion, were a studied negation of that period of her life. If she had denied being married to Haskett she could hardly have stood more convicted of duplicity than in this obliteration of the self which had been his wife.

Waythorn started up, checking himself in the analysis of her motives. What right had he to create a fantastic effigy of her and then pass judgment on it? She had spoken vaguely of her first marriage as unhappy, had hinted, with becoming reticence, that Haskett had wrought havoc among her young illusions. . . . It was a pity for Waythorn's peace of mind that Haskett's very inoffensiveness shed a new light on the nature of those illusions. A man would rather think that his wife has been brutalised by her first husband than that the process has been reversed.

IV

"Mr. Waythorn, I don't like that French governess of Lily's."

Haskett, subdued and apologetic, stood before Waythorn in the library, revolving his shabby hat in his hand.

Waythorn, surprised in his armchair over the evening paper, stared back perplexedly at his visitor.

"You'll excuse my asking to see you," Haskett continued. "But this is my last visit, and I thought if I could have a word with you it would be a better way than writing to Mrs. Waythorn's lawyer."

Waythorn rose uneasily. He did not like the French governess either; but that was irrelevant.

"I am not so sure of that," he returned stiffly; "but since you wish it I will give your message to—my wife." He always hesitated over the possessive pronoun in addressing Haskett.

The latter sighed. "I don't know as that will help much. She didn't like it when I spoke to her."

Waythorn turned red. "When did you see her?" he asked.

"Not since the first day I came to see Lily—right after she was taken sick. I remarked to her then that I didn't like the governess."

Waythorn made no answer. He remembered distinctly that, after that first visit, he had asked his wife if she had seen Haskett. She had lied to him then, but she had respected his wishes since; and the incident cast a curious light on her character. He was sure she would not have seen Haskett that first day if she had divined that Waythorn would object, and the fact that she did not divine it was almost as disagreeable to the latter as the discovery that she had lied to him.

"I don't like the woman," Haskett was repeating with mild persistency. "She ain't straight, Mr. Waythorn—she'll teach the child to be underhand. I've noticed a change in Lily—she's too anxious to please—and she don't always tell the truth. She used to be the straightest child, Mr. Waythorn—" He broke off, his voice a little thick. "Not but what I want her to have a stylish education," he ended.

Waythorn was touched. "I'm sorry, Mr. Haskett; but frankly, I don't quite see what I can do."

Haskett hesitated. Then he laid his hat on the table, and advanced to the hearth-rug, on which Waythorn was standing. There was nothing aggressive in his manner, but he had the solemnity of a timid man resolved on a decisive measure.

"There's just one thing you can do, Mr. Waythorn," he said. "You can remind Mrs. Waythorn that, by the decree of the courts, I am entitled to have a voice in Lily's bringing up." He paused, and went on more deprecatingly: "I'm not the kind to talk about enforcing my rights, Mr. Waythorn. I don't know as I think a man is entitled to rights he hasn't known how to hold on to; but this business of the child is different. I've never let go there—and I never mean to."

The scene left Waythorn deeply shaken. Shame-facedly, in indirect ways, he had been finding out about Haskett; and all that he had learned was favorable. The little man, in order to be near his daughter, had sold out his share in a profitable business in Utica, and accepted a modest clerkship in a New York manufacturing house. He boarded in a shabby street and had few acquaintances. His passion for Lily filled his life. Waythorn felt that this exploration of Haskett was like groping about with a dark-lantern in his wife's past; but he saw now that there were recesses his lantern had not explored. He had never enquired into the exact circumstances of his wife's first matrimonial rupture. On the surface all had been fair. It was she who had obtained the divorce, and the courts had given her the child. But Waythorn knew how many ambiguities such a verdict might cover. The mere fact that Haskett retained a right over his daughter implied an unsuspected compromise. Waythorn was an idealist. He always refused to recognise unpleasant contingencies till he found himself confronted with them, and then he saw them followed by a spectral train of consequences. His next days were thus haunted, and he determined to try to lay the ghosts by conjuring them up in his wife's presence.

When he repeated Haskett's request a flame of anger passed over her face; but she subdued it instantly and spoke with a slight quiver of outraged motherhood.

"It is very ungentlemanly of him," she said.

The word grated on Waythorn. "That is neither here nor there. It's a bare question of rights."

She murmured: "It's not as if he could ever be a help to Lily—"

Waythorn flushed. This was even less to his taste. "The question is," he repeated, "what authority has he over her?"

She looked downward, twisting herself a little in her seat. "I am willing to see him—I thought you objected," she faltered.

In a flash he understood that she knew the extent of Haskett's claims. Perhaps it was not the first time she had resisted them.

"My objecting has nothing to do with it," he said coldly; "if Haskett has a right to be consulted you must consult him."

She burst into tears, and he saw that she expected him to regard her as a victim.

Haskett did not abuse his rights. Waythorn had felt miserably sure that he would not. But the governess was dismissed, and from time to time the little man demanded an interview with Alice. After the first outbursts she accepted the situation with her usual adaptability. Haskett had once reminded Waythorn of the piano-tuner, and Mrs. Waythorn, after a month or two, appeared to class him with that domestic familiar. Waythorn could not but respect the father's tenacity. At first he had tried to cultivate the suspicion that Haskett might be "up to" something, that he had an object in securing a foothold in the house. But in his heart Waythorn was sure of Haskett's single-mindedness; he even guessed in the latter a mild contempt for such advantages as his relation with the Waythorns might offer. Haskett's sincerity of purpose made him invulnerable, and his successor had to accept him as a lien on the property.

Mr. Sellers was sent to Europe to recover from his gout, and Varick's affairs hung on Waythorn's hands. The negotiations were prolonged and complicated; they necessitated frequent conferences between the two men, and the interests of the firm forbade Waythorn's suggesting that his client should transfer his business to another office.

Varick appeared well in the transaction. In moments of relaxation his coarse streak appeared, and Waythorn dreaded his geniality; but in the office he was concise and clear-headed, with a flattering deference to Waythorn's judgment. Their business relations being so affably established, it would have been absurd for the two men to ignore each other in society. The first time they met in a drawing-room, Varick took up their intercourse in the same easy key, and his hostess's grateful glance obliged Waythorn to respond to it. After that they ran across each other frequently, and one evening at a ball Waythorn, wandering through the remoter rooms, came upon Varick seated beside his wife. She coloured a little, and faltered in what she was saying; but Varick nodded to Waythorn without rising, and the latter strolled on.

In the carriage, on the way home, he broke out nervously: "I didn't know you spoke to Varick."

Her voice trembled a little. "It's the first time—he happened to be standing near me; I didn't know what to do. It's awkward, meeting everywhere—and he said you had been very kind about some business."

"That's different," said Waythorn.

She paused a moment. "I'll do just as you wish," she returned pliantly. "I thought it would be less awkward to speak to him when we meet."

Her pliancy was beginning to sicken him. Had she really no will of her own—no theory about her relation to these men? She had accepted Haskett—did she mean to accept Varick? It was "less awkward," as she had said, and her instinct was to evade difficulties or to circumvent them. With sudden vividness Waythorn saw how the instinct had developed. She was "as easy as an old shoe"—a shoe that too many feet had worn. Her elasticity was the result of tension in too many different directions. Alice Haskett—Alice Varick—Alice Waythorn—she had been each in turn, and had left hanging to each name a little of her privacy, a little of her personality, a little of the inmost self where the unknown god abides.

"Yes—it's better to speak to Varick," said Waythorn wearily.

V

The winter wore on, and society took advantage of the Waythorns' acceptance of Varick. Harassed hostesses were grateful to them for bridging over a social difficulty, and Mrs. Waythorn was held up as a miracle of good taste. Some experimental spirits could not resist the diversion of throwing Varick and his former wife together, and there were those who thought he found a zest in the propinquity. But Mrs. Waythorn's conduct remained irreproachable. She neither avoided Varick nor sought him out. Even Waythorn could not but admit that she had discovered the solution of the newest social problem.

He had married her without giving much thought to that problem. He had fancied that a woman can shed her past like a man. But now he saw that Alice was bound to hers both by the circumstances which forced her into continued relation with it, and by the traces it had left on her nature. With grim irony Waythorn compared himself to a member of a syndicate. He held so many shares in his wife's personality and his predecessors were his partners in the business. If there had been any element of passion in the transaction he would have felt less deteriorated by it. The fact that Alice took her change of husbands like a change of weather reduced the situation to mediocrity. He could have forgiven her for blunders, for excesses; for resisting Haskett, for yielding to Varick; for anything but her acquiescence and her tact. She reminded him of a juggler tossing knives; but the knives were blunt and she knew they would never cut her.

And then, gradually, habit formed a protecting surface for his sensibilities. If he paid for each day's comfort with the small change of his illusions, he grew daily to value the comfort more and set less store upon the coin. He had drifted into a dulling propinquity with Haskett and Varick and he took refuge in the cheap revenge of satirising the situation. He even began to reckon up the advantages which accrued from it, to ask himself if it were not better to own a third of a wife who knew how to make a man happy than a whole one who had lacked opportunity to acquire the art. For it *was* an art, and made up, like all others, of concessions, eliminations, and embellishments; of lights judiciously thrown and shadows skillfully softened. His wife knew exactly how to manage the lights, and he knew exactly to what training she owed her skill. He even tried to trace the source of his obligations, to discriminate between the influences which had combined to produce his domestic happiness: he perceived that Haskett's commonness had made Alice worship good breeding, while Varick's liberal construction of the marriage bond had taught her to value the conjugal virtues; so that he was directly indebted to his predecessors for the devotion which made his life easy if not inspiring.

From this phase he passed into that of complete acceptance. He ceased to satirise himself because time dulled the irony of the situation and the joke lost its humour with its sting. Even the sight of Haskett's hat on the hall table had ceased to touch the springs of epigram. The hat was often seen there now, for it had been decided that it was better for Lily's father to visit her than for the little girl to go to his boarding-house. Waythorn, having acquiesced in this arrangement, had been surprised to find how little difference it made. Haskett was never obtrusive, and the few visitors who met him on the stairs were unaware of his identity. Waythorn did not know how often he saw Alice, but with himself Haskett was seldom in contact.

One afternoon, however, he learned on entering that Lily's father was waiting to see him. In the library he found Haskett occupying a chair in his usual provisional way. Waythorn always felt grateful to him for not leaning back.

"I hope you'll excuse me, Mr. Waythorn," he said rising. "I wanted to see Mrs. Waythorn about Lily, and your man asked me to wait here till she came in."

"Of course," said Waythorn, remembering that a sudden leak had that morning given over the drawing-room to the plumbers.

He opened his cigar-case and held it out to his visitor, and Haskett's acceptance seemed to mark a fresh stage in their intercourse. The spring evening was chilly, and Waythorn invited his guest to draw up his chair to the fire. He meant to find an excuse to leave Haskett in a moment; but he was tired and cold, and after all the little man no longer jarred on him.

The two were enclosed in the intimacy of their blended cigar-smoke when the door opened and Varick walked into the room. Waythorn rose abruptly. It was the first time Varick had come to the house, and the surprise of seeing him, combined with the singular inopportuneness of his arrival, gave a new edge to Waythorn's blunted sensibilities. He stared at his visitor without speaking.

Varick seemed too preoccupied to notice his host's embarrassment.

"My dear fellow," he exclaimed in his most expansive tone, "I must apologise for tumbling in on you in this way, but I was too late to catch you down town, and so I thought—"

He stopped short, catching sight of Haskett, and his sanguine colour deepened to a flush which spread vividly under his scant blond hair. But in a moment he recovered himself and nodded slightly. Haskett returned the bow in silence, and Waythorn was still groping for speech when the footman came in carrying a tea-table.

The intrusion offered a welcome vent to Waythorn's nerves. "What the deuce are you bringing this here for?" he said sharply.

"I beg your pardon, sir, but the plumbers are still in the drawing-room, and Mrs. Waythorn said she would have tea in the library." The footman's perfectly respectful tone implied a reflection on Waythorn's reasonableness.

"Oh, very well," said the latter resignedly, and the footman proceeded to open the folding tea-table and set out its complicated appointments. While this interminable process continued the three men stood motionless, watching it with a fascinated stare, till Waythorn, to break the silence, said to Varick: "Won't you have a cigar?"

He held out the case he had just tendered to Haskett, and Varick helped himself with a smile. Waythorn looked about for a match, and finding none, proffered a light from his own cigar. Haskett, in the background, held his ground mildly, examining his cigar-tip now and then, and stepping forward at the right moment to knock its ashes into the fire.

The footman at last withdrew, and Varick immediately began: "If I could just say half a word to you about this business—"

"Certainly," stammered Waythorn; "in the dining-room—"

But as he placed his hand on the door it opened from without, and his wife appeared on the threshold.

She came in fresh and smiling, in her street dress and hat, shedding a fragrance from the boa which she loosened in advancing.

"Shall we have tea in here, dear?" she began; and then she caught sight of Varick. Her smile deepened, veiling a slight tremor of surprise.

"Why, how do you do?" she said with a distinct note of pleasure.

As she shook hands with Varick she saw Haskett standing behind him. Her smile faded for a moment, but she recalled it quickly, with a scarcely perceptible side-glance at Waythorn.

"How do you do, Mr. Haskett?" she said, and shook hands with him a shade less cordially.

The three men stood awkwardly before her, till Varick, always the most self-possessed, dashed into an explanatory phrase.

"We—I had to see Waythorn a moment on business," he stammered, brick-red from chin to nape.

Haskett stepped forward with his air of mild obstinacy. "I am sorry to intrude; but you appointed five o'clock—" he directed his resigned glance to the time-piece on the mantel.

She swept aside their embarrassment with a charming gesture of hospitality.

"I'm so sorry—I'm always late; but the afternoon was so lovely." She stood drawing off her gloves, propitiatory and graceful, diffusing about her a sense of ease and familiarity in which the situation lost its grotesqueness. "But before talking business," she added brightly, "I'm sure every one wants a cup of tea."

She dropped into her low chair by the tea-table, and the two visitors, as if drawn by her smile, advanced to receive the cups she held out.

She glanced about for Waythorn, and he took the third cup with a laugh.

(1904)

Testing Your Understanding—Unit V

"Orientation" by Daniel Orozco

✓ **Paragraphs 1–9**
CHECKING YOUR COMPREHENSION

Choose the best answer for each of the following questions.

1. In paragraph 3, what information is not revealed?
   a. The author only included what the "tour guide" says.
   b. Workers shouldn't ask too many questions.
   c. Employees need to work overtime to finish their work.
   d. The employees work an eight-hour workday.

2. It can be inferred that the speaker
   a. is the new worker's supervisor.
   b. has worked in the office for a significant amount of time.
   c. enjoys working in this office.
   d. is a woman who is frustrated about giving this office tour.

Identify the following sentences as true or false.

3. John LaFountaine occasionally uses the women's room by mistake.

4. Albert Bosch likes Ellie Tapper, who likes Curtis Lance.

5. Jamie Pierce's father continually humiliates and hurts Jamie's mother.

Answer the following questions.

6. What is the protocol for making a phone call in the office?

7. What does the author suggest regarding Russell Nash's weight gain?

Define the following words as they are used in the story.

8. civil

9. forays

10. tedious

Discussion and Critical Thinking Question

1. Discuss how you would feel if you were the one being given the tour of your new workplace. So far in the story, is there anything that would make you skeptical about taking the job?

Paragraphs 10–18
CHECKING YOUR COMPREHENSION

Choose the best answer for each of the following questions.

1. The word "nothing" at the end of paragraph 13 refers to the fact that Larry Bagdikian would have
   a. no children left alive.
   b. the narrator, Larry's close friend, to help him through hard times.
   c. no financial burden.
   d. his job even if his family were to suffer.

2. The tone of paragraph 14 is
   a. upbeat.
   b. somber.
   c. formal.
   d. humorous.

Identify the following statements as true or false.

3. The narrator is afraid of Cohn Heavey.

4. Barry Hacker's wife works in the office.

5. Larry Bagdikian's daughters have a degenerative muscle disease.

Answer the following questions.

6. Why would the office have a Floor Evacuation Review, an Escape Route Quiz, Biannual Fire Drills, and an Annual Earthquake Drill if the speaker states that "these things never happen"?

7. Explain why the reader should presume that the speaker and the new employee are walking through the office as this conversation is taking place.

Define the following words as they are used in the story.

8. dependents

9. rescind

10. ambient

Discussion and Critical Thinking Question

1. Discuss why it is so ironic that the speaker makes comments about going to the symphony and the ballpark with his fellow employees.

Paragraphs 19–27
CHECKING YOUR COMPREHENSION

1. What evidence is given regarding Matthew Payne's presence?
    a. He introduced himself to the new employee.
    b. The speaker's assurance.
    c. He is in charge of the Supplies Cabinet.
    d. No evidence is given.

2. It is ironic that the new employee is told the location of the blades for the shedder because
    a. it makes sense that they are kept in Section Four with the razor blades.
    b. Curtis Lane would have to go into the closet to get them.
    c. she will not remember where they are located.
    d. the speaker explained that shredding is not part of her job.

Identify the following statements as true or false.

3. Gwendolyn Stich tries to portray herself as a very happy person.

4. The view from the photocopy machine faces southwest and overlooks the park.

Answer the following questions.

5. What is the difference between lunch and break?

6. As a new employee, explain which paragraph in this section has the most significant information.

Define the following words as they are used in the text.

7. compulsion

8. carnage

Discussion and Critical Thinking Questions

1. How do you think the new employee felt after the orientation?

2. Discuss the fact that bizarre and questionable information was so understated in the story. How does this impact the story as a whole?

"The Other Two" by Edith Wharton

Sections I and II
CHECKING YOUR COMPREHENSION

Choose the best answer for each of the following questions.

1. What was Mr. Waythorn's assumption regarding Mr. Hassett?
   a. Mrs. Waythorn had married him when she was seventeen.
   b. Mr. Hassett was boring and dull.
   c. Mr. Hassett was not a good person.
   d. Mr. Waythorn had no assumptions regarding Mr. Hassett.

2. When Waythorn's friends found out that he was going to marry Mrs. Varick
   a. they stopped talking to him.
   b. they were hesitant to accept her since she'd been married twice before.
   c. they were happy for him that he finally found a woman that he could love.
   d. they knew he was lonely and felt he was lucky that she had accepted his proposal.

Identify the following statements as true or false.

3. Lily was Mrs. Waythorn's child from her first marriage who was stricken by typhoid.

4. Mr. Waythorn was upset that Mr. Varick spoke to him when they ran into each other.

5. Mr. Waythorn was upset that Seller's illness would cause him a greater workload.

Answer the following questions.

6. Why had Mr. Hassett's lawyer written to Mrs. Waythorn?

7. What was so ironic about Mr. Waythorn leaving his house earlier than usual and running into Mr. Varick?

Define the following words as they are used in the text.

8. agitation   11. dispatching

9. decisive   12. adjuring

10. ballast   13. mused

Discussion and Critical Thinking Question

1. Discuss why the author had Mrs. Waythorn pour cognac into Mr. Waythorn's coffee by accident. What significance does this action have to the storyline?

Sections III and IV
CHECKING YOUR COMPREHENSION

Choose the best answer for each of the following questions.

1. During Mr. Waythorn's meeting with Mr. Varick,
   a. Varick bullied Waythorn into submission.
   b. they set up another meeting for the next day.
   c. both men remained cordial and business-like.
   d. Waythorn made numerous comments about his wife.

2. Hassett discussed all of the following with Mr. Waythorn EXCEPT:
   a. that he expected a say in raising Lily.
   b. that he didn't care for Lily's governess.
   c. that Lily's illness left her weak and feeble.
   d. that he didn't want to involve his lawyer again.

Identify the following statements as true or false.

3. Waythorn was honored that he was called upon by Sellers to take care of Varick's business.

4. Mr. Seller's quick recovery dismissed any further meetings between Waythorn and Varick.

5. Waythorn realized that Hassett's main concern was the well-being of Lily and was not interested in romancing Mrs. Waythorn.

Answer the following questions.

6. What had Waythorn inferred regarding Mr. Hassett's physical stature?

7. Why did Waythorn agree that it was better for his wife to speak to Varick?

Define the following words as they are used in the text.

8. swaddled   11. forbade

9. obdurate   12. pliancy

10. farthing   13. vividness

Discussion and Critical Thinking Question

1. Discuss why when Mrs. Waythorn "burst into tears," Mr. Waythorn "saw that she expected him to regard her as a victim." What is the author revealing regarding Mrs. Waythorn?

Section V
CHECKING YOUR COMPREHENSION

Choose the best answer for each of the following questions.

1. The Waythorns socially
   a. avoided Varick when they saw him at parties.
   b. accepted Varick's presence in public.
   c. spoke to hostesses prior to parties to ensure that Varick would not be present.
   d. avoided all parties since they were made to feel like social outcasts.

2. The reader can conclude that Varick and Hassett met previously since
   a. Varick was Lily's step-father at one point.
   b. they both worked for Mr. Sellers.
   c. they greeted each other like they were good friends.
   d. Waythorn noted that he saw them eating lunch together in town.

Identify the following statements as true or false.

3. Waythorn believed that being Alice's third husband had its benefits.

4. Waythorn was upset to find Hassett waiting for him in the library.

5. Varick often visited the Waythorn residence.

Answer the following questions.

6. Explain the juggling analogy that the author uses to describe Alice Waythorn's relationship with Mr. Hassett, Mr. Varick, and Mr. Waythorn.

7. Why did Hassett continue to visit the Waythorn residence even after Lily was cured of typhoid?

Define the following words as they are used in the text.

8. propinquity

9. satirise

10. epigram

11. sanguine

12. obstinacy

> ## Discussion and Critical Thinking Question
>
> 1. Discuss why Alice Waythorn did not feel threatened when having tea with her two ex-husbands and her current husband. What information did you learn as you read the story that would lead you to understand why Alice felt this uncomfortable situation would work out well?

Chapter Review
END OF CHAPTER ANALYSIS

1. Compare the narrator in Orozco's "Orientation" to the narrator in Wharton's "The Other Two."

2. Explain the concept of movement as it relates to both stories and how it affects the pace of the stories.

Group Project

1. Both short stories involve the idea of knowing one's place in society. Choose a time during your life that you felt suppressed and discuss the different ways to overcome and deal with such situations.

Journal Ideas

1. Write a letter to the new employee in "Orientation," giving advice as to how you would deal with working with the other people in the office.

2. Pretend you are Mr. Waythorn and write an entry in a diary about your experiences dealing with your wife's ex-husbands. Be sure to include the thoughts, feelings, and emotions that you think Mr. Waythorn would be experiencing.

Organizing Information

When reading literature, it is important to be able to pull out the sequence of events in the story. To make sure you understand what you are reading, it is important to reflect and connect to what you have read as well. Lastly, oftentimes we have questions about what we read. Some of these questions may need to be answered by a fellow classmate or an instructor, while other questions may be rhetorical and can't be answered but are ideas you are wondering at that point in the story. See the chart below and choose one of the stories to complete the chart. The first entry using "The Other Two" has been done for you.

What I Read	What I Think About What I Read	Questions I Have About What I Read
Mr. Waythorn, recently married, was waiting for his wife to join him in the drawing room. She was upstairs looking in on her daughter, Lily, who was stricken with typhoid while her mother and her new stepfather were away on their honeymoon.	I think it must have been hard for Lily to get so sick while her mother was away. I am sure she would have been more at ease if her mother was by her side. I also think that at twelve it may be hard for Lily to accept that her mother's attention is now on a new man in her life and not focused on her. I wonder if Lily gets along with Mr. Waythorn.	How serious of a disease is typhoid? Can someone die from it? What medicine cures it? Where is Lily's father? Does she get to see him often? Is Lily happy that her mother remarried? Does Mr. Waythorn have any children of his own?

Unit VI: Psychology

From

Samuel E. Wood

Ellen Green Wood

Denise Boyd

Mastering the World of Psychology

Third Edition

Chapter 10:
Health and Stress

An Introduction to Psychology

Psychology is defined as the scientific study of human and animal behavior and mental processes. This occurs through the orderly investigation into a problem that involves collecting and analyzing data, drawing conclusions, and communication findings. Psychology is concerned with explaining how a number of separate facts are related.

Introduction to psychology courses are often required at most liberal arts colleges and universities. A degree in psychology will prepare students to enter careers in such fields as business, public relations, staff training, human resources, mental health therapy, research, and education.

Strategies for Reading Psychology Texts

When reading a psychology textbook, it is necessary to define all terms and understand their relationships to one another. It is also helpful to note the similarities and differences between related ideas. This can be done by utilizing Venn diagrams and concept maps. It is essential to pay attention to two specific factors as new concepts are introduced in a psychology textbook – the theorist who conceived the idea and the impact the idea has on prior beliefs in the field. Applying the concepts introduced to your life and to the world around you will help you understand them better. Be sure that you are able to give examples of the concepts, ideas, and theories that are introduced in the text.

10 HEALTH AND STRESS

SOURCES OF STRESS

RESPONDING TO STRESS

HEALTH AND ILLNESS

LIFESTYLE AND HEALTH

What comes to mind when you hear the word *bully?* Perhaps you think of a school setting in which one child says to another, "Give me your lunch money, or I'll beat you up." But bullying extends beyond the school playground. Thus, psychologists have recently begun to study the phenomenon of bullying in the workplace.

Most researchers define a workplace bully as an employee who behaves in ways that cause harm

to targeted co-workers. The tactics employed by bullies may include yelling and name calling as well as covert behaviors such as withholding information. In researchers' terminology, *targets* are the unfortunate victims of these behaviors. The institutional relationship between a bully and a target can be of any type, but bullying is probably most obvious when bullies are the targets' supervisors. In their book, *The Bully at Work,* psychologists Gary and Ruth Namie (2000) describe four types of "bully-bosses." See if you recognize any of them. (Note that although the Namies developed these types with bosses in mind, they could be applied to organizational leaders or any situation in which one person bullies another.)

According to the Namies, the Constant Critic is often the darling of upper management, thanks to his or her ability to wheedle performance improvements out of supervisees. The Constant Critic's tactics usually include inundating supervisees with massive amounts of information and then criticizing them for their failure to memorize every word of every memo he or she has ever generated. Constant Critics are also known for nitpicking and for making unreasonable, perfectionist demands of those whom they supervise. Predictably, supervisees are often blamed by Constant Critics for their own failures, and most are willing to lie to higher-level managers to be certain that the blame falls on the targeted supervisee.

Named for a World War II artillery rocket that emitted a distinctive whining sound before exploding, the Screaming Mimi's behavior often resembles that of his or her namesake. The sound of a slamming door often announces that the Screaming Mimi is in a volatile mood. This kind of bully-boss intimidates supervisees with angry, foot-stomping outbursts, verbal abuse, and threats. Screaming Mimis also constantly interrupt supervisees during conversations and meetings. These interruptions often take on a hostile tone. Screaming Mimis use intimidating nonverbal behaviors such as violating supervisees' personal space as well. They justify unreasonable demands with statements that are reminiscent of authoritarian parents: "Do it because I'm your boss, and I said so."

A third kind of bully boss, the Gatekeeper, must be in control at all times. Gatekeepers often institute policies that require their approval of all allocations of resources. For example, they may keep frequently needed supplies in a locked cabinet in their offices. A supervisee who requests a new box of paper clips from the Gatekeeper is likely to have to listen to a lecture on the cost of paper clips. In addition, Gatekeepers include minor infractions (e.g., "on several occasions Mr. X was more than five minutes late for a meeting") in supervisees' performance evaluations. To intimidate a target, Gatekeepers often invoke the "silent treatment" and make it clear that they expect all supervisees to help them isolate the target. A Gatekeeper may also "accidentally" delete a supervisee's name from the department e-mail list. Then, when the "deleted" supervisee misses a meeting, the Gatekeeper reports the infraction to higher-ups with comments such as "How can you expect me to accomplish anything with such irresponsible people in my department?"

The Two-Headed Snake variety of bully-boss uses friendliness to get close to targets. The target of a Two-Headed Snake believes that the Snake is a friend, when, in reality, the Snake often makes disparaging remarks about the target to other supervisees and to higher-level managers. Two-Headed Snakes also use what the Namies call a "divide and conquer" strategy. They bestow favors on employees who are on the same level as the target for gathering information about the target. For example, a confederate of the Two-Headed Snake might encourage the target to make critical remarks about the supervisor that the confederate then reports back to the Snake.

Working under any type of bully-boss can be extremely stressful. Researchers have found that targets are prone to anxiety and depression. Long-term exposure to bullying tactics may even lead to posttraumatic stress disorder (Matthiesen & Einarsen, 2004). Targets may also experience physical symptoms such as frequent headaches and fatigue (Meyers, 2006).

The targets of bully-bosses often feel helpless because they fear that speaking out will lead to retaliation. Many times, these fears are justified (Cortina & Magley, 2003). Moreover, employees who complain about bullies are often told that they are overly sensitive. In effect, they are told to "get over it." Seeing bully-bosses promoted or given awards only adds to the frustration that many of their targets feel.

According to the Namies, there are some effective coping strategies that the target of a bully-boss can use to regain his or her psychological health. First, say the Namies, targets should give the bully's behavior a name—*bullying, intimidation, psychological harassment,* or whatever term the target thinks best fits. Second, the target should listen to his or her body's "fight-or-flight" message and do one or the other. The Namies recommend taking time off from work and consulting with a mental health professional to decide which option (stay and fight versus move on to another organization) is best. They also recommend that the target use some of this time off to gather data about the impact of the bully-boss's behavior on the organization. This data may include information about employee turnover, absenteeism, or stress-related health costs. Even if the target decides to move on, say the Namies, he or she should present this information to the bully-boss's supervisor. The Namies' work with the victims of workplace bullies indicates that those who expose the bully before leaving their jobs recover from the effects of having been bullied more quickly than those who remain silent about their reason for resigning.

---

stress

The physiological and psychological response to a condition that threatens or challenges a person and requires some form of adaptation or adjustment.

fight-or-flight response

A response to stress in which the sympathetic nervous system and the endocrine glands prepare the body to fight or flee.

SOURCES OF STRESS

What do you mean when you say you are "stressed out"? Most psychologists define **stress** as the physiological and psychological response to a condition that threatens or challenges an individual and requires some form of adaptation or adjustment. Stress is associated with the **fight-or-flight response**, in which the body's sympathetic nervous system and the endocrine glands prepare the body to fight or escape from a threat (see Chapter 2). Most of us frequently experience other kinds of **stressors**, stimuli or events that are capable of producing physical or emotional stress.

10.1 *What was the Social Readjustment Rating Scale designed to reveal?*

stressor

Any stimulus or event capable of producing physical or emotional stress.

Social Readjustment Rating Scale (SRRS)

Holmes and Rahe's measure of stress, which ranks 43 life events from most to least stressful and assigns a point value to each.

LIFE CHANGES

Researchers Holmes and Rahe (1967) developed the **Social Readjustment Rating Scale (SRRS)** to measure stress by ranking different life events from most to least stressful and assigning a point value to each event. Life events that produce the greatest life changes and require the greatest adaptation are considered the most stressful, regardless of whether the events are positive or negative. The 43 life events on the scale range from death of a spouse (assigned 100 stress points) to minor law violations such as getting a traffic ticket (11 points). Find your life stress score by completing *Try It.*

Holmes and Rahe claim that there is a connection between the degree of life stress and major health problems. People who score 300 or more on the SRRS, the researchers say, run about an 80% risk of suffering a major health problem within the next two years. Those who score between 150 and 300 have a 50% chance of becoming ill within a two-year period (Rahe et al., 1964). More recent research has shown that the weights given to life events by Holmes and Rahe continue to be appropriate for adults in North America and that SRRS scores are correlated with a variety of health indicators (Dohrenwend, 2006; Faisal-Cury et al., 2004; Hobson & Delunas, 2001; Scully, Tosi, & Banning, 2000).

Some researchers have questioned whether a high score on the SRRS is a reliable predictor of future health problems (Krantz, Grunberg, & Baum, 1985; McCrae, 1984). One of the main shortcomings of the SRRS is that it assigns a point value to each life change without taking into account how an individual copes with that stressor. One study found that SRRS scores did reliably predict disease progression in multiple sclerosis patients (Mohr et al., 2002). But the patients who used more effective coping strategies displayed less disease progression than did those who experienced similar stressors but coped poorly with them.

Even positive life events, such as getting married, can cause stress.

 **FINDING A LIFE STRESS SCORE**

To assess your level of life changes, check all of the events that have happened to you in the past year. Add up the points to derive your life stress score. (Based on Holmes & Masuda, 1974.)

Rank	Life Event	Life Change Unit Value	Your Points	Rank	Life Event	Life Change Unit Value	Your Points
1	Death of spouse	100	___	25	Outstanding personal achievement	28	___
2	Divorce	73	___	26	Spouse beginning or stopping work	26	___
3	Marital separation	65	___	27	Beginning or ending school	26	___
4	Jail term	63	___	28	Change in living conditions	25	___
5	Death of close family member	63	___	29	Revision of personal habits	24	___
6	Personal injury or illness	53	___	30	Trouble with boss	23	___
7	Marriage	50	___	31	Change in work hours or conditions	20	___
8	Getting fired at work	47	___	32	Change in residence	20	___
9	Marital reconciliation	45	___	33	Change in schools	20	___
10	Retirement	45	___	34	Change in recreation	19	___
11	Change in health of family member	44	___	35	Change in church activities	19	___
12	Pregnancy	40	___	36	Change in social activities	18	___
13	Sex difficulties	39	___	37	Taking out loan for lesser purchase (e.g., car or TV)	17	___
14	Gain of new family member	39	___	38	Change in sleeping habits	16	___
15	Business readjustment	39	___	39	Change in number of family get-togethers	15	___
16	Change in financial state	38	___	40	Change in eating habits	15	___
17	Death of close friend	37	___	41	Vacation	13	___
18	Change to different line of work	36	___	42	Christmas	12	___
19	Change in number of arguments with spouse	35	___	43	Minor violation of the law	11	___
20	Taking out loan for major purchase (e.g., home)	31	___		**Life stress score:**		___
21	Foreclosure of mortgage or loan	30	___				
22	Change in responsibilities at work	29	___				
23	Son or daughter leaving home	29	___				
24	Trouble with in-laws	29	___				

mypsychlab Where learning comes to life!

GO TO www.mypsychlab.com
to view an "It" video related to this topic.

DAILY HASSLES

Which is more stressful—major life events or those little problems and frustrations that seem to crop up every day? Richard Lazarus believes that the little stressors, which he calls **hassles**, cause more stress than major life events do. (Lazarus & DeLongis, 1983). Daily hassles include irritating, frustrating experiences such as standing in line, being stuck in traffic, waiting for an appliance or utility repair technician to come to your home, and so on. Relationships are another frequent source of hassles, such as happens when another person misunderstands us or when co-workers or customers are hard to get along with. Likewise, environmental conditions such as traffic noise and pollution are among the daily hassles reported by city dwellers (Moser & Robin, 2006).

To illustrate the usefulness of Lazarus's approach, Kanner and others (1981) developed the Hassles Scale to assess various categories of hassles. Unlike the Holmes and Rahe scale, the Hassles Scale takes into account the facts that items may or may not represent stressors to individuals and that the amount of stress produced by an item varies from person to person. People completing the scale indicate the items that have been a hassle for them and rate those items for severity on a 3-point scale. Table 10.1 on page 324 shows the hassles most frequently reported by college students in Lazarus's original study in the late 1970s. Do you think they are still relevant to students today?

10.2 What roles do hassles and uplifts play in the stress of life, according to Lazarus?

hassles

Little stressors, including the irritating demands that can occur daily, that may cause more stress than major life changes do.

TABLE 10.1   The Ten Most Common Hassles for College Students

HASSLE	PERCENTAGE OF TIMES CHECKED
1. Troubling thoughts about future	76.6
2. Not getting enough sleep	72.5
3. Wasting time	71.1
4. Inconsiderate smokers	70.7
5. Physical appearance	69.9
6. Too many things to do	69.2
7. Misplacing or losing things	67.0
8. Not enough time to do the things you need to do	66.3
9. Concerns about meeting high standards	64.0
10. Being lonely	60.8

Source: Kanner et al. (1981).

DeLongis, Folkman, & Lazarus (1988) studied 75 American couples over a 6-month period and found that daily stress (as measured on the Hassles Scale) related significantly to present and future "health problems such as flu, sore throat, headaches, and backaches" (p. 486). Research also indicates that minor hassles that accompany stressful major life events, such as those measured by the SRRS, are better predictors of a person's level of psychological distress than the major events themselves (Pillow, Zautra, & Sandlar, 1996).

According to Lazarus, **uplifts**, or positive experiences in life, may neutralize the effects of many hassles. Lazarus and his colleagues also constructed an Uplifts Scale. As with the Hassles Scale, people completing this scale make a cognitive appraisal of what they consider to be an uplift. Research has demonstrated links among hassles, uplifts, and a personal sense of well-being. It appears that a hectic daily schedule increases hassles, decreases uplifts, and diminishes their subjective sense of how well they feel (Erlandsson & Eklund, 2003). However, items viewed as uplifts by some people may actually be stressors for others. For middle-aged people, uplifts are often health- or family-related (Pinquart & Sorensen, 2004). For college students uplifts often take the form of having a good time (Kanner et al., 1981).

uplifts

The positive experiences in life, which may neutralize the effects of many hassles.

10.3 How do choice-related conflicts and lack of control contribute to stress?

MAKING CHOICES

What happens when you have to decide which movie to see or which new restaurant to try? Simply making a choice, even among equally desirable alternatives (an **approach-approach conflict**), can be stressful. Some approach-approach conflicts are minor, such as deciding which movie to see. Others can have major consequences, such as the conflict between building a promising career or interrupting that career to raise a child. In an **avoidance-avoidance conflict**, a person must choose between two undesirable alternatives. For example, you may want to avoid studying for an exam, but at the same time you want to avoid failing the test. An **approach-avoidance conflict** involves a single choice that has both desirable and undesirable features. The person facing this type of conflict is simultaneously drawn to and repelled by a choice—for example, wanting to take a wonderful vacation but having to empty a savings account to do so.

Situations in which we perceive ourselves to have no choice can be stressful as well. What happens, for example, when a student who is approaching graduation needs to take a certain course but finds that all the sections are full or that it won't be offered for another year? If you have had such an experience, then you won't be surprised to learn that humans who are warned of a stressor before it occurs and have a chance to prepare themselves for it experience less stress than those who must cope with an unexpected stressor.

approach-approach conflict

A conflict arising from having to choose between equally desirable alternatives.

avoidance-avoidance conflict

A conflict arising from having to choose between undesirable alternatives.

approach-avoidance conflict

A conflict arising when the same choice has both desirable and undesirable features.

Our physical and psychological well-being is profoundly influenced by the degree to which we feel a sense of control over our lives (Rodin & Salovey, 1989). Langer and Rodin (1976) studied the effects of control on nursing-home residents. Residents in one group were given some measure of control over their lives, such as choices in arranging their rooms and in the times they could see movies. They showed improved health and well-being and had a lower death rate than another group who were not given such control. Within 18 months, 30% of the residents given no choices had died, compared with only 15% of those who had been given some control over their lives. Control is important for cancer patients, too. Some researchers suggest that a sense of control over their daily physical symptoms and emotional reactions may be even more important for cancer patients than control over the course of the disease itself (Thompson et al., 1993).

Several studies suggest that we are less subject to stress when we have the power to do something about it, whether we exercise that power or not (John, 2004). Glass and Singer (1972) subjected two groups of participants to the same loud noise. Participants in one group were told that they could, if necessary, terminate the noise by pressing a switch. These participants suffered less stress, even though they never did exercise the control they were given. Friedland and others (1992) suggest that when people experience a loss of control because of a stressor, they are motivated to try to reestablish control in the stressful situation. Failing this, they often attempt to increase their sense of control in other areas of their lives.

STRESS IN THE WORKPLACE

> **10.4** For people to function effectively and find satisfaction on the job, what nine variables should fall within their comfort zone?

Have you ever had a boss who was difficult to work with? Perhaps you have had the misfortune to have worked under a supervisor who fit one of the "bully-boss" profiles that were discussed at the beginning of the chapter. If so, then you are well acquainted with the phenomenon of work-related stress. Of course, difficult bosses are only one source of on-the-job stress, and the amount and sources of stress differ across workers and employers. Albrecht (1979) suggested that if people are to function effectively and find satisfaction on the job, the following nine variables must fall within their comfort zone (see also Figure 10.1):

- *Workload.* Too much or too little to do can cause people to feel anxious, frustrated, and unrewarded.
- *Clarity of job description and evaluation criteria.* Anxiety arises from confusion about job responsibilities and performance criteria or from a job description that is too rigidly defined to leave room for individual initiative.

FIGURE 10.1 Variables in Work Stress
For a person to function effectively and find satisfaction on the job, these nine variables should fall within the person's comfort zone.

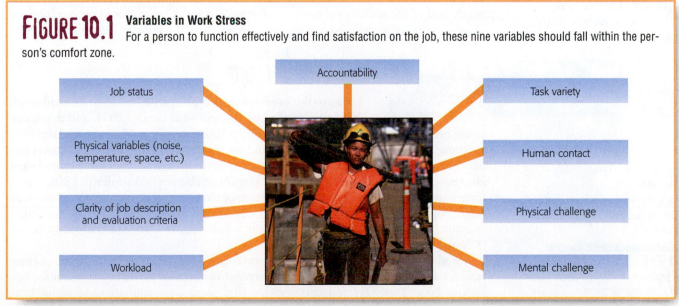

Accountability

Job status

Task variety

Physical variables (noise, temperature, space, etc.)

Human contact

Clarity of job description and evaluation criteria

Physical challenge

Workload

Mental challenge

Source: Albrecht (1979).

- *Physical variables.* Temperature, noise, humidity, pollution, amount of workspace, and the physical positions (standing or sitting) required to carry out job duties should fall within a person's comfort zone.
- *Job status.* People with very low-paying, low-status jobs may feel psychological discomfort; those with celebrity status often cannot handle the stress that fame brings.
- *Accountability.* Accountability overload occurs when people have responsibility for the physical or psychological well-being of others but only a limited degree of control (air-traffic controllers, emergency room nurses and doctors); accountability underload occurs when workers perceive their jobs as meaningless.
- *Task variety.* To function well, people need a comfortable amount of variety and stimulation.
- *Human contact.* Some workers have virtually no human contact on the job (forest-fire lookouts); others have almost continuous contact with others (welfare and employment office workers). People vary greatly in how much interaction they enjoy or even tolerate.
- *Physical challenge.* Jobs range from being physically demanding (construction work, professional sports) to requiring little to no physical activity. Some jobs (firefighting, police work) involve physical risk.
- *Mental challenge.* Jobs that tax people beyond their mental capability, as well as those that require too little mental challenge, can be frustrating.

Which of the nine work stress variables do you think cause the most stress for restaurant servers?

Workplace stress can be especially problematic for women because of sex-specific stressors, including sex discrimination and sexual harassment in the workplace and difficulties in combining work and family roles. These added stressors have been shown to increase the negative effects of occupational stress on the health and well-being of working women (Swanson, 2000).

Job stress can have a variety of consequences. Perhaps the most frequently cited is reduced effectiveness on the job. But job stress can also lead to absenteeism, tardiness, accidents, substance abuse, and lower morale (Wilhelm et al., 2004). Chronic stress can also lead to work-related **burnout** (Freudenberger & Richelson, 1981). People with burnout lack energy, feel emotionally drained, and are pessimistic about the possibility of changing their situations. People who feel that their work is unappreciated are more subject to burnout than others. For example, one survey suggested that nearly half of the social workers in the United Kingdom suffer from burnout, and the sense of being unappreciated was the best predictor of the condition (Evans et al., 2006).

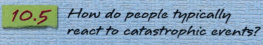

10.5 *How do people typically react to catastrophic events?*

burnout

Lack of energy, exhaustion, and pessimism that results from chronic stress.

posttraumatic stress disorder (PTSD)

A prolonged and severe stress reaction to a catastrophic event or to severe, chronic stress.

CATASTROPHIC EVENTS

Catastrophic events such as the terrorist attacks of September 11, 2001, the deadly Indian Ocean tsunami of 2004, and the devastating hurricanes that hit the Gulf Coast of the United States in 2005 are stressful both for those who experience them directly and for people who learn of them via news media. Most people are able to manage the stress associated with such catastrophes. However, for some, these events lead to **posttraumatic stress disorder (PTSD)**, a prolonged and severe stress reaction to a catastrophic event (such as a plane crash or an earthquake) or to severe, chronic stress (such as that experienced by soldiers engaged in combat or residents of neighborhoods in which violent crime is a daily occurrence) (Kilpatrick et al., 2003).

Studies show that the effects of such traumatic events can linger for years, particularly for those who have some kind of personal connection to them. For example, surveys of New York City residents indicate that some were continuing to suffer from symptoms of PTSD up to two years after the terrorist attacks of 2001 (Adams &

Boscarino, 2006). Moreover, PTSD sometimes does not appear until many years after an event has been experienced, and in some cases, it is triggered by the anniversary of a traumatic event. For example, mental health professionals in the United States reported that the number of World War II veterans seeking treatment from the Veterans Administration for war-related symptoms of PTSD increased substantially in the years that followed the fiftieth anniversary of the war's end in 1945 (Johnston, 2000). Researchers hypothesize that age-related changes in the brain lessened some older veterans' ability to manage the emotions that were associated with traumatic combat experiences, an effect that was particularly marked in veterans who also suffered from dementia.

People with PTSD often have flashbacks, nightmares, or intrusive memories that make them feel as though they are actually reexperiencing the traumatic event. They suffer increased anxiety and startle easily, particularly in response to anything that reminds them of the trauma (Green, Lindy, & Grace, 1985). Many survivors of war or catastrophic events experience *survivor guilt* because they lived while others died; some feel that perhaps they could have done more to save others. Extreme combat-related guilt in Vietnam veterans is a risk factor for suicide or preoccupation with suicide (Hendin & Haas, 1991). One study of women with PTSD revealed that they were twice as likely as women without PTSD to experience first-onset depression and three times as likely to develop alcohol problems (Breslau et al., 1997). PTSD sufferers also experience cognitive difficulties, such as poor concentration (Vasterling et al., 2002).

SOCIAL SOURCES OF STRESS

10.6 How do racism, socioeconomic status, and unemployment affect health?

There are many sources of stress that are associated with variations in social status. For example, members of ethnic minority groups are exposed to stressors that rarely affect the lives of those in the so-called dominant group. Likewise, aspects of economic status, such as poverty and unemployment, are also characterized by unique sources of stress.

Racism. Some theorists have proposed that a phenomenon called *historical racism*—experienced by members of groups that have a history of repression—can also be a source of stress (Troxel et al., 2003). Researchers interested in the effects of historical racism have focused primarily on African Americans. Many of these researchers claim that the higher incidence of high blood pressure among African Americans is attributable to stress associated with historical racism. Surveys have shown that African Americans experience more race-related stress than members of other minority groups do (Utsey et al., 2002). Those African Americans who express the highest levels of concern about racism display higher levels of cardiovascular reactivity to experimentally induced stressors, such as sudden loud noises, than do peers who express less concern (Bowen-Reid & Harrell, 2002). At least one study has demonstrated a correlation between African Americans' perceptions of racism and hypertension (Din-Dzietham et al., 2004). Researchers found that African Americans who reported the highest levels of race-related stressors in their workplaces were more likely to have high blood pressure than workers who reported fewer such stressors.

African Americans are also more likely than members of other minority groups to have a strong sense of ethnic identity, a factor that helps moderate the effects of racial stress (Utsey et al., 2002). But some studies show that personal characteristics, such as hostility, may increase the effects of racial stress (Fang & Myers, 2001; Raeikkoenen, Matthews, & Saloman, 2003). So, the relationship between historical racism and cardiovascular health is probably fairly complex and varies considerably across individuals. Moreover, some researchers believe that the association must be studied more thoroughly in other historically oppressed groups, such as Native Americans, before firm conclusions can be drawn (Belcourt-Dittloff & Stewart, 2000).

A strong sense of ethnic identity helps African Americans cope with the stress that may arise from living with racism.

socioeconomic status
A collective term for the economic, occupational, and educational factors that influence an individual's relative position in society.

Socioeconomic Status. The term **socioeconomic status** is often used to refer to differences in income levels, but it includes much more than just financial resources. Occupation and education are also important components of socioeconomic status, as is the more subjective variable of social status. These variables interact to influence the status that is assigned to an individual, and these interactions can vary differently from one setting to another. For example, in some neighborhoods, police officers have low status even though they may have more education and higher incomes than the people who live in the communities they serve. In other neighborhoods, police officers have high status despite having less education and lower incomes than many members of the community. Thus, socioeconomic status is a fairly complex variable.

Despite these complexities, large-scale studies of health and other variables of interest often rely on data such as income and educational level to sort people into socioeconomic status categories. When this technique is used, as you can probably predict, people who are low in socioeconomic status are usually found to more frequently suffer from stress-related health conditions such as colds and the flu. In addition, health risk factors such as high levels of LDL cholesterol are typically more common among them (Goodman et al., 2005).

Closer scrutiny of the variables associated with socioeconomic status reveals other factors that help us interpret links between socioeconomic status and health. For example, one frequent finding is that people of lower socioeconomic status have higher levels of stress hormones than people of higher status (Cohen, Doyle, & Baum, 2006). Looking further into this relationship, researchers have identified several behavioral and social factors among such people that help to explain the relationship between status and stress hormones. These factors included higher rates of smoking, more limited social networks, and less regular patterns of eating as compared to people at higher levels of socioeconomic status. This is not to say that these factors apply to everyone who has a low income, but they are found more frequently among those who are economically disadvantaged. Their presence affects the averages of health variables among low-income groups, thus creating correlations between socioeconomic status and these variables.

Unemployment. Finally, unemployment is another aspect of socioeconomic status that is related to stress and health. People who are forced out of their jobs experience heightened risks of stress-related illnesses in the months that follow (Crowley, Hayslip, & Hobdy, 2003; He, Colantonio, & Marshall, 2003; Isaksson et al., 2004). These effects are found among people of low, middle, and high socioeconomic status, by the way. This consistency is the result of the financial strain that accompanies the loss of income and the uncertainty about the future that is part of the experience of looking for a new job. These aspects of unemployment are stressful no matter how much money people made in their former jobs. However, unemployment is also stressful because it diminishes people's sense of control over what happens to them. And as you learned earlier in this chapter, perceived control is a good predictor of responses to stress.

RESPONDING TO STRESS

How do you respond to stress? Psychologists have different views of the ways in which people respond to stressful experiences. Each approach can help us gain insight into our own experiences and, perhaps, deal more effectively with stress.

general adaptation syndrome (GAS)
The predictable sequence of reactions (alarm, resistance, and exhaustion stages) that organisms show in response to stressors.

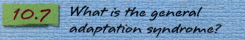 **10.7** What is the general adaptation syndrome?

THE GENERAL ADAPTATION SYNDROME

Hans Selye (1907–1982), the researcher most prominently associated with the effects of stress on health, established the field of stress research. At the heart of Selye's concept of stress is the **general adaptation syndrome (GAS)**, the predictable sequence of reactions that organisms show in response

FIGURE 10.2   The General Adaptation Syndrome

The three stages in Selye's general adaptation syndrome are (1) the alarm stage, during which there is emotional arousal and the defensive forces of the body are mobilized for fight or flight; (2) the resistance stage, in which intense physiological efforts are exerted to resist or adapt to the stressor; and (3) the exhaustion stage, when the organism fails in its efforts to resist the stressor.

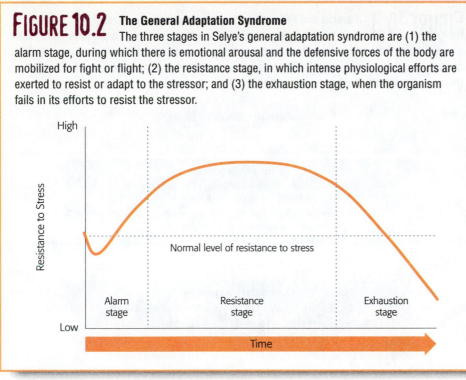

Source: Selye (1956).

to stressors. It consists of three stages: the alarm stage, the resistance stage, and the exhaustion stage (Selye, 1956). (See Figure 10.2)

The first stage of the body's response to a stressor is the **alarm stage**, in which the adrenal cortex releases hormones called *glucocorticoids* that increase heart rate, blood pressure, and blood-sugar levels, supplying a burst of energy that helps the person deal with the stressful situation (Pennisi, 1997). Next, the organism enters the **resistance stage**, during which the adrenal cortex continues to release glucocorticoids to help the body resist stressors. The length of the resistance stage depends both on the intensity of the stressor and on the body's power to adapt. If the organism finally fails in its efforts to resist, it reaches the **exhaustion stage**, at which point all the stores of deep energy are depleted, and disintegration and death follow.

Selye found that the most harmful effects of stress are due to the prolonged secretion of glucocorticoids, which can lead to permanent increases in blood pressure, suppression of the immune system, weakening of muscles, and even damage to the hippocampus (Stein-Behrens et al., 1994). Thanks to Selye, the connection between extreme, prolonged stress and certain diseases is now widely accepted by medical experts.

LAZARUS'S COGNITIVE THEORY OF STRESS

Is it the stressor itself that upsets us, or the way we think about it? Richard Lazarus (1966; Lazarus & Folkman, 1984) contends that it is not the stressor that causes stress but rather a person's perception of it. According to Lazarus, when people are confronted with a potentially stressful event, they engage in a cognitive process that involves a primary and a secondary appraisal. A **primary appraisal** is an evaluation of the meaning and significance of the situation—whether its effect on one's well-being is positive, irrelevant, or negative. An event appraised as stressful could involve (1) harm or loss—that is, damage that has already occurred; (2) threat, or the potential for harm or loss; or (3) challenge—that is, the opportunity to grow or to gain. An appraisal of threat, harm, or loss can occur in relation to anything important to you—a friendship, a part of your body, your

alarm stage
The first stage of the general adaptation syndrome, in which the person experiences a burst of energy that aids in dealing with the stressful situation.

resistance stage
The second stage of the general adaptation syndrome, when there are intense physiological efforts to either resist or adapt to the stressor.

exhaustion stage
The third stage of the general adaptation syndrome, which occurs if the organism fails in its efforts to resist the stressor.

10.8 What are the roles of primary and secondary appraisals when a person is confronted with a potentially stressful event?

primary appraisal
A cognitive evaluation of a potentially stressful event to determine whether its effect is positive, irrelevant, or negative.

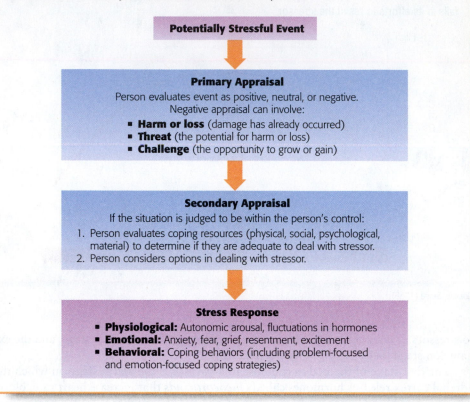

FIGURE 10.3 **Lazarus and Folkman's Psychological Model of Stress**
Lazarus and Folkman emphasize the importance of a person's perceptions and appraisal of stressors. The stress response depends on the outcome of the primary and secondary appraisals, whether the person's coping resources are adequate to cope with the threat, and how severely the resources are taxed in the process.

Potentially Stressful Event

Primary Appraisal
Person evaluates event as positive, neutral, or negative.
Negative appraisal can involve:
- **Harm or loss** (damage has already occurred)
- **Threat** (the potential for harm or loss)
- **Challenge** (the opportunity to grow or gain)

Secondary Appraisal
If the situation is judged to be within the person's control:
1. Person evaluates coping resources (physical, social, psychological, material) to determine if they are adequate to deal with stressor.
2. Person considers options in dealing with stressor.

Stress Response
- **Physiological:** Autonomic arousal, fluctuations in hormones
- **Emotional:** Anxiety, fear, grief, resentment, excitement
- **Behavioral:** Coping behaviors (including problem-focused and emotion-focused coping strategies)

Source: Folkman (1984).

secondary appraisal

A cognitive evaluation of available resources and options prior to deciding how to deal with a stressor.

coping

Efforts through action and thought to deal with demands that are perceived as taxing or overwhelming.

problem-focused coping

A direct response aimed at reducing, modifying, or eliminating a source of stress.

property, your finances, your self-esteem. When people appraise a situation as involving threat, harm, or loss, they experience negative emotions such as anxiety, fear, anger, and resentment (Folkman, 1984). An appraisal that sees a challenge, on the other hand, is usually accompanied by positive emotions such as excitement, hopefulness, and eagerness.

During **secondary appraisal**, if people judge the situation to be within their control, they make an evaluation of available resources—physical (health, energy, stamina), social (support network), psychological (skills, morale, self-esteem), material (money, tools, equipment), and time. Then, they consider the options and decide how to deal with the stressor. The level of stress they feel is largely a function of whether their resources are adequate to cope with the threat, and how severely those resources will be taxed in the process. Figure 10.3 summarizes the Lazarus and Folkman psychological model of stress. Research supports their claim that the physiological, emotional, and behavioral reactions to stressors depend partly on whether the stressors are appraised as challenging or threatening.

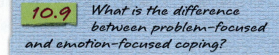
10.9 *What is the difference between problem-focused and emotion-focused coping?*

COPING STRATEGIES

If you're like most people, the stresses you have experienced have helped you develop some coping strategies. **Coping** refers to a person's efforts through action and thought to deal with demands perceived as taxing or overwhelming. **Problem-focused coping** is direct; it consists of reducing, modifying, or eliminating the source of stress itself. If you are getting a poor grade in history and appraise this as a threat, you may study harder, talk over your problem with your professor, form a study group with other class members, get a tutor, or drop the course (see the *Explain It*).

Explain It WHY DO POP QUIZZES FACILITATE LEARNING?

What happens when your professor walks into class and announces in a seemingly gleeful tone, "Good morning, class. We're going to start today with a pop quiz"? On hearing these words, you think back to your decision to watch a poker tournament on television instead of reading your assigned chapter, and your heart rate increases dramatically. This is a sure sign that your sympathetic nervous system has triggered the fight-or-flight response, and you are in the throes of a stressful experience. But you suppress the urge you feel to run from the room by resolving never to be caught off guard again in this particular class. The next time you are tempted to while away an evening in front of the television, you force yourself to study instead. How do the various types of coping come into play in this series of events?

As you have learned, emotion-focused coping is the strategy we use when we are faced with a stressor about which we can do little. Being faced with a pop quiz for which you are unprepared is just such a situation. To counter the fight-or-flight response, you modify your thinking about the situation in an effort to indirectly quell the tumultuous emotions you are experiencing. That's why your resolution to be better prepared next time around makes you feel better.

Problem-focused coping addresses the actual stressor and attempts to modify it. Obviously, resolving to be better prepared won't get the job done. You have to actually follow through on your goal. If you do, then you are engaging in problem-focused coping. In so doing, you are exerting some degree of control over the future appearance of this particular stressor. Recall from our discussion of controllability earlier in the chapter that we cope more effectively with stressors over which we believe we have control.

What do these coping strategies have to do with learning? To find out, we have to examine what might happen the next time your professor announces a pop quiz, assuming that you have kept your resolution to prepare for class. If you have read the assigned material, your emotional response to the quiz announcement is likely to be less intense than it was when you were unprepared. However, it is unlikely that you will perform well on the quiz unless you have actually learned the material. In other words, pop quizzes give prepared students feedback about the effectiveness of their study strategies. Presumably, if you took the time to prepare, but you are disappointed by your quiz grade, you will take steps to not only prepare for class but also to be certain that you are effectively processing what you read. This, of course, is exactly what professors are trying to get you to do when they employ pop quizzes as an instructional strategy. And research suggests that, whether professors count pop quizzes as regular grades or use them for extra credit, they are effective both for motivating students to prepare for class and for helping them learn (Ruscio, 2001; Thorne, 2000).

Emotion-focused coping involves reappraising a stressor to reduce its emotional impact. Research has shown that emotion-focused coping can be a very effective way of managing stress (Austenfeld & Stanton, 2004). If you lose your job, you may decide that it isn't a major tragedy and instead view it as a challenge, an opportunity to find a better job with a higher salary. Despite what you may have heard, ignoring a stressor—one form of emotion-focused coping—can be an effective way of managing stress. Researchers studied 116 people who had experienced heart attacks (Ginzburg, Soloman, & Bleich, 2002). All of the participants reported being worried about suffering another attack. However, those who tried to ignore their worries were less likely to exhibit anxiety-related symptoms such as nightmares and flashbacks. Other emotion-focused strategies, though, such as keeping a journal in which you write about your worries and track how they change over time, may be even more effective (Pennebaker & Seagal, 1999; Solano et al., 2003).

A combination of problem-focused and emotion-focused coping is probably the best stress-management strategy (Folkman & Lazarus, 1980). For example, a heart patient may ignore her anxiety (emotion-focused coping) while conscientiously adopting recommended lifestyle changes such as increasing exercise (problem-focused coping).

Review and Reflect on page 332 summarizes the key aspects of the various theories concerning humans' response to stress.

emotion-focused coping
A response involving reappraisal of a stressor to reduce its emotional impact.

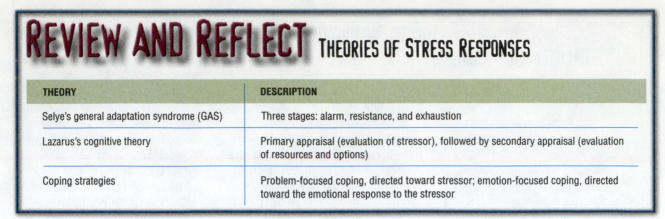

REVIEW AND REFLECT THEORIES OF STRESS RESPONSES

THEORY	DESCRIPTION
Selye's general adaptation syndrome (GAS)	Three stages: alarm, resistance, and exhaustion
Lazarus's cognitive theory	Primary appraisal (evaluation of stressor), followed by secondary appraisal (evaluation of resources and options)
Coping strategies	Problem-focused coping, directed toward stressor; emotion-focused coping, directed toward the emotional response to the stressor

HEALTH AND ILLNESS

Have you heard the term *wellness* and wondered exactly what was meant by it? This word is associated with a new approach to thinking about health, used by both professionals and laypersons. This approach encompasses a growing emphasis on lifestyle, preventive care, and the need to maintain wellness rather than thinking of health matters only when the body is sick. Health psychologists are discovering how stress, through its influence on the immune system, may affect people's health. They are also examining how personal and demographic factors are related to both illness and wellness.

10.10 How do the biomedical and biopsychosocial models differ in their approaches to health and illness?

biomedical model
A perspective that explains illness solely in terms of biological factors.

biopsychosocial model
A perspective that focuses on health as well as illness and holds that both are determined by a combination of biological, psychological, and social factors.

TWO APPROACHES TO HEALTH AND ILLNESS

For many decades, the predominant view in medicine was the **biomedical model**, which explains illness in terms of biological factors. Today, physicians and psychologists alike recognize that the **biopsychosocial model** provides a fuller explanation of both health and illness (see Figure 10.4) (Engel, 1977, 1980; Schwartz, 1982). This model considers health and illness to be determined by a combination of biological, psychological, and social factors.

Growing acceptance of the biopsychosocial approach has given rise to a new subfield, **health psychology**, which is "the field within psychology devoted to understanding psychological influences on how people stay healthy, why they become ill, and how they respond when they do get ill" (Taylor, 1991, p. 6). Health psychology is particularly important today because several prevalent diseases, including heart disease and cancer, are related to unhealthy lifestyles and stress (Taylor & Repetti, 1997).

10.11 What are the Type A, Type B, and Type D behavior patterns?

CORONARY HEART DISEASE

To survive, the heart muscle requires a steady, sufficient supply of oxygen and nutrients carried by the blood. Coronary heart disease is caused by the narrowing or the blockage of the coronary arteries, the arteries that supply blood to the heart muscle. Although coronary heart disease remains the leading cause of death in the United States, responsible for 24% of all deaths, deaths due to this cause have declined 50% during the past 30 years (National Center for Health Statistics, 2005).

A health problem of modern times, coronary heart disease is largely attributable to lifestyle and is therefore an important field of study for health psychologists. A *sedentary lifestyle*—one that includes a job at which one spends most of the time sitting and less than 20 minutes of exercise three times per week—is the primary modifiable risk factor

health psychology
The subfield within psychology that is concerned with the psychological factors that contribute to health, illness, and recovery.

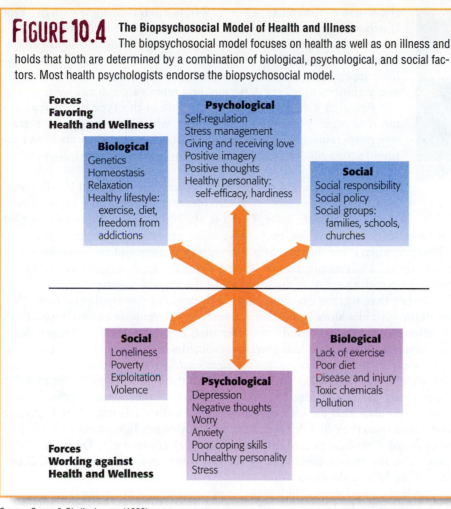

FIGURE 10.4 The Biopsychosocial Model of Health and Illness
The biopsychosocial model focuses on health as well as on illness and holds that both are determined by a combination of biological, psychological, and social factors. Most health psychologists endorse the biopsychosocial model.

Source: Green & Shellenberger (1990).

contributing to death from coronary heart disease (Gallo et al., 2003). Other modifiable risk factors are high serum cholesterol level, cigarette smoking, and obesity.

Though not modifiable, another important risk factor is family history. The association between family history and coronary heart disease is both genetic and behavioral. For instance, individuals whose parents have high blood pressure, but who have not yet developed the disorder themselves, exhibit the same kinds of emotional reactivity and poor coping strategies as their parents (Frazer, Larkin, & Goodie, 2002).

High levels of stress and job strain have also been associated with increased risk for coronary heart disease and stroke (Brydon, Magid, & Steptoe, 2006; Rosengren, Tibblin, & Wilhelmsen, 1991; Siegrist et al., 1990). Apparently, the effects of stress enter the bloodstream almost as if they were injected intravenously. Malkoff and others (1993) report that after an experimental group of participants had experienced laboratory-induced stress, their blood platelets (special clotting cells) released large amounts of a substance that promotes the buildup of plaque in blood vessels and may lead to heart attack and stroke. No changes were found in the blood platelets of unstressed control-group participants.

Personality type is also associated with an individual's risk of heart disease. After extensive research, cardiologists Meyer Friedman and Ray Rosenman (1974) concluded that there are two types of personality: Type A, associated with a high rate of coronary heart disease, and Type B, commonly found in persons unlikely to develop heart disease.

People with the **Type A behavior pattern** have a strong sense of time urgency and are impatient, excessively competitive, hostile, and easily angered. They are "involved in a chronic, incessant struggle to achieve more and more in less and less time"

Type A behavior pattern

A behavior pattern marked by a sense of time urgency, impatience, excessive competitiveness, hostility, and anger; considered a risk factor in coronary heart disease.

Hostility is a key component of the Type A behavior pattern.

Type B behavior pattern

A behavior pattern marked by a relaxed, easygoing approach to life, without the time urgency, impatience, and hostility of the Type A pattern.

Type D behavior pattern

People who exhibit chronic emotional distress combined with a tendency to suppress negative emotions.

(Friedman & Rosenman, 1974, p. 84). In contrast, people with the Type B behavior pattern are relaxed and easygoing and are not driven by a sense of time urgency. They are not impatient or hostile and are able to relax without guilt. They play for fun and relaxation rather than to exhibit superiority over others. Yet, a Type B individual may be as bright and ambitious as a Type A person, and more successful as well.

Research indicates that the lethal core of the Type A personality is not time urgency but anger and hostility, which fuel an aggressive, reactive temperament (Smith & Ruiz, 2002). These associations have been found across cultures and in both men and women (Mohan, 2006; Olson et al., 2005).

However, careful studies have shown that anger and hostility may be part of a larger complex of variables that includes other forms of emotional distress (Kubzansky et al., 2006; Olson et al., 2005). When anger and hostility are considered as single variables, both prove to be predictive of coronary heart disease. However, when other distress variables, such as anxiety and cynicism, are added to them, statistical analyses suggest that it is the whole cluster of negative emotions that best predicts heart disease rather than any one of the variables alone.

The finding that negative emotions collectively predict coronary disease better than any one of the variables alone has led some researchers to propose a new classification, Type D behavior pattern ("D" for distress; Denollet, 1997). People with this profile exhibit a chronic pattern of emotional distress combined with a tendency to suppress negative emotions. In one study of men who were enrolled in a rehabilitative therapy program after having had a heart attack, those with the Type D profile were found to have four times the risk of death as other patients in the program (Sher, 2004). Researchers speculate that the high mortality rate of individuals with Type D personality may come from their body's heightened tendency to produce an inflammatory response to invasive medical procedures such as surgery (Pedersen & Denollet, 2003). However, more research is needed before the physiology associated with Type D personality will be fully understood.

Whatever the physiological link between personality and coronary disease, its relationship to both health behaviors and social support may turn out to be equally important. For example, individuals who, like those with Type D personality, tend to have a negative view of life, are less likely to abstain from tobacco after completing a smoking cessation program (Hooten et al., 2005). Furthermore, researchers have found that Type D personality in the partners of patients who have coronary heart disease impair these partners' ability to be supportive (Pedersen, van Domburg, & Theuns, 2004). As you can see, the ramifications of personality for heart disease may turn out to be quite comprehensive. Hostility not only is highly predictive of coronary heart disease but also is associated with ill health in general (Miller et al., 1996).

10.12 *How do psychological factors influence cancer patients' quality of life?*

CANCER

Cancer is the second leading cause of death in the United States, accounting for 22% of all deaths (National Center for Health Statistics, 2004a). Cancer strikes frequently in the adult population, and about 30% of Americans—more than 75 million people—will develop cancer at some time in their lives. The young are not spared the scourge of cancer, for it takes the lives of more children aged 3 to 14 than any other disease.

Cancer, a collection of diseases rather than a single illness, can invade cells in any part of a living organism—humans, other animals, and even plants. Normal cells in all parts of the body divide, but fortunately they have built-in instructions about when to stop dividing. Unlike normal cells, cancer cells do not stop dividing. And, unless caught in time and destroyed, they continue to grow and spread, eventually killing the organism. Health psychologists point out that an unhealthy diet, smoking, excessive alcohol consumption, promiscuous sexual behavior, or becoming sexually active in the early teens (especially for females) are all behaviors that increase the risk of cancer.

The more than 1 million people in the United States who are diagnosed with cancer each year have the difficult task of adjusting to a potentially life-threatening disease and the chronic stressors associated with it. Thus, researchers claim that cancer patients need more than medical treatment. Their therapy should include help with psychological and behavioral factors that can influence their quality of life. Carver and others (1993) found that 3 months and 6 months after surgery, breast cancer patients who maintained an optimistic

This group of cancer patients is involved in art therapy, which is believed to lower the stress level associated with having a serious illness.

outlook, accepted the reality of their situation, and maintained a sense of humor experienced less distress. Patients who engaged in denial—refusal to accept the reality of their situation—and had thoughts of giving up experienced much higher levels of distress. Dunkel-Schetter and others (1992) found that the most effective elements of a strategy for coping with cancer were social support (such as through self-help groups), a focus on the positive, and distraction. Avoidant coping strategies such as fantasizing, denial, and social withdrawal were associated with more emotional distress.

THE IMMUNE SYSTEM AND STRESS

10.13 What are the effects of stress on the immune system?

Composed of an army of highly specialized cells and organs, the immune system works to identify and search out and destroy bacteria, viruses, fungi, parasites, and any other foreign matter that may enter the body. The key components of the immune system are white blood cells known as **lymphocytes**, which include B cells and T cells. *B cells* are so named because they are produced in the bone marrow. *T cells* derive their name from the thymus gland where they are produced. All cells foreign to the body, such as bacteria, viruses, and so on, are known as *antigens*. B cells produce proteins called *antibodies,* which are highly effective in destroying antigens that live in the bloodstream and in the fluid surrounding body tissues (Paul, 1993). For defeating harmful foreign invaders that have taken up residence inside the body's cells, however, T cells are critically important.

lymphocytes

The white blood cells—including B cells and T cells—that are the key components of the immune system.

Psychoneuroimmunology is a field of study in which psychologists, biologists, and medical researchers combine their expertise to learn the effects of psychological factors—emotions, thinking, and behavior—on the immune system (Fleshner & Laudenslager, 2004). Researchers now know that the immune system is not just a means for fighting off foreign invaders. Rather, it is an incredibly complex, interconnected defense system working with the brain to keep the body healthy (Ader, 2000).

psychoneuroimmunology

(sye-ko-NEW-ro-IM-you-NOLL-oh-gee) A field in which psychologists, biologists, and medical researchers combine their expertise to study the effects of psychological factors on the immune system.

Psychological factors, emotions, and stress are all related to immune system functioning (Robles, Glaser, & Kiecolt-Glaser, 2005). The immune system exchanges information with the brain, and what goes on in the brain can apparently enhance or suppress the immune system. Periods of high stress are correlated with increased symptoms of many infectious diseases, including oral and genital herpes, mononucleosis, colds, and flu. Stress may also decrease the effectiveness of certain kinds of vaccines (Miller et al., 2004; Moynihan et al., 2004) and decrease levels of the immune system's B and T cells. Kiecolt-Glaser and others (1996) found that elderly men and women experiencing chronic stress as a result of years of caring for a spouse with Alzheimer's disease showed an impaired immune response to flu shots. Physicians have long observed that stress and anxiety can worsen autoimmune diseases. And "if fear can produce relapses [in autoimmune diseases], then even the fear of a relapse may become a self-fulfilling prophecy" (Steinman, 1993, p. 112). Stress is also associated with an increase in illness behaviors—reporting physical symptoms and seeking medical care (Cohen & Herbert, 1996; Cohen & Williamson, 1991).

Stress has the power to suppress the immune system long after the stressful experience is over. An experimental group of medical students who were enduring the stress of major exams was compared with a control group of medical students who were on vacation from classes and exams. When tested for the presence of disease-fighting antibodies, participants in the exam group, but not those in the control group, had a significant reduction in their antibody count because of the stress. The lowered antibody count was still present 14 days after the exams were over. At that point, the students were not even aware that they were still stressed and reported feeling no stress (Deinzer et al., 2000).

In addition to academic pressures, poor marital relationships and sleep deprivation have been linked to lowered immune response (Kiecolt-Glaser et al., 1987; Maier & Laudenslager, 1985). Several researchers have reported that severe, incapacitating depression is also related to lowered immune system activity (Herbert & Cohen, 1993; Robles et al., 2006). For several months after the death of a spouse, the widow or widower suffers weakened immune system function and is at a higher risk of mortality. Severe bereavement weakens the immune system, increasing a person's chance of suffering from a long list of physical and mental ailments for as long as two years following a partner's death (Prigerson et al., 1997).

10.14 *What personal and social factors are associated with health and resistance to stress?*

REDUCING THE IMPACT OF STRESS AND ILLNESS

There are several personal factors that seem to offer protection against the effects of stress and illness. People who are generally optimistic tend to cope more effectively with stress, which in turn may reduce their risk of illness (Seligman, 1990). An important characteristic shared by optimists is that they generally expect good outcomes. Such positive expectations help make them more stress-resistant than pessimists, who tend to expect bad outcomes. Similarly, individuals who are optimistic seem to be able to find positives even in the darkest of circumstances (Rini et al., 2004). An especially lethal form of pessimism is hopelessness. A longitudinal study of a large number of Finnish men revealed that participants who reported feeling moderate to high hopelessness died from all causes at two to three times the rates of those reporting low or no hopelessness (Everson et al., 1996).

In addition, studying male executives with high levels of stress, psychologist Suzanne Kobasa (1979; Kobasa, Maddi, & Kahn, 1982) found three psychological characteristics that distinguished those who remained healthy from those who had a high incidence of illness. The three qualities, which she referred to collectively as **hardiness**, are *commitment, control,* and *challenge.* Hardy individuals feel a strong sense of commitment to both their work and their personal life. They see themselves not as victims of whatever life brings but as people who have control over consequences and outcomes. They act to solve their own problems, and they welcome challenges in life, viewing them not as threats but as opportunities for growth and improvement. Other researchers have found that the dimensions of hardiness are related to the subjective sense of well-being among the elderly (Smith, Young, & Lee, 2004).

hardiness

A combination of three psychological qualities—commitment, control, and challenge—shared by people who can handle high levels of stress and remain healthy.

Another personal factor that contributes to resistance to stress and illness is religious faith (Dedert et al., 2004; Miller & Thresen, 2003). A meta-analysis of 42 separate studies combined data on some 126,000 individuals and revealed that religious involvement is positively associated with measures of physical health and lower rates of cancer, heart disease, and stroke (McCullough et al., 2000). Why is religious involvement linked to health? Researchers are currently examining a number of hypotheses (Powell, Shahabi, & Thresen, 2003). One proposal is that individuals who frequent religious services experience proportionately more positive emotions than those who do not attend.

Other aspects of social involvement contribute to health as well. In one study, researchers gave volunteers nasal drops containing a cold virus. Within the next few days, symptoms of the viral infection rose sharply in some of the 151 women and 125 men who participated in the study, but less so or not at all in others. Participants with a rich social life in the form of frequent interactions with others—spouses, children, parents, co-workers, friends, and volunteer and religious groups—seemed to enjoy a powerful shield of protection against the virus infection. This pattern of protection held across age and racial groups, for both sexes, at all educational levels, and at every season of the year (Ader, 2000; Cohen et al., 1997).

Religious involvement may also provide people with a stronger form of social support than is available to those who are not religious (Seeman et al., 2003). **Social support** is support provided, usually in time of need, by a spouse, other family members, friends, neighbors, colleagues, support groups, or others. It can involve tangible aid, information, and advice, as well as emotional support. It can also be viewed as the feeling of being loved, valued, and cared for by those toward whom we feel a similar obligation.

A strong social support network can help a person recover faster from an illness.

social support

Tangible and/or emotional support provided in time of need by family members, friends, and others; the feeling of being loved, valued, and cared for by those toward whom we feel a similar obligation.

Social support appears to have positive effects on the body's immune system as well as on the cardiovascular and endocrine systems (Holt-Lunstad et al., 2003; Miller, Cohen, & Ritchey, 2002; Moynihan et al., 2004; Uchino, Cacioppo, & Kiecolt-Glaser, 1996). Social support may help encourage health-promoting behaviors and reduce the impact of stress so that people are less likely to resort to unhealthy methods of coping, such as smoking or drinking. Further, social support has been shown to reduce depression and enhance self-esteem in individuals who suffer from chronic illnesses such as kidney disease (Symister & Friend, 2003). A large study of soldiers who had enlisted in the U.S. Army showed that a high level of social support from peers was an essential ingredient in reducing stress (Bliese & Castro, 2000). People with social support recover more quickly from illnesses and lower their risk of death from specific diseases. Social support may even increase the probability of surviving a heart attack because it buffers the impact of stress on cardiovascular function (Steptoe, 2000).

GENDER AND HEALTH

10.15 How do males and females differ with regard to health?

Most medical research in the past, primarily funded by the U.S. government, rejected women as participants in favor of men (Matthews et al., 1997). One area where the failure to study women's health care needs has been particularly evident is in research examining mortality risk following open-heart surgery. Women are more likely to die after such surgery than are men. To date, studies have shown that the gender gap in surgical survival narrows with age, but researchers are still investigating why women's postsurgical mortality rate is higher than men's (Vaccarino et al., 2002).

In general, however, men have higher death rates from all causes than women do, although women tend to be less healthy. These seemingly contradictory findings have puzzled researchers for decades (Rieker & Bird, 2005). The finding that women are more likely than men are to seek medical care explains some of this difference (Addis & Mahalik, 2003). However, differences in care seeking fall short of fully explaining gender differences in illness and death.

In recent years, researchers have begun to examine how the progression of potentially fatal diseases varies across gender (Case & Paxson, 2004). For example, lung diseases that are caused by smoking afflict women and men about equally. However, for unknown reasons, men with these diseases are more seriously ill, as indicated by gender differences in the frequency of hospitalization, and males are more likely to die from them than are women. Researchers are looking at physiological gender differences such as hormone levels in search of explanations for these patterns. Some have also pointed out that interactions among gender differences in the physiological, psychological, and social domains must be examined as well (Rieker & Bird, 2005).

RACE AND HEALTH

Like gender, racial categories are associated with different patterns of health outcomes. Remember as you read that the methods used to collect health statistics often obscure important variations among subgroups of the five major groups—White Americans, African Americans, Hispanic Americans, Asian Americans and Pacific Islanders, and Native Americans—whose health is tracked by government agencies. Here are a few highlights from the many findings in this area.

Group Differences in Health. African Americans have higher rates of many chronic conditions than do White Americans. For example, they have higher rates of diabetes, arthritis, and high blood pressure (National Center for Health Statistics, 2005). African Americans are 40% more likely than White Americans to die of heart disease and 30% more likely to die of cancer. Even when African and White Americans of the same age suffer from similar illnesses, the mortality rate of African Americans is higher (CDC, 2003a). And the rate of AIDS is more than three times higher among African Americans than among White Americans.

Hispanic Americans account for more than 20% of new tuberculosis cases in the United States (CDC, 2003a). Hypertension and diabetes are also more prevalent among Hispanic Americans than among non-Hispanic White Americans, but heart problems are less prevalent (CDC, 2005a). Rates of diabetes are also dramatically higher among Native Americans than for other groups (CDC, 2005a). In addition, the infant mortality rate among Native Americans is two times higher than among Whites (CDC, 2005a).

Asian Americans are comparatively healthy. However, there are wide disparities among subgroups. For example, Vietnamese women are five times more likely to suffer from cervical cancer than White women are (CDC, 2005a). Similarly, the overall age-adjusted death rate for Asian American males is 40% lower than that for White American males, but their death rate from stroke is 8% higher.

Among Native Americans, cancer rates are higher than they are among other groups (NCHS, 2005). Public health officials attribute this difference to high smoking rates among Native Americans. As a result, Native Americans not only get more cancers than people in other groups, but about 10% of them also suffer from chronic lung diseases. Rates of diabetes are also dramatically higher among Native Americans than for other groups (CDC, 2003a).

Explaining Group Differences. How can such differences be explained? One health-related factor that distinguishes racial groups is the incidence of poverty (Franks, Gold, & Fiscella, 2003). About a quarter of African Americans, Native Americans, and Hispanic Americans live in poverty (U.S. Census Bureau, 2004b). Thus, we might conclude that variables related to poverty—nutritional status, access to health care, and education, for example—explain racial differences in health.

However, studies that provide us with a closer look at the links among race, income, and health suggest otherwise. For instance, in one study, researchers found that the general health of African American and White children from middle-class families was quite similar; however, the African American children had much higher rates of asthma than did the White children in the study (Weitzman, Byrd, & Auinger, 2005). Large-scale studies of health trends also show that poor White Americans and African Americans have similar rates of health-related activity limitations in old age (NCHS, 2005). However, the rate of such limitations is nearly 50% less among older Hispanic Americans who live in poverty.

As these findings illustrate, group differences in socioeconomic factors do not fully account for group differences in health, so what other variables might contribute to them? Bioethics professor Pilar Ossorio and sociologist Troy Duster suggest that the phenomenon of *racial patterning* underlies such differences (Ossorio & Duster, 2005). Racial patterning is the tendency of groups of people to maintain their collective identities through shared behavior patterns (e.g., diet). Moreover, groups tend to share certain aspects of living conditions that may have health consequences as well (e.g., the concentration of Hispanic Americans in the desert regions of the southwestern United States). As a result of these patterns, risk and protective factors occur at different rates in different groups.

LIFESTYLE AND HEALTH

Thanks to the proliferation of computers all over the world and to the availability of the World Wide Web, people who live in the industrialized nations of the world have something very important in common with those who live in the remotest regions of the developing world: a penchant for turning to the Internet for information about health (see the *Apply It;* Borzekowski, Fobil, & Asante, 2006; Fogel et al., 2002). If you have searched the Net for health information, you know that any health-related search term will turn up dozens of Web sites that remind you of what you probably already know: For most of us, health enemy number one is our own habits—lack of exercise, too little sleep, alcohol or drug abuse, an unhealthy diet, and overeating. What can make someone change an unhealthy lifestyle? Perhaps vanity is the key. Researchers have found that people are more likely to adopt healthy behaviors if they believe behavioral change will make them look better or appear more youthful than if they simply receive information about the health benefits of the suggested change (Mahler et al., 2003). Still, there are some health-threatening behaviors that carry such grave risks that everyone ought to take them seriously. The most dangerous unhealthy behavior of all is smoking.

Apply It — INTERPRETING HEALTH INFORMATION ON THE INTERNET

How reliable is the information available on the Internet? In a large-scale study of health-related Web sites sponsored by the American Medical Association, researchers found that the quality of information varied widely from one site to another (Eysenbach et al., 2002). A study of Internet-based advice for managing children's fever sponsored by the British Medical Association found that most Web sites contained erroneous information. Moreover, in a follow-up study done four years later, the researchers found that about half of the sites were no longer available; those that remained showed little improvement in the quality of information.

Despite these difficulties, physicians' organizations acknowledge the potential value of the Internet in helping patients learn about and manage their own health. And because so many older adults are using the Internet to learn about health issues, the American Association of Retired Persons (2002) has published a list of points to keep in mind when surfing the Web for health information and advice:

- *Remember that there are no rules governing what is published on the Internet.* Unlike scientific journal articles, which are usually written and reviewed by experts in the field, Internet articles can be posted by anyone, without review of any kind. Without expert knowledge, it is extremely difficult to tell whether the information and advice these articles contain are valid.

- *Consider the source.* Generally, Web sites sponsored by medical schools, government agencies, and public health organizations are reliable. Others, especially those promoting a health-related product, should be considered suspect.

- *Get a second opinion.* Ask your health care provider about Internet-based information or read what's available from several different sources on the topic.

- *Examine references.* Sites that refer to credible sources (e.g., books, other Web sites) that you can find on the Internet or in a library or bookstore are probably more reliable than sites that offer no references to support their advice.

- *How current is the information?* Health-related information changes frequently. Be certain that you are reading the most current findings and recommendations.

- *Is it too good to be true?* As in all areas of life, if something sounds too good to be true (e.g., a vitamin that cures cancer), it probably is. Try to find experimental, placebo-controlled studies that support any claims.

Using these guidelines, you can become a better consumer of Internet-based health information.

SMOKING AND HEALTH

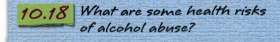

10.17 Why is smoking the most dangerous health-threatening behavior?

Smoking remains the foremost cause of preventable diseases and deaths in the United States (U.S. Department of Health and Human Services, 2000). That message appears to be taking root because the prevalence of smoking among American adults has been decreasing and is currently less than 25% (National Center for Health Statistics, 2005). Moreover, smoking is more likely to be viewed as a socially unacceptable behavior now than in the past (Chassin et al., 2003). But there are wide variations in smoking habits according to gender and ethnic group. The highest rates of smoking are found among Native American men (33%) and women (31%), while the lowest rates are reported for Asian American men (17%) and women (6%) (NCHS, 2005).

Even though the prevalence of smoking is decreasing, every year more than 1 million young Americans become regular smokers, and more than 400,000 American adults die from diseases related to tobacco use (U.S. Department of Health and Human Services, 2000). Smoking increases the risk for heart disease, lung cancer, other smoking-related cancers, and emphysema. It is now known that smoking suppresses the action of T cells in the lungs, increasing susceptibility to respiratory tract infections and tumors (McCue et al., 2000).

Other negative consequences from smoking include the widespread incidence of chronic bronchitis and other respiratory problems; the deaths and injuries from fires caused by smoking; and the low birth weight and retarded fetal development in babies born to smoking mothers. Furthermore, mothers who smoke during pregnancy tend to have babies who are at greater risk for anxiety and depression and are five times more likely to become smokers themselves (Cornelius et al., 2000). And millions of nonsmokers engage in *passive smoking* by breathing smoke-filled air—with proven ill effects. Research indicates that nonsmokers who are regularly exposed to *second hand smoke* have twice the risk of heart attack of those who are not exposed (National Center for Chronic Disease Prevention and Health Promotion, 2006).

There are many ways to quit smoking, but overall success rates for these methods, or for smoking cessation in general, can be somewhat misleading. There are many variables that affect success rates other than the desire to quit and the cessation method that a person chooses. Thus, if a study shows that only 20% of smokers using nicotine replacement, such as patches or chewing gum, succeed, reasons other than the purely physical aspects of nicotine addiction may be to blame (Rose, 2006).

The circumstances in smokers' lives may affect the outcome of their attempts to quit smoking. In one study involving more than 600 college students, researchers found that those who perceived that their lives were not very stressful had more success than other participants who felt more stress (Norman et al., 2006). Participants' overall success rate over the 18-month-long study was only 18%, but the low-perceived-stress group achieved a success rate of 52%. By contrast, only 13% of participants who perceived their lives to be highly stressful managed to quit in 18 months. The implication of these findings for others who want to quit smoking is that the often-heard recommendation that they choose a "quit date" is probably good advice. Planning a quit date to coincide with times of reduced stress, such as immediately after final exams, might be better than trying to quit at times of great stress.

ALCOHOL ABUSE

10.18 What are some health risks of alcohol abuse?

Do you use alcohol regularly? Many Americans do. Recall from Chapter 4 that *substance abuse* is defined as continued use of a substance that interferes with a person's major life roles at home, in school, at work, or elsewhere and contributes to legal difficulties or any psychological problems (American Psychiatric Association, 2000a). Alcohol is perhaps the most frequently abused substance of all, and the health costs of alcohol abuse are staggering—in fatalities, medical bills, lost work, and family problems.

When consumed to excess, alcohol can damage virtually every organ in the body, but it is especially harmful to the liver. Moreover, even a person who has never previously had a drink in his or her life can die from ingesting too much alcohol over a short period of time (see Table 10.2). One Norwegian longitudinal study involving more than 40,000 male participants found that the rate of death prior to age 60 was significantly higher among alcoholics than nonalcoholics (Rossow & Amundsen, 1997). Alcoholics are about three times as likely to die in automobile accidents or of heart disease as nonalcoholics, and they have twice the rate of deaths from cancer.

Damage to the brains of alcoholics has been found by researchers using MRI scans (Dauringac et al., 2005). CT scans also show brain shrinkage in a high percentage of alcoholics, even in those who are young and in those who show normal cognitive functioning (Lishman, 1990). Moreover, heavy drinking can cause cognitive impairment that continues for several months after the drinking stops (Sullivan et al., 2002). The only good news in recent studies is that some of the effects of alcohol on the brain seem to be partially reversible with prolonged abstinence.

Since the late 1950s, the American Medical Association has maintained that alcoholism is a disease and that once an alcoholic, always an alcoholic. According to this view, even a small amount of alcohol can cause an irresistible craving for more, leading alcoholics to lose control of their drinking (Jellinek, 1960). Thus, total abstinence is seen as the only acceptable and effective method of treatment. Alcoholics Anonymous (AA) also endorses both the disease concept and the total abstinence approach to treatment. And there is a drug that may make abstinence somewhat easier. Researchers report that the drug acamprosate helps prevent relapse in recovering alcoholics (Mason et al., 2006).

Some studies suggest a genetic influence on alcoholism and lend support to the disease model. For example, neuroscientist Henri Begleiter and his colleagues have accumulated a large body of evidence suggesting that the brains of alcoholics respond differently to visual and auditory stimuli than those of nonalcoholics (Hada et al., 2000,

TABLE 10.2 Alcohol Poisoning

How much alcohol does it take to cause alcohol poisoning?
- This varies according to weight and tolerance for alcohol.
- Eight to ten drinks in one hour is sufficient to induce alcohol poisoning in anyone.

Are there any quick ways to sober up?
- No. There is no way to speed up elimination of alcohol from the body.
- Coffee, cold showers, walking it off, and sleeping it off don't work.

What are the signs of alcohol poisoning?
- Confusion, stupor, coma, or person can't be roused
- No response to pinching the skin
- Vomiting while asleep
- Seizures
- Slow breathing (fewer than 8 breaths per minute)
- Irregular breathing (10 seconds or more between breaths)
- Low body temperature, bluish skin, paleness

What should I do if I think someone has alcohol poisoning?
- Call 911.
- Stay with the person.
- Keep the person from choking on vomit.
- Tell paramedics how much and what type of alcohol the person drank.

Source: National Highway and Traffic Safety Administration (2007).

2001; Prabhu et al., 2001). Further, many relatives of alcoholics, even children and adults who have never consumed any alcohol in their lives, display the same types of response patterns (Kamarajan et al., 2006; Zhang et al., 2001). The relatives of alcoholics who do display these patterns are more likely to become alcoholics themselves or to suffer from other types of addictions (Anokhin et al., 2000; Beirut et al., 1998). Consequently, Begleiter has suggested that the brain-imaging techniques he uses in his research may someday be used to determine which relatives of alcoholics are genetically predisposed to addiction (Porjesz et al., 1998).

10.19 *What is the difference between bacterial and viral STDs?*

SEXUALLY TRANSMITTED DISEASES

What is the most common infectious disease in the United States? You might be surprised to learn that it is *chlamydia*, a sexually transmitted disease (CDC, 2005d). **Sexually transmitted diseases (STDs)** are infections spread primarily through sexual contact. Each year, approximately 15 million Americans contract an STD. The incidence of many STDs has increased dramatically over the past 30 years or so. This trend can be partly explained by more permissive attitudes toward sex and increased sexual activity among young people, some of whom have had several sexual partners by the time they graduate from high school (look back at Figure 8.4 on page 262). Another factor is the greater use of nonbarrier methods of contraception, such as the birth control pill, which do not prevent the spread of STDs. Barrier methods, such as condoms and vaginal spermicide, provide some protection against STDs.

Chlamydia is one of many **bacterial STDs**, diseases that can be cured by antibiotics. It can be transmitted through many kinds of physical contact involving the genitals as well as actual intercourse (CDC, 2005d). Women are about three times as likely as men to suffer from chlamydia. The prevalence of another bacterial STD, *gonorrhea,* has declined considerably in recent years, but the strains that exist today are far more resistant to antibiotics than those that existed decades ago (CDC, 2005d). One of the long-term effects of both chlamydia and gonorrhea is *pelvic inflammatory disease,* an infection of the female reproductive tract that can cause infertility.

Another bacterial STD is *syphilis,* which can lead to serious mental disorders and death if it is not treated in the early stages of infection. At one time, syphilis had been almost completely eradicated. However, in 2004, about 8,000 cases were reported to the Centers for Disease Control and Prevention (CDC, 2005d). Most of these cases involved homosexual males who live in urban areas (CDC, 2005d). Educating such men about the dangers of syphilis and measures that may be taken to prevent its transmission has become a major focus of public health officials in recent years.

Unlike STDs caused by bacteria, **viral STDs** cannot be treated with antibiotics and are considered to be incurable. One such disease is *genital herpes,* a disease that can be acquired through either intercourse or oral sex. The Centers for Disease Control and Prevention reports that 20% of the adult population in the United States is infected with herpes (CDC, 2001a). Outbreaks of the disease, which include the development of painful blisters on the genitals, occur periodically in most people who carry the virus.

A more serious viral STD is *genital warts* caused by infection with *human papillomavirus (HPV).* The primary symptom of the disease, the presence of growths on the genitals, is not its most serious effect, however. HPV is strongly associated with cervical cancer (CDC, 2003c). Studies indicate that, in the United States, 25% of women in their twenties and 10% of women older than the age of 30 are infected with HPV (Stone et al., 2002).

Recently, the Food and Drug Administration approved a vaccine that officials believe will protect young women against four types of HPV (CDC, 2006a). However, the vaccine is licensed for use only in females between the ages of 9 and 26, and researchers do not yet know how long the vaccine's protective effects will last. Moreover, officials point out that there are other forms of HPV against which the vaccine offers no protection. For these reasons, public health officials state that women who get the vaccine should continue to be vigilant about safe sex practices and routine medical screening.

The most feared STD is **acquired immune deficiency syndrome (AIDS)**, caused by infection with the **human immunodeficiency virus (HIV)**. The virus attacks the immune sys-

---

sexually transmitted diseases (STDs)
Infections that are spread primarily through intimate sexual contact.

bacterial STDs
Sexually transmitted diseases that are caused by bacteria and can be treated with antibiotics.

viral STDs
Sexually transmitted diseases that are caused by viruses and are considered to be incurable.

acquired immune deficiency syndrome (AIDS)
A devastating and incurable illness that is caused by infection with the human immunodeficiency virus (HIV) and progressively weakens the body's immune system, leaving the person vulnerable to opportunistic infections that usually cause death.

human immunodeficiency virus (HIV)
The virus that causes AIDS.

Try It — AIDS QUIZ

Answer *true* or *false* for each statement.

1. AIDS is a single disease. (true/false)
2. AIDS symptoms vary widely from country to country and even from risk group to risk group. (true/false)
3. Those at greatest risk for getting AIDS are people who have sex without using condoms, drug users who share needles, and infants born to AIDS-infected mothers. (true/false)
4. AIDS is one of the most highly contagious diseases. (true/false)
5. One way to avoid contracting AIDS is to use an oil-based lubricant with a condom. (true/false)

Answers:

1. *False:* AIDS is not a single disease. Rather, a severely impaired immune system leaves a person with AIDS highly susceptible to a whole host of infections and diseases.
2. *True:* In the United States and Europe, AIDS sufferers may develop Kaposi's sarcoma (a rare form of skin cancer), pneumonia, and tuberculosis. In Africa, people with AIDS usually waste away with fever, diarrhea, and symptoms caused by tuberculosis.
3. *True:* Those groups are at greatest risk. Screening of blood donors and testing of donated blood have greatly reduced the risk of contracting AIDS through blood transfusions. Today, women make up the fastest-growing group of infected people worldwide, as AIDS spreads among heterosexuals, especially in Africa.
4. *False:* AIDS is not among the most highly infectious diseases. You cannot get AIDS from kissing, shaking hands, or using objects handled by people who have AIDS.
5. *False:* Do not use oil-based lubricants, which can eat through condoms. Latex condoms with an effective spermicide are safer. Learn the sexual history of any potential partner, including HIV test results. Don't have sex with prostitutes.

mypsychlab Where learning comes to life!

GO TO www.mypsychlab.com to view an "It" video related to this topic.

tem until it is essentially nonfunctional. Although the first case was diagnosed in this country in 1981, there is still no cure for AIDS. Test your knowledge about AIDS in *Try It*.

The long search for effective treatments for HIV, chronicled in Figure 10.5 on page 344, has produced two major victories. First, the discovery that drugs such as AZT can prevent the transmission of HIV from a pregnant woman to her fetus has saved thousands of lives. During the 1990s, nearly 2,000 infants were diagnosed with HIV each year. Thanks to widespread prenatal HIV screening and to the availability of these preventive drugs, just under 100 infants were diagnosed with HIV in 2004 (CDC, 2006c).

Second, the advent of *antiretroviral drugs* has probably prevented millions of deaths from AIDS by interfering with HIV's ability to invade healthy cells, the process through which HIV destroys its victims' immune systems. At present, the United Nations, aided by the World Bank, governments throughout the industrialized world, corporations, charitable foundations, and celebrity spokespersons, such as U2 singer Bono, is working to provide the funding needed to supply antiretroviral drugs to developing regions in which HIV-infection rates are particularly high, such as sub-Saharan Africa (Global Fund to Fight AIDS, Tuberculosis, and Malaria, 2005; Merson, 2006).

Researchers believe that HIV is transmitted primarily through the exchange of blood, semen, or vaginal secretions during sexual contact or when IV (intravenous) drug users share contaminated needles or syringes. Figure 10.6 on page 345 illustrates the proportion of AIDS cases attributable to each means of transmitting the disease. Although HIV/AIDS rates are higher among men who have sex with men, it is a mistake to think of it as a men's disease. About 30% of AIDS sufferers are women (CDC, 2004b).

What are the psychological effects on people who struggle to cope with this fearsome disease? The reaction to the news that one is HIV-positive is frequently shock, bewilderment, confusion, or disbelief. Stress reactions to the news are typically so common and so acute that experts strongly recommend pretest counseling so that those who do test positive may know in advance what to expect (Maj, 1990). Another common reaction is anger—at past or present sexual partners, family members, health care professionals, or society in general. Often, a person's response includes guilt, a sense that one is being punished for homosexuality or drug abuse. Other people exhibit denial,

FIGURE 10.5   Milestones from the History of HIV/AIDS

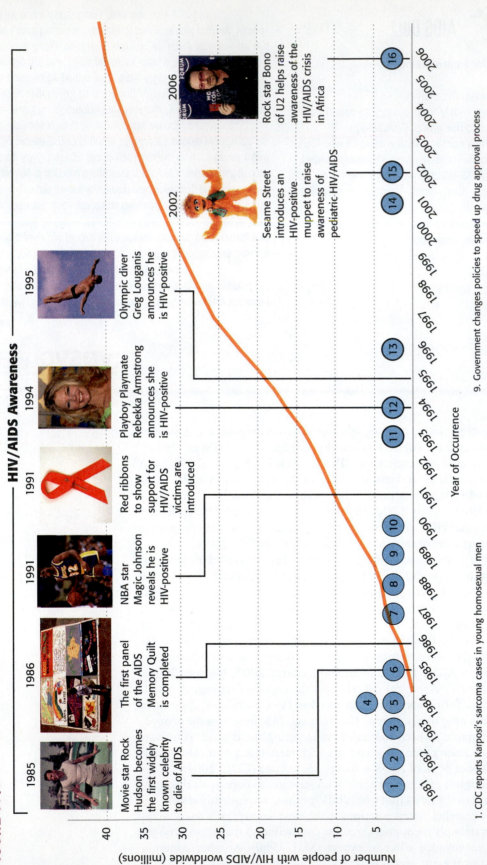

HIV/AIDS Awareness

1985 — Movie star Rock Hudson becomes the first widely known celebrity to die of AIDS

1986 — The first panel of the AIDS Memory Quilt is completed

1991 — NBA star Magic Johnson reveals he is HIV-positive

1991 — Red ribbons to show support for HIV/AIDS victims are introduced

1994 — Playboy Playmate Rebekka Armstrong announces she is HIV-positive

1995 — Olympic diver Greg Louganis announces he is HIV-positive

2002 — Sesame Street introduces an HIV-positive muppet to raise awareness of pediatric HIV/AIDS

2006 — Rock star Bono of U2 helps raise awareness of the HIV/AIDS crisis in Africa

Number of people with HIV/AIDS worldwide (millions)

40 / 35 / 30 / 25 / 20 / 15 / 10 / 5

Year of Occurrence

1981 1982 1983 1984 1985 1986 1987 1988 1989 1990 1991 1992 1993 1994 1995 1996 1997 1998 1999 2000 2001 2002 2003 2004 2005 2006

1. CDC reports Karposi's sarcoma cases in young homosexual men
2. CDC names and defines Acquired Immune Deficiency Syndrome (AIDS)
3. Officials warn public about infection risk associated with blood transfusions
4. Researchers identify HIV as cause of AIDS
5. Officials issue advisories about infection risk associated with IV-drug use
6. Blood banks begin screening supplies for HIV
7. FDA approves experimental drugs for AIDS
8. CDC mails brochure about HIV/AIDS to every home in the United States
9. Government changes policies to speed up drug approval process
10. FDA approves AZT treatment for children with HIV
11. Government launches large-scale studies on women with HIV/AIDS
12. FDA approves AZT for pregnant women with HIV
13. HIV/AIDS cases decline for the first time since 1982 in the U.S.
14. Lower-cost generic drugs for HIV/AIDS become available
15. FDA approves first finger-prick test for HIV
16. FDA approves triple-drug therapy

Source: CDC (2001).

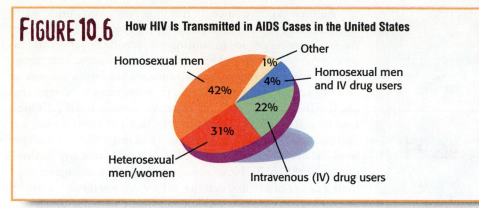

FIGURE 10.6 How HIV Is Transmitted in AIDS Cases in the United States

Homosexual men 42%

Other 1%

Homosexual men and IV drug users 4%

22%

Heterosexual men/women 31%

Intravenous (IV) drug users

Source: CDC (2004)

ignoring medical advice and continuing to act as if nothing has changed in their lives. Then, of course, there is fear—of death; of mental and physical deterioration; of rejection by friends, family, and co-workers; of sexual rejection; of abandonment. Experiencing emotional swings ranging from shock to anger to guilt to fear can lead to serious clinical depression and apathy (Tate et al., 2003). Once apathy sets in, HIV-positive patients may become less likely to comply with treatment (Dorz et al., 2003).

To cope psychologically, AIDS patients, those infected with HIV, and their loved ones need education and information about the disease. They can be helped by psychotherapy, self-help groups, and medications such as antidepressants and anti-anxiety drugs. Self-help groups and group therapy may serve as an extended family for some patients.

DIET AND EXERCISE

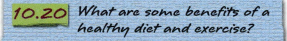

10.20 What are some benefits of a healthy diet and exercise?

In Chapter 9, you learned about obesity as it relates to the primary motive of hunger and that a BMI in excess of 30 is considered obese. Obesity increases a person's chances of developing several chronic diseases (CDC, 2006e). These conditions include high blood pressure, type 2 diabetes, gallbladder disease, arthritis, and respiratory disorders. In addition, people who are obese are more likely to develop coronary heart disease and to have elevated levels of LDL cholesterol (the bad cholesterol that is associated with heart disease).

Health problems may also develop in people whose diets have insufficient amounts of particular nutrients (CDC, 2006e). For example, a diet that is deficient in iron leads to *anemia,* a condition that impairs the blood's ability to deliver oxygen to the body's organs. Likewise, a diet that lacks sufficient calcium may cause degeneration of the bones. And pregnant women whose diets lack folic acid are more likely to deliver infants with spinal defects.

People who regularly consume fast foods are at risk for both obesity and specific nutritional deficiencies. Thus, nutrition experts recommend that such food be eaten infrequently or not at all. To help consumers achieve this goal, experts have also developed several strategies for improving overall diet quality. One simple approach is the "5-a-day" plan in which people are advised to try to eat at least five servings of fruits and vegetables every day. Another involves reading the labels of processed foods and avoiding those that are high in saturated fats, trans fats, and sodium, all of which are associated with high levels of LDL cholesterol. Labels can also guide people to foods that are high in monosaturated fats, a type of fat that may increase levels of HDL cholesterol (the good cholesterol).

Studies show that regular exercise also pays rich dividends in the form of physical and mental fitness. However, many people still express reluctance to exercise. More than 30% of Americans get no exercise at all (National Center for Health Statistics, 2004a). Some simply prefer not to be physically active; others blame such factors as the cost of joining a health club or even the unpredictability of the weather for their lack of physical activity (Salmon et al., 2003). Such individuals are missing out on one of the simplest and most effective ways of enhancing one's health.

Regular aerobic exercise improves cardiovascular fitness in people of all ages.

aerobic exercise

(ah-RO-bik) Exercise that uses the large muscle groups in continuous, repetitive action and increases oxygen intake and breathing and heart rates.

Aerobic exercise (such as running, swimming, brisk walking, bicycling, rowing, and jumping rope) is exercise that uses the large muscle groups in continuous, repetitive action and increases oxygen intake and breathing and heart rates. To improve cardiovascular fitness and endurance and to lessen the risk of heart attack, an individual should perform aerobic exercise regularly—five times a week for 20 to 30 minutes (CDC, 2006b). Less than 20 minutes of aerobic exercise three times a week has "no measurable effect on the heart," and more than 3 hours per week "is not known to reduce cardiovascular risk any further" (Simon, 1988, p. 3). However, individuals who engage in more than 3 hours of aerobic activity each week are more successful at losing excess weight and keeping it off than are those who exercise less (Votruba, Horvitz, & Schoeller, 2000).

In case you are not yet convinced, consider the following benefits of exercise (Fiatarone et al., 1988):

- Increases the efficiency of the heart, enabling it to pump more blood with each beat, and reduces the resting pulse rate and improves circulation
- Raises levels of HDL (the good blood cholesterol), which (1) helps rid the body of LDL (the bad blood cholesterol) and (2) removes plaque buildup on artery walls
- Burns up extra calories, enabling you to lose weight or maintain your weight
- Makes bones denser and stronger, helping to prevent osteoporosis in women
- Moderates the effects of stress
- Gives you more energy and increases your resistance to fatigue
- Benefits the immune system by increasing natural killer cell activity

Exercise also appears to moderate the effects of aging on the body. Strength training, for example, has been found to reduce *sarcopenia,* an age-related process in which the muscles deteriorate (CDC, 2006b). Such training appears to prevent the loss of bone mass, or *osteoporosis,* as well. Moreover, physical exercise helps seniors with balance, coordination, and stamina.

10.21 *What are the benefits and risks associated with alternative medicine?*

alternative medicine

Any treatment or therapy that has not been scientifically demonstrated to be effective.

ALTERNATIVE MEDICINE

Americans spend billions of dollars each year on unconventional treatments—herbs, massage, self-help groups, megavitamins, folk remedies, and homeopathy—for a variety of illnesses and conditions. In one such survey, the National Science Foundation (NSF, 2002) found that 88% of Americans believe that there are valid ways of preventing and curing illnesses that are not recognized by the medical profession. Moreover, a growing number of people are turning to alternative health care providers for treatment of their mental health problems (Simon et al., 2004). And college-educated Americans are more likely to use unconventional treatments than those who have less education.

The National Science Foundation (2002) defines **alternative medicine** as any treatment or therapy that has not been scientifically demonstrated to be effective. Even a simple practice such as taking vitamins sometimes falls into this category. For instance, if you take Vitamin C to protect yourself against the common cold, you are using alternative medicine because Vitamin C has not been scientifically proven to prevent colds.

Most patients who use alternative treatments do not inform their physicians about them. Health professionals cite this tendency toward secrecy as a major risk factor in the use of alternative medicine (Yale-New Haven Hospital, 2003). They point out that many therapies, especially those that involve food supplements, have pharmacological effects that can interfere with treatments prescribed by physicians. Consequently, individuals who use alternative treatments should tell their physicians about them. While doctors may be skeptical about the utility of the alternative treatments, they need to have this information about their patients to practice conventional medicine effectively. Moreover, faith in an alternative treatment may cause an individual to delay seeking necessary conventional medical treatment.

Although it is true that some alternative therapies may be helpful in both preventing and treating illness, most health professionals agree that lifestyle changes bring greater health benefits than do any methods of alternative medicine. Unfortunately, many people resist making lifestyle changes because they see them as taking too long to be effective or being too difficult to carry out. However, Table 10.3 shows that the benefits of various lifestyle changes, some of which are fairly easy to achieve, can be well worth the effort.

Many individuals turn to vitamins and other nutritional supplements to improve their health and fight disease. These substances can interact with prescription medications, so health care professionals strongly recommend that patients inform their doctors if they are taking some kind of supplement.

TABLE 10.3 Benefits of Lifestyle Changes

LIFESTYLE CHANGE	BENEFITS
If overweight, lose just 10 pounds.	34% reduction in triglyceride levels; 16% decrease in total cholesterol; 18% increase in HDL ("good" cholesterol); significant reduction in blood pressure; decreased risk of diabetes, sleep apnea, and osteoarthritis (Still, 2001).
Add 20 to 30 grams of fiber to your diet each day.	Improved bowel function; reduced risk of colon cancer and other digestive system diseases; decrease in total cholesterol; reduced blood pressure; improved insulin function in both diabetics and non-diabetics (HCF, 2003).
Engage in moderate physical activity every day (e.g., walk up and down stairs for 15 minutes; spend 30 minutes washing a car).	Reduced feelings of anxiety and sadness; increased bone density; reduced risk of diabetes, heart disease, high blood pressure, and many other life-shortening diseases (CDC, 1999).
Stop smoking at any age, after any number of years of smoking.	*Immediate:* improved circulation; reduced blood level of carbon monoxide; stabilization of pulse rate and blood pressure; improved sense of smell and taste; improved lung function and endurance; reduced risk of lung infections such as pneumonia and bronchitis. *Long-term:* reduced risk of lung cancer (declines substantially with each year of abstinence); decreased risk of other smoking-related illnesses such as emphysema and heart disease; decreased risk of cancer recurrence in those who have been treated for some form of cancer (National Cancer Institute, 2000).

In the section of this chapter that discussed stress, you learned that exerting control over controllable stressors can help you cope. The same is true of health. And, although the list of lifestyle changes in Table 10.3 may be intimidating, you need not make all of them to improve your chances of a healthy future. You might consider starting with just one. Even if you never make another change, you are likely to live longer and be healthier than you would have otherwise been.

CHAPTER 10 SUMMARY

SOURCES OF STRESS p. 322

10.1 What was the Social Readjustment Rating Scale designed to reveal? p. 322
The SRRS assesses stress in terms of life events, positive or negative, that necessitate change and adaptation. Holmes and Rahe found a relationship between degree of life stress (as measured on the scale) and major health problems.

10.2 What roles do hassles and uplifts play in the stress of life, according to Lazarus? p. 323
According to Lazarus, daily hassles typically cause more stress than major life changes. Positive experiences in life—or uplifts—can neutralize the effects of many of the hassles, however.

10.3 How do choice-related conflicts and lack of control contribute to stress? p. 324
In an approach-approach conflict, a person must decide between equally desirable alternatives. In an avoidance-avoidance conflict, the choice is between two undesirable alternatives. In an approach-avoidance conflict, a person is both drawn to and repelled by a single choice. Stressors that are unpredictable and uncontrollable have greater impact than those that are predictable and controllable.

10.4 For people to function effectively and find satisfaction on the job, what nine variables should fall within their comfort zone? p. 325
The nine variables that should fall within a worker's comfort zone are workload, clarity of job description and evaluation criteria, physical variables, job status, accountability, task variety, human contact, physical challenge, and mental challenge.

10.5 How do people typically react to catastrophic events? p. 326
Most people cope quite well with catastrophic events. However, some people develop posttraumatic stress disorder (PTSD), a prolonged, severe stress reaction, often characterized by flashbacks, nightmares, or intrusive memories of the traumatic event.

10.6 How do racism, socioeconomic status, and unemployment affect health? p. 327
Some researchers believe that African Americans have higher levels of high blood pressure than members of other groups because of stress due to historical racism. People of low socioeconomic status have more stress-related health problems than those of higher status. Perceived status may predict these outcomes better than objective status. Unemployment is another status variable that is related to health.

RESPONDING TO STRESS p. 328

10.7 What is the general adaptation syndrome? p. 328
The general adaptation syndrome (GAS) proposed by Selye is the predictable sequence of reactions that organisms show in response to stressors. It consists of the alarm stage, the resistance stage, and the exhaustion stage.

10.8 What are the roles of primary and secondary appraisals when a person is confronted with a potentially stressful event? p. 329
Lazarus maintains that, when confronted with a potentially stressful event, a person engages in a cognitive appraisal process consisting of (1) a primary appraisal, to evaluate the relevance of the situation to one's well-being (whether it will be positive, irrelevant, or negative), and (2) a secondary appraisal, to evaluate one's resources and determine how to cope with the stressor.

10.9 What is the difference between problem-focused and emotion-focused coping? p. 330
Problem-focused coping is a direct response, aimed at reducing, modifying, or eliminating the source of stress; emotion-focused coping involves reappraising a stressor in an effort to reduce its emotional impact.

HEALTH AND ILLNESS p. 332

10.10 How do the biomedical and biopsychosocial models differ in their approaches to health and illness? p. 332
The biomedical model focuses on illness rather than on health and explains illness in terms of biological factors. The biopsychosocial model focuses on health as well as on illness and holds that both are determined by a combination of biological, psychological, and social factors.

10.11 What are the Type A, Type B, and Type D behavior patterns? p. 332
The Type A behavior pattern, often cited as a risk factor for coronary heart disease, is characterized by a sense of time urgency, impatience, excessive competitive drive, hostility, and easily aroused anger. The Type B behavior pattern is characterized by a relaxed, easy-going approach to life, without the time urgency, impatience, and hostility of the Type A pattern. People with Type D behavior patterns experience high levels of negative emotions that they usually suppress.

10.12 How do psychological factors influence cancer patients' quality of life? p. 334
Cancer patients can improve their quality of life by maintaining an optimistic outlook, accepting the reality of their situation, and maintaining a sense of humor. Social support and psychotherapy can help them do so.

10.13 What are the effects of stress on the immune system? p. 335
Stress has been associated with lowered immune response and with increased symptoms of many infectious diseases.

10.14 What personal and social factors are associated with health and resistance to stress? p. 336
Personal factors related to health and resistance to stress are optimism, hardiness, religious involvement, and social support.

10.15 How do males and females differ with regard to health? p. 337

Women are more likely than men to die following heart surgery. Generally, though, men are more likely to die from most diseases than women are, but women are generally less healthy. When men and women have the same diseases, men are often more seriously ill. Researchers suspect these patterns may be due to the unique physiology of each gender.

10.16 How does racial patterning contribute to health differences across groups? p. 338

Racial patterning produces correlations between race and health through its influence on group differences in health-related behavior patterns.

LIFESTYLE AND HEALTH p. 339

10.17 Why is smoking the most dangerous health-threatening behavior? p. 340

Smoking is considered the most dangerous health-related behavior because it is directly related to more than 400,000 deaths each year, including deaths from heart disease, lung cancer, respiratory diseases, and stroke.

10.18 What are some health risks of alcohol abuse? p. 340

Alcohol abuse damages virtually every organ in the body, including the liver, stomach, skeletal muscles, heart, and brain. Alcoholics are three times as likely to die in motor vehicle accidents as nonalcoholics.

10.19 What is the difference between bacterial and viral STDs? p. 342

Bacterial STDs can be treated and, in most cases, cured with antibiotics. Viral STDs are considered to be incurable.

10.20 What are some benefits of a healthy diet and exercise? p. 345

Obesity is related to many chronic health conditions. Nutrient deficiencies also cause problems. Regular aerobic exercise reduces the risk of cardiovascular disease, increases muscular strength, moderates the effects of stress, makes bones denser and stronger, and helps one maintain a desirable weight.

10.21 What are the benefits and risks associated with alternative medicine? p. 346

Alternative medicine, or the use of any treatment that has not been proven scientifically to be effective, can benefit individuals who find alternative treatments that are effective. However, many patients increase their risk of poor outcomes by not telling their physicians about their use of alternative treatments. And some people delay seeking necessary conventional medical treatment because they believe that alternative approaches will work.

KEY TERMS

mypsychlab™ *Resources*

Selye's General Adaptation Syndrome
Coping Strategies and Their Effects
Sources of HIV Infection in Adults

How Stressed Are You?
Stress and Health

9/11 Post Traumatic Stress Disorder
Coping with Stress
Gender Differences in Stress Vulnerability
Smoking Damage
Alcoholism
Marathon Heart

CHAPTER 10 STUDY GUIDE

Answers to all the Study Guide questions are provided at the end of the book.

SECTION ONE: CHAPTER REVIEW

SOURCES OF STRESS (pp. 322–328)

1. On the Social Readjustment Rating Scale, only negative life changes are considered stressful. (true/false)

2. The Social Readjustment Rating Scale takes account of the individual's perceptions of the stressfulness of the life change in assigning stress points. (true/false)

3. According to Lazarus, hassles typically account for more life stress than major life changes. (true/false)

4. Lazarus's approach to measuring hassles and uplifts considers individual perceptions of stressful events. (true/false)

5. Travis cannot decide whether to go out or stay home and study for his test. What kind of conflict does he have?
   a. approach-approach
   b. avoidance-avoidance
   c. approach-avoidance
   d. ambivalence-ambivalence

6. What factor or factors increase stress, according to research on the topic?
   a. predictability of the stressor
   b. unpredictability of the stressor
   c. predictability of and control over the stressor
   d. unpredictability of and lack of control over the stressor

7. Sources of workplace stress for women include
   a. sexual harassment.
   b. discrimination.
   c. balancing family and work demands.
   d. all of the above.

8. Victims of catastrophic events usually panic. (true/false)

9. Posttraumatic stress disorder is a prolonged and severe stress reaction that results when a number of common sources of stress occur simultaneously. (true/false)

10. The group that has received the most attention from researchers interested in the association between stress and racism is
    a. Native Americans.
    b. Hispanic Americans.
    c. Asian Americans.
    d. African Americans.

RESPONDING TO STRESS (pp. 328–331)

11. The stage of the general adaptation syndrome marked by intense physiological efforts to adapt to the stressor is the (alarm, resistance) stage.

12. Susceptibility to illness increases during the (alarm, exhaustion) stage of the general adaptation syndrome.

13. Selye focused on the (psychological, physiological) aspects of stress; Lazarus focused on the (psychological, physiological) aspects of stress.

14. During secondary appraisal, a person
    a. evaluates his or her coping resources and considers options for dealing with the stressor.
    b. determines whether an event is positive, neutral, or negative.
    c. determines whether an event involves loss, threat, or challenge.
    d. determines whether an event causes physiological or psychological stress.

15. Coping aimed at reducing, modifying, or eliminating a source of stress is called (emotion-focused, problem-focused) coping; that aimed at reducing an emotional reaction to stress is called (emotion-focused, problem-focused) coping.

16. People typically use a combination of problem-focused and emotion-focused coping when dealing with a stressful situation. (true/false)

HEALTH AND ILLNESS (pp. 332–339)

17. The biomedical model focuses on _____; the biopsychosocial model focuses on _____.
    a. illness; illness
    b. health and illness; illness
    c. illness; health and illness
    d. health and illness; health and illness

18. Most research has pursued the connection between the Type A behavior pattern and
    a. cancer.
    b. coronary heart disease.
    c. stroke.
    d. ulcers.

19. Recent research suggests that the most toxic component of the Type A behavior pattern is
    a. hostility.
    b. impatience.
    c. a sense of time urgency.
    d. perfectionism.

20. Viral STDs are those that can be effectively treated with antibiotics. (true/false)

21. HIV eventually causes a breakdown in the _____ system.
    a. circulatory
    b. vascular
    c. immune
    d. respiratory

22. The incidence of AIDS in the United States is highest among
    a. homosexuals and IV drug users.
    b. homosexuals and hemophiliacs.
    c. homosexuals and bisexuals.
    d. heterosexuals, IV drug users, and hemophiliacs.

23. Lowered immune response has been associated with
    a. stress.
    b. depression.
    c. stress and depression.
    d. neither stress nor depression.

24. Some research suggests that optimists are more stress-resistant than pessimists. (true/false)

25. Which of the following is not a dimension of psychological hardiness?

a. a feeling that adverse circumstances can be controlled and changed
b. a sense of commitment and deep involvement in personal goals
c. a tendency to look on change as a challenge rather than a threat
d. close, supportive relationships with family and friends

26. Social support tends to reduce stress but is unrelated to health outcomes. (true/false)

LIFESTYLE AND HEALTH (pp. 339–347)

27. Which is the most important factor leading to disease and death?
a. unhealthy lifestyle
b. a poor health care system
c. environmental hazards
d. genetic disorders

28. Which health-compromising behavior is responsible for the most deaths?
a. overeating
b. smoking
c. lack of exercise
d. excessive alcohol use

29. (Alcohol, Smoking) damages virtually every organ in the body.

30. To improve cardiovascular fitness, aerobic exercise should be done
a. 15 minutes daily.
b. 1 hour daily.
c. 20 to 30 minutes daily.
d. 20 to 30 minutes three or four times a week.

31. Alternative health treatments have proven to be just as effective as traditional approaches to illness. (true/false)

SECTION TWO: THE BIOPSYCHOSOCIAL MODEL OF HEALTH AND ILLNESS

List at least two forces for each of the following:

1. Biological forces favoring health and wellness _____
   _____

2. Biological forces working against health and wellness _____
   _____

3. Psychological forces favoring health and wellness _____
   _____

4. Psychological forces working against health and wellness _____
   _____

5. Social forces favoring health and wellness _____
   _____

6. Social forces working against health and wellness _____
   _____

SECTION THREE: FILL IN THE BLANK

1. Medicine has been dominated by the _____ model, which focuses on illness rather than on health, whereas the _____ model asserts that both health and illness are determined by a combination of biological, psychological, and social factors.

2. The field of psychology that is concerned with the psychological factors that contribute to health, illness, and recovery is known as _____ _____.

3. The fight-or-flight response is controlled by the _____ and the endocrine glands.

4. The first stage of the general adaptation syndrome is the _____ stage.

5. The stage of the general adaptation syndrome during which the adrenal glands release hormones to help the body resist stressors is called the _____ stage.

6. Lazarus's theory is considered a _____ theory of stress and coping.

7. Noelle knew that her upcoming job interview would be difficult, so she tried to anticipate the kinds of questions she would be asked and practiced the best possible responses. Noelle was practicing _____ coping.

8. The most feared disease related to the immune system is _____.

9. The primary means of transmission of HIV is through sexual contact between _____.

10. Daily _____ are the "irritating, frustrating, distressing demands and troubled relationships that plague us day in and day out."

11. Tiffany is a psychologist who works with biologists and medical researchers to determine the effects of psychological factors on the immune system. Tiffany works in the field of _____.

12. People with the Type _____ behavior pattern have a strong sense of time urgency and are impatient, excessively competitive, hostile, and easily angered.

13. The effects of alcohol on _____ may continue for several months after an alcoholic stops drinking.

14. _____ appraisal is an evaluation of the significance of a potentially stressful event according to how it will affect one's well-being–whether it is perceived as irrelevant or as involving harm, loss, threat, or challenge.

15. African Americans may have a greater incidence of _____ _____ _____ than White Americans because of the stress associated with historical racism.

16. A _____ is any event capable of producing physical or emotional stress.

17. Cole wants to get a flu shot, but he is also very afraid of needles. He is faced with an _____ _____ conflict.

SECTION FOUR: COMPREHENSIVE PRACTICE TEST

1. Stress consists of the threats and problems we encounter in life. (true/false)

2. Hans Selye developed the
   a. diathesis stress model.
   b. general adaptation syndrome model.
   c. cognitive stress model.
   d. conversion reaction model.

3. The fight-or-flight response is seen in the _____ stage of the general adaptation syndrome.
   a. alarm
   c. resistance
   b. exhaustion
   d. arousal

4. Lack of exercise, poor diet, and disease and injury are considered to be _____ forces that work against health and wellness.
   a. environmental
   c. biological
   b. psychological
   d. social

5. Charlotte has been looking for new bedroom furniture and has found two styles that she really likes. She is trying to decide which one she will purchase. Charlotte is experiencing an _____ conflict.
   a. approach-approach
   b. approach-avoidance
   c. avoidance-avoidance
   d. avoidance-approach

6. People's sense of control over a situation can have an important beneficial influence on how a stressor affects them even if they do not exercise that control. (true/false)

7. Posttraumatic stress disorder leaves some people more vulnerable to future mental health problems. (true/false)

8. Which of the following is not a variable in work stress?
   a. workload
   b. clarity of job description
   c. perceived equity of pay for work
   d. task variety

9. Research indicates that African Americans who are highly concerned about _____ are more sensitive to stressors than their peers who are less concerned.

10. Religious faith helps people cope with negative life events. (true/false)

11. Lazarus's term for the positive experiences that can serve to cancel out the effects of day-to-day hassles is
    a. stress assets.
    b. coping mechanisms.
    c. uplifts.
    d. appraisals.

12. Type B behavior patterns seem to be more correlated with heart disease than do Type A behavior patterns. (true/false)

13. B cells produce antibodies that are effective in destroying antigens that live _____ the body cells; T cells are important in the destruction of antigens that live _____ the body cells.
    a. outside; inside
    b. inside; outside

14. AIDS is caused by HIV, often called the AIDS virus. (true/false)

15. HIV weakens the immune system by attacking T cells. (true/false)

SECTION FIVE: CRITICAL THINKING

1. In your view, which is more effective for evaluating stress: the Social Readjustment Rating Scale or the Hassle Scale? Explain the advantages and disadvantages of each.

2. Prepare two arguments: one supporting the position that alcoholism is a genetically inherited disease, and the other supporting the position that alcoholism is not a medical disease but results from learning.

3. Choose several stress-producing incidents from your life and explain what problem-focused and emotion-focused coping strategies you used. From the knowledge you have gained in this chapter, list other coping strategies that might have been more effective.

Testing Your Understanding—Unit VI

Mastering the World of Psychology, Third Edition
Chapter 10: Health and Stress

✓ **Pages 170–178**
CHECKING YOUR COMPREHENSION

Choose the best answer for each of the following questions.

1. According to the text, both Gatekeeper Bullies and Two-Headed Snake Bullies
   a. are loud and demonstrative.
   b. nitpick and make unreasonable demands.
   c. turn their employees against each other.
   d. believe in fight-or-flight.

2. The Social Readjustment Rating Scale (SRRS) is a predictor of
   a. a person's ability to handle coping with disease.
   b. a person's chances to survive a major health problem.
   c. a person's cognitive sympathetic response to stress.
   d. a person's risk of suffering major health problems.

3. The primary purpose of Figure 10.1 is to
   a. describe the variables that all workers experience.
   b. compare the variables that workers experiences every 24 hours.
   c. list the variables that contribute to workers' effectiveness and satisfaction.
   d. show distinction among the variables that workers must avoid for success.

Identify the following statements as true or false.

4. The text infers that those who suffer from posttraumatic stress disorder (PTSD) are unable to live normal lives.

5. Hassles and uplifts may neutralize the effects of one another.

6. Table 10.1 reveals how often college students experienced common hassles.

7. To calculate your Life Stress Score it is necessary to acknowledge the activities that have occurred within the last 24 months.

Answer the following questions.

8. Explain the relationship between social status and socioeconomic status.

9. Describe the differences between the approach-approach conflict and the avoidance-avoidance conflict.

10. Explain the three stages of Selye's general adaption syndrome (GAS).

Define each term as it is used in the chapter.

11. historical racism

12. survivor guilt

13. glucocorticoids

14. coping

15. stressors

Discussion and Critical Thinking Questions

1. The ability to navigate today's technology in the workplace has become a problem for some employees. Should technological knowledge be added as a variable to Albrecht's work stress variables? How could the absence of technological skills stress an employee?

2. Race relations in the United States have improved tremendously over the past few decades. Do you believe that historical racism, as it is explained in the text, is as predominant as in the past? Any there any types of social stress that are not included in the text that you feel play a large part in today's society?

3. After finding your own Life Stress Score, discuss if you feel your score represents the amount of stress you feel in your life.

Pages 178–189
CHECKING YOUR COMPREHENSION

Choose the best answer for each of the following questions.

1. According to the text, what do the biomedical model and the biopsychosocial model have in common?
   a. They both take social factors into consideration.
   b. They both include the use of health psychology.
   c. They both take biological factors into consideration.
   d. They both have been recognized by physicians for many decades.

2. What factor is NOT mentioned in aiding the reduction of the impact of stress and illness?
   a. religious faith
   b. a vitamin regimen
   c. an optimistic outlook
   d. a rich social life

3. What do the authors infer regarding individuals who are Type D?
   a. They allow their negative emotions to interfere with their daily actions.
   b. They are not able to deal with external factors as well as those with Type B.
   c. They are able to compensate for their unconstructive behavior through therapy.
   d. They go through life hostile and angered by those around them.

Identify the following statements as true or false.

4. An individual's personality type can change depending on their circumstances.

5. Hardiness is prevalent in healthy male executives who handle stress well.

6. Research has found that while women are less healthy than the males in our society, they are more likely to seek medical attention when it is needed.

Answer the following questions.

7. Explain the three components of hardiness.

8. Describe the effect social support has on people with illness.

9. Explain the concept of racial patterning.

Define each term as it is used in the chapter.

10. antibodies

11. antigens

12. coping

13. psychoneuroimmunology

14. lymphocytes

Discussion and Critical Thinking Questions

1. The text infers that individuals can control many factors that attribute to coronary heart disease. What questions would you ask someone who has been told he/she is at risk of coronary heart disease, and what advice would you give him/her?

2. Examine Type A, B, and D personality pattern behaviors. After coming to a decision regarding the shortcomings of each type of personality, discuss how you feel each shortcoming can be counteracted in people's everyday lives.

3. Discuss which factors in the biopsychosocial model (noted in Figure 10.4) would be the hardest to combat if a person found out that he/she (1) lost a job, (2) had cancer, or (3) was getting divorced?

Pages 189–197
CHECKING YOUR COMPREHENSION

Choose the best answer for each of the following questions.

1. According to the text, what is not mentioned regarding babies born to mothers who smoke?
   a. They are more likely to become smokers themselves.
   b. They are at a greater risk for anxiety and depression.
   c. They have widespread incidence of chronic bronchitis and other respiratory problems.
   d. They have low birth rates and retarded fetal development.

2. Which of the following facts was not stated by the authors in the text?
   a. AIDS is a disease that is transmitted eight times more easily from men to women.
   b. AIDS is currently epidemic and is believed to have originated in Africa.
   c. AIDS rates are higher among men who have sex with men.
   d. AIDS is sometimes accompanied with serious clinical depression.

3. Health professionals agree that
   a. aerobic exercise is a fundamental activity of alternative medicine.
   b. research has shown alternative medicine is helpful in fighting disease.
   c. lifestyle changes are more beneficial than alternative medicine.
   d. alternative medicine makes bones denser and stronger, preventing osteoporosis.

Identify the following statements as true or false.

4. The text states that even a small amount of alcohol can damage a person's liver.

5. Nonbarrier methods of contraception have decreased the spread of STDs.

6. The National Center for Health Statistics reported that 30% of all Americans do not exercise.

Answer the following questions.

7. What is the major difference between viral STDs and bacterial STDs?

8. List the seven benefits of exercise that are mentioned in the text.

9. What types of treatments or therapies are considered alternative medicine?

Define each term as it is used in the chapter.

10. passive

11. longitudinal study

12. degeneration

13. endurance

14. conventional

Discussion and Critical Thinking Questions

1. The text notes that there are both benefits and detriments of alternative medicine. Discuss whether you think alternative medicine's positive attributes outweigh its negative attributes.

2. What are your thoughts regarding the introduction of an HIV-positive Muppet on Sesame Street? Do you feel it is necessary to include such harsh realities in children's television?

✔ **Chapter Review**
END OF CHAPTER ANALYSIS

1. After reading the chapter, you should be able to answer all of the following questions EXCEPT:
   a. What are some ways to prevent coronary heart disease?
   b. What is the relationship between the immune system and stress?
   c. How does a person's cultural background affect his or her personality type?
   d. How does long-term tobacco and alcohol use affect an individual's health?

2. In order to learn the bold/highlighted words/concepts in the chapter's margins, it is important to do all of the following EXCEPT:
   a. memorize each definition word for word.
   b. recognize the relationship between the concept and the main point of the chapter.
   c. be able to verbalize each definition in your own words.
   d. compare and contrast the words/concepts that are related.

3. Which of the following visuals in the chapter is used to show sequence?
   a. Figure 10.4, The Biopsychosocial Model of Health and Illness
   b. Table 10.3, Benefits of Lifestyle Changes
   c. Figure 10.5, Milestones from the History of HIV/AIDS
   d. Figure 10.1, Variables in Work Stress

Group Projects

1. After taking the AIDS Quiz (p. 191), review any questions you answered incorrectly. Discuss with your group the AIDS education you received from school and other institutions. Come up with some ideas that our government and educational systems can use in order to prevent people in today's society from being plagued with this disease.

2. As a group, create a survey that would cover the different factors mentioned in the chapter regarding a healthy lifestyle. After surveying other students on campus (either in your other classes, in the dorms, etc.), make some generalizations regarding the surveyed students' healthy lifestyles and ways the college can help with these changes.

3. In our society there are many organizations that teach the public about the connection between health and stress, such as the American Heart Association (www.americanheart.org) and the Campaign for Tobacco-Free Kids (www.tobaccofreekids.org). Investigate one of these websites or any other organization's website that deals with the topics covered in the chapter and discuss the similarities and differences regarding the information you find.

Journal Ideas

1. Write a letter to a character in a book you recently read and explain how some of the negative activities in their life are detrimental to their health. Using the information in the chapter, advise them how they can change their poor habits and the benefits these changes will make to their lives.

2. After reviewing the information in the text about Type A, Type B, and Type D behavior patterns, write about which category you fit into and at least three situations that occurred recently that prove your findings.

Organizing Information

Textbook chapters provide section headings to make the students aware that a different topic is being introduced. In this textbook, the authors ask questions (see p. 168) that will be answered in the chapter. Write the questions on the front of index cards and then after reviewing the text, write the answers in your own words on the back of the cards. You can use these cards to review information yourself or have someone else quiz you. The first one is done for you below.

Front of Index Card

Chapter 10: Health and Stress

Sources of Stress:

10.1: What was the Social Readjustment Scale designed to reveal?

Back of Index Card

Chapter 10: Health and Stress

Page 170

Sources of Stress:

10.1: What was the Social Readjustment Scale designed to reveal?

Answer: The SRRS is used to show how much stress a person has in their life and how this stress affects major health problems. Research has noted, though, that it doesn't take into account a person's coping skills, but other research has shown that the SRRS is pretty accurate.

Credits

Photo Credits

Page 4: Courtesy IBM Corporation
Page 7: Mark Richards/PhotoEdit Inc.
Page 14: Steve Cole/Getty Images
Page 23: Diego Azubel/epa/Corbis
Page 24: Courtesy IBM Corporation
Pages 37–38: Paula Nadelstern
Page 42: Pearson Education
Page 57: Paula Nadelstern
Page 71: Chad Ehlers/Stock Connection
Page 73: Photo Disc
Page 78: Gg/estockPhoto
Page 82, top to bottom: Scala/Art Resource, NY; The Granger Collection
Page 83, clockwise from top: From *"Perspective, Jan Vredeman de Vries."* Reprinted by Permission of Dover Publications, Inc.; M.C. Escher's *"Belvedere"* © 2003 Cordon Art B.V.-Baarn-Holland. All Rights Reserved; Historical Picture Archive/Corbis
Page 84, left to right: The Granger Collection; John R. Jones/Papilio/Corbis
Page 86, clockwise from top left: The Granger Collection; Tate, London/Art Resource, NY; Ann Burns, Professor of Mathematics, Long Island University, C.W. Post Campus
Page 88: Courtesy of Paul J. Steinhardt, Princeton University
Page 95, top to bottom: Michele Burgess/Corbis; Scala/Art Resource, NY
Page 97: Photo Disc
Page 99: PhotoLink/Getty Images
Pages 114–115: Christine Pemberton/Omni-Photo
Page 116: Courtesy of Illinois Historic Preservation Agency
Page 117: Werner Forman/Art Resource, NY
Page 119: Library of Congress
Page 120: Library of Virginia
Page 121: Abby Aldrich Rockefeller Folk Art Museum, The Colonial Williamsburg Foundation, Williamsburg, VA
Page 123: The Colonial Williamsburg Foundation

Page 125: Attributed to Freake-Gibbs, *The Mason Children—David, Joanna, & Abigail,* c. 1670, Fine Arts Museum of San Francisco. Gift of Mr. and Mrs. John D. Rockefeller 3rd (1979.7.3)
Page 128: Photo by Mark Sexton/Peabody Essex Museum
Page 130: *Mrs. Elizabeth Freake and Baby Mary* (detail), c. 1670, Worcester Art Museum, Worcester, MA. Gift of Mr. and Mrs. Albert W. Rice.
Page 131: 20th Century Fox/Kobal Collection
Page 133: Unidentified artist, *Landscape (View of a Town),* Worcester Art Museum, Worcester, MA. Gift of Dr. and Mrs. Kinnicut.
Page 135: *Portrait of an Unidentified Woman (Formerly Edward Hyde, Viscount Cornbury),* 18th century. © Collection of the New-York Historical Society (Acc. No. 1952.80) /Bridgeman Art Library
Page 170: Gideon Mendel/Corbis
Page 171: Rachel Epstein/PhotoEdit Inc.
Page 172: Michael Greenlar/The Image Works
Page 175: Spencer Grant/PhotoEdit Inc.
Page 176: Paul A. Souders/Corbis
Page 177: Ariel Skelley/Corbis
Page 184: Jose Luis Pelaez Inc./Corbis
Page 185: Chris Fitzgerald/The Image Works
Page 187: Ronnie Kaufman/Corbis
Page 194, left to right: Hulton Archive/Getty Images; Stephen Chernin/Getty Images; NBAE/Getty Images; Frank Trapper/Corbis; Getty Images; AP Images; Pierre Verdy/AFP/Getty Images
Page 196: Sonda Dawes/The Image Works
Page 197: Brand X Pictures/Jupiter Images